# Language and Literary Form in French Caribbean Writing

Contemporary French and Francophone Cultures, 31

# Contemporary French and Francophone Cultures

## Series Editors

EDMUND SMYTH
*Manchester Metropolitan University*

CHARLES FORSDICK
*University of Liverpool*

## Editorial Board

JACQUELINE DUTTON
*University of Melbourne*

LYNN A. HIGGINS
*Dartmouth College*

MIREILLE ROSELLO
*University of Amsterdam*

MICHAEL SHERINGHAM
*University of Oxford*

DAVID WALKER
*University of Sheffield*

This series aims to provide a forum for new research on modern and contemporary French and francophone cultures and writing. The books published in *Contemporary French and Francophone Cultures* reflect a wide variety of critical practices and theoretical approaches, in harmony with the intellectual, cultural and social developments which have taken place over the past few decades. All manifestations of contemporary French and francophone culture and expression are considered, including literature, cinema, popular culture, theory. The volumes in the series will participate in the wider debate on key aspects of contemporary culture.

## Recent titles in the series:

CELIA BRITTON

# Language and Literary Form in French Caribbean Writing

LIVERPOOL UNIVERSITY PRESS

First published 2014 by
Liverpool University Press
4 Cambridge Street
Liverpool
L69 7ZU

British Library Cataloguing-in-Publication data
A British Library CIP record is available

ISBN 978-1-78138-036-9 cased

Typeset by Carnegie Book Production, Lancaster
Printed and bound by CPI Group (UK) Ltd, Croydon CR0 4YY

# Contents

# Acknowledgements

Earlier versions of most of the chapters in this book have previously been published as journal articles or chapters in edited books. Thus chapter 1 appeared in *Paragraph* 32.2 (2009), pp. 168–81; chapter 3 is based on a much shorter article published under the same title in the *ASCALF Yearbook* 1 (1996), pp. 15–23; chapter 4 is a revised version of 'Exile, Incarceration and the Homeland: Jewish References in French Caribbean Novels' in Michelle Keown, David Murphy and James Procter (eds), *Comparing Postcolonial Diasporas*, (Basingstoke: Palgrave Macmillan, 2009), pp. 149–67; chapter 5 appeared in *French Cultural Studies* 15.1 (2004), pp. 35–47; and chapter 6, under the title 'The De-Construction of Subjectivity in Daniel Maximin's *L'Île et une nuit*' in *Paragraph* 24.3 (2001), pp. 44–58. Chapter 7 was published as '*Discours* and *histoire*, magical and political discourse in Édouard Glissant's *Le Quatrième Siècle*', *French Cultural Studies* 5.14 (1994), pp. 151–62; chapter 8 as 'Collective narrative voice in three novels by Édouard Glissant' in S. Haigh (ed.), *An Introduction to Francophone Caribbean Writing: Guadeloupe and Martinique* (Oxford: Berg, 1999), pp. 135–48; chapter 9 as 'Fictions of identity and identities of fiction in Glissant's *Tout-monde*', *ASCALF Yearbook* 4 (2000), pp. 47–59; and chapter 10 as 'Transnational Languages in Glissant's "Tout-monde"' in Mary Gallagher (ed.), *World Writing: Poetics, Ethics, Globalization* (Toronto: University of Toronto Press, 2008), pp. 62–85. In all cases the original texts have been revised for inclusion in this volume. I am very grateful to all the original publishers for giving me permission to reprint the articles in question.

I also wish to thank the ever-supportive Anthony Cond at Liverpool University Press; Maryse Condé for kindly allowing me to publish my interview with her; and Charles Forsdick, Mary Gallagher and Eli Park Sorensen for their very valuable comments on the manuscript. As my teaching career has now come to an end, I would like to dedicate this book to the students whom I taught at Kings College London, Reading University, Aberdeen University and University College London, and who taught me so much.

# Abbreviations

DA    *Le Discours antillais*

IP    *L'Intention poétique*

IPD   *Introduction à une poétique du divers*

NRM   *Une Nouvelle Région du monde*

PR    *Poétique de la Relation*

TM    *Tout-monde*

TTM   *Traité du tout-monde*

# Introduction

This book brings together articles and book chapters written over the last twenty years. They cover different types of writing – mainly fiction, but also essays and articles, and literary manifestoes; they also vary widely in scope, from readings of one particular text to more general studies of literary genres or movements. But they all share a common focus on the linguistic and/or formal aspects of literary texts.

Part I looks at issues of genre, intertextuality and discourse in relation to a number of French Caribbean writers. The first three chapters are all concerned with the reactions of French Caribbean writers to the ways in which they are seen by European audiences: the problems of asserting difference without lapsing into the stereotypes of exoticism. Thus chapter 1 analyses the ambiguous relationship to primitivism of the review *Tropiques* in the 1940s, in the context of French surrealism, African-American literature and European ethnography.[1] Chapter 2 continues this concern with genre in the phenomenon of 'auto-exoticism' – the internalization and reproduction by French Caribbean writers of the colonial other's exotic vision of their culture – as diagnosed by René Ménil in the 1950s and then, thirty years later, treated rather differently by Patrick Chamoiseau and Raphaël Confiant; this also involves issues of language, in the latters' promotion of Creole over French and their emphasis on integrating distinctively oral language into literary texts. Chapter 3 focuses more directly on the reception of French Caribbean literature by metropolitan readers, exploring the oddly literalized notion of consumption that is used to market this literature – 'eating' the text – and, again, the internalized reproduction of this in the texts themselves. Not only the content of the representations but also, and especially, their *language* is presented as 'edible'. The remaining chapters of Part I are more detailed studies of individual texts. Chapter 4 analyses French Caribbean and Jewish intertextual relations in Gisèle Pineau's *L'Exil selon Julia* and Simone and André Schwarz-Bart's *Un Plat de porc aux bananes vertes*. Maryse Condé's deliberate breaking of the 'rules' of literary discourse in *Traversée de la mangrove* is the subject of Chapter 5; and an interview with the author forms an Appendix to the book. Chapter 6 discusses postcolonial feminist theories of narrative agency in relation to Daniel Maximin's *L'Île et une nuit*.[2]

Part II is devoted to the novels and essays of Édouard Glissant, who explored questions of language and poetics throughout his career. He more than any other French Caribbean writer has influenced my understanding of the issues that form the subject of this book – hence his prominence in it. The ideas developed in his essays also inform his novels, whose structure and language, as well as their themes, embody his attempt to create a means of expression that would address the unrepresentability of Caribbean history (the discursive structure of *Le Quatrième Siècle*, chapter 7) and the problem of social solidarity in Martinique (his evolving use of collective narrative voice in *Malemort, La Case du commandeur* and *Mahagony*, chapter 8). In his later work the boundary between theoretical and literary writing becomes increasingly porous: in *Tout-monde*, for example, where the generic interplay between fiction and autobiography also involves his theorization of identity (chapter 9). Chapter 10 discusses his theories of language and of how languages interact in a globalized world; and Chapter 11 his presentation of the relationship between the work of art and the real in *Une Nouvelle Région du monde*.[3]

It would be fair to say that criticism of postcolonial literature has until recently somewhat neglected the formal aspects of the texts it analyses. One major exception to this, however, is encapsulated in the notion of 'writing back to the centre' that underpinned the very early project of *The Empire Writes Back*[4] and has subsequently been developed in Helen Tiffin's concept of 'counter-discourse', which she defines as a 'postcolonial subversion and appropriation of the dominant European discourses'.[5] In placing the emphasis firmly on the parodic, intertextual dimension of literary texts, this approach is, clearly, committed to questions of form and genre. But in practice it has not proved very productive; apart from Tiffin's own analyses of J.M. Coetzee's *Foe* in relation to *Robinson Crusoe* and Jean Rhys' *Wide Sargasso Sea* in relation to *Jane Eyre*, and the various postcolonial remakes of *The Tempest* with Caliban as the hero, it would appear that not many postcolonial literary texts are accessible to this type of analysis.[6] But there is now a new concern with the far more general question of the *literariness* of postcolonial literature. The first major example of this was Gayatri Spivak's *Death of a Discipline*[7] – the text of three lectures given in 2000 – which stresses the need for postcolonial studies to return to the skills of close reading and attention to language and form that characterized the more old-fashioned tradition of (European based) Comparative Literature, and to extend these to the reading of subaltern literatures. Adopting Derrida's notion of *teleopoiesis* (*Death*, p. 31), Spivak argues that literature has the unique capacity to foster an imaginative process of 'othering' in which, rather than objectifying the other, the reader sees the world from the other's point of view: postcolonial theory must 'reclaim the role of teaching literature as training the imagination – the great inbuilt instrument of othering' (*Death*, p. 13). Nicholas Harrison's *Postcolonial Criticism*, published in 2003, accords a similar importance to the specificity of the literary and its irreducibility to historical or social analysis; more recent examples include Eli Park Sorensen's *Postcolonial Studies and the Literary* and the collection of essays edited by Jane Hiddlestone and Patrick Crowley, *Postcolonial Poetics: Genre and Form*.[8] Although all of these assert the scarcity of previous work in this area – Dominique Combe, for instance, in the preface to *Postcolonial Poetics*, writes: 'we have to recognize that literary form and genre, as such, are seldom taken into account by most postcolonial critical essays; probably because these originated in cultural studies and often revolve around the social sciences rather than literature' (p. viii) – it seems clear that attention to the language and literary form of postcolonial writing is becoming an important area of research.

This has meant, among other things, renegotiating the relationship between postcolonial literary texts and the political. Postcolonial literature, because of the situation in which it is produced and consumed, is usually assumed to have an inescapable political dimension not necessarily present in other kinds of literature.[9] Thus, writers of the kind of essays cited by Combe above have sometimes felt that, given the urgency of the themes of much of the literature – inequality and the struggle for political liberation – there is something rather reactionary or dilettante in concentrating solely on their formal and stylistic aspects. As Sorensen puts it in the opening sentence of his book: 'Until recently, thinking about aesthetics, literariness and literary form within the field of postcolonial studies would have seemed hopelessly reactionary and contradictory' (p. x); he later remarks: 'Facing the overwhelming task of voicing the history of the oppressed, it may appear not only as a superfluous luxury for writers, critics and readers to dwell on aspects such as literary form and the specificity of literature, but equally troublesome as well in an ethical sense' (p. 4). Perhaps because of this, critics who do focus on the formal features of texts almost always consider them in conjunction with the social context and political themes of the works in question. They vary, however, in the types and degrees of connectedness that they posit between the two levels.

Thus, while Harrison argues strongly that literature should not be read as making political statements, he also emphasizes its 'worldliness', to use Edward Said's phrase – i.e., its inextricable involvement in 'historical and ideological problematics [...] The work of narrative fiction, I have argued, can never be *wholly* or "purely" literary' (*Postcolonial Criticism*, p. 147, italics original). But he identifies a certain tension between the work's literariness and its engagement with what might broadly be called political realities. Harrison sees ambiguity and indeterminacy of meaning as a dominant characteristic of the literary; whereas, if one follows the influential arguments of theorists such as Peter Hallward and Chris Bongie, political principles, commitments and actions are necessarily unambiguous: politics is a matter of 'taking sides'.[10]

In somewhat similar vein, Sorensen criticizes the tendency of anglophone postcolonial criticism to assume that the conspicuously formal experiments of avant-garde postcolonial literature – in the work of Salman Rushdie, for example – can automatically be equated with political subversion or resistance (*Postcolonial Studies*, pp. 8–11), whereas realist texts are conversely assumed to be politically conservative. This represents a more sophisticated position than the orthodox view that left-wing political commitment in literature goes together with realism,[11] and it is perhaps more characteristic of anglophone than francophone postcolonial criticism; francophone literature has no equivalent to the dominance of Salman Rushdie, for instance.[12] But Sorensen's insistence that there is no easy automatic correlation between the formal features of a text and its possible political significance is equally valid for francophone postcolonial literature.

Like Harrison, Jane Hiddlestone emphasizes

> the ways in which the analysis of a text's poetics highlights ambivalence [...] ambiguity is conceived to be a key part of a text's poetic function, since poetic form, through the use of allusion and suggestion, serves precisely to open up meaning rather than to define and close it down. (*Postcolonial Poetics*, p. 3)

But whereas for Harrison the literariness of the text is necessarily separate from its political interpretations, she sees the work's formal features as having a less conflictual, more instrumental relation with the political – not, however, in the sense of expressing defined political positions, but rather of questioning them: 'it is through the use of poetic experimentation that writers open up their readers' understanding of postcolonial experiences rather than providing them with answers' (p. 3). Formal analysis thus enables us to approach the political in a new way, 'to articulate a more nuanced understanding of the ways in which form and genre can engage with the political' (p. 1);[13] she continues: 'This turn to the aesthetic is by no means a gesture of disengagement from the political context of colonialism and its aftermath, but constitutes a renewed effort to analyse how texts offer multiple distinct ways of responding to political and historical questions' (p. 1).

I would certainly want to subscribe to this aim, at least to the extent of claiming that the chapters of this book treat language and form not as ends in themselves, but as offering a particular way of illuminating the themes and social context of the works. However, the nature of this connection varies considerably between one text and another, and what the formal features relate to is not always political in the proper sense of the word. In some cases it is: chapters 7 and 8 examine links between the textual and the political, that is, the significance of literary textual features in enabling a politicized grasp of history in *Le Quatrième Siècle,* and the construction of a collective narrative voice in Glissant's 'roman du Nous' as a contribution to the political project of building a national community. But other chapters discuss rather different kinds of connection. For instance, in chapters 1 and 2, while the novels by Chamoiseau and Confiant which I describe at the end of chapter 2 have a similar kind of relationship to the political as those of Glissant, I am mainly concerned to analyse *political* discourses which have literature as their object: both *Tropiques* and *Éloge de la créolité*[14] are committed to creating a collective sense of pride on the part of Martinicans in their cultural identity, and both *Éloge* as a whole and many of the texts in *Tropiques* read as political manifestoes; Ménil's discussions of literature in *Antilles déjà jadis,* also, are explicitly Marxist and anti-colonial. Chapter 3 looks rather at the ideological dimension of the reception and marketing of postcolonial novels for a metropolitan readership. In my other chapters, the articulation is between the textual and the cultural or ideological, as distinct from the strictly political. Thus in chapter 5 Condé's 'irreverence' is not directed at the postcolonial condition, but works to dismantle ideological stereotypes in a far more diffuse sense. Chapter 6 moves from formal questions of narrative agency to a more general Lacanian reconceptualization of the subject in Maximin's novel. The intertextual links between the Jewish and the Caribbean experience in the texts discussed in chapter 4 lead on to a broader exploration of the historical and cultural differences in their vision of the 'homeland'. Glissant explores a far more all-pervasive notion of intertextuality between the text and the landscape in *Une Nouvelle Région du monde*, as I discuss in chapter 11, and his theorizations of language and of the relation between the text and the real, as indeed his political experiments with narrative voice, are always informed by his overarching *philosophical* reworking of the concept of identity.

Unlike most of the current generation of researchers in francophone studies, I came to the field having already worked for twenty years in linguistics, avant-garde French literature (the *nouveau roman* in particular), structuralist and post-structuralist literary and film theory. This background has influenced my approach to francophone Caribbean texts, not only in my dominant focus on language and textuality, but also in the theoretical works that I have drawn on in several of the chapters here. There is some discussion of certain aspects of postcolonial theory in this book: of work on exoticism in chapter 2 and discursive agency in chapter 6, for example, and of the commodification of the postcolonial as theorized by Graham Huggan, in chapters 2 and 3 – Huggan's work makes possible a reframing of the debates surrounding *créolité* in the 1990s.[15] I consider in some detail the influence on Glissant of Gilles Deleuze and Félix Guattari, whose *Kafka. Pour une littérature mineure* has made a fairly influential contribution to postcolonial theory (my interest, however, is not in this text, but in their *Mille Plateaux*, and Deleuze's *Différence et répétition*).[16] However, postcolonial theory is certainly not dominant in this book, whose theoretical points of reference – their eclecticism reflecting the length of time over which the original essays were written – are rather Barthes, Bakhtin, Kristeva, Althusser, Lacan, Saussure, Benveniste, Hegel and Merleau-Ponty.[17] This therefore raises the question: how does the focus of my book relate to postcolonial theory?

Postcolonial theory has an important relationship with poststructuralist theory. Some strands of the former have been just as hostile to poststructuralism as some metropolitan anglophone literary criticism.[18] But the three founding figures of postcolonial theory, Said, Spivak and

Bhabha, are profoundly and explicitly influenced by Foucault, Lacan and Derrida. The so-called 'linguistic turn' of poststructuralism greatly increased, in various ways, the importance of language, discourse and textuality in theorizations of society and subjectivity. In the work of Foucault and Lacan particularly, the claim that analysis of the textual illuminates the social is fundamental. For Foucault the subject is constructed in discourse, and Lacan's psychoanalytic theory owes a great deal to the linguistics of Saussure, Jakobson and Benveniste: in his Symbolic Order, the psyche is determined by the structures of language – the subject is 'subject to the signifier'.[19] However, Foucault's concept of discourse is fairly distant from concrete language use; and in practice the uses that Said and Spivak make of his work, and even the extensive use that other postcolonial theorists also make of Foucauldian discursive agency, tend not to result in very detailed, concrete textual analysis.[20] The enormous amount of literary analysis that has been inspired by Lacan is, on the whole, more textually orientated; but Bhabha's use of him is not – in fact, it is not centrally concerned with literature in any sense. In other words, postcolonial theory's appropriations of poststructuralism have tended to underexploit the latter's investment in language.

This is perhaps all the more surprising in that one aspect of language is a crucial problem in postcolonial theory: the colonized subject's difficult relation to the colonial language. For obvious reasons it is a particularly acute problem for postcolonial writers and intellectuals, and has been much discussed by them.[21] But it also affects colonial subjects more generally, through the education system, or in dealings with other colonial authorities, or in migration to the metropole (Fanon's *Peau noire, masques blancs* analyses this eloquently[22]). As such, it is a prominent theme in many postcolonial novels. But as far as I am aware there is nothing in orthodox postcolonial theory that provides as precise and illuminating a framework for analysis of the subject's relationship to the language s/he speaks as Benveniste's seminal *Problèmes de linguistique générale*, especially chapter 21, 'De la subjectivité dans le langage'.[23] Indeed, his concept of the *sujet d'énonciation* has been widely used in structuralist and poststructuralist literary criticism. I have tried to show here what it can contribute to a reading of a postcolonial novel, *Le Quatrième Siècle*.

In a very different way, Mikhail Bakhtin offers another perspective on the question of the subject's position in language, approaching it not from a Western intellectual tradition but from that of dissident Soviet Marxism. He emphasizes the fundamentally *social* nature of language, so that, in his formulation, it is not only the alienated colonial subject whose language does not 'belong' to him, but *any* speaker, who inevitably finds that 'Our practical everyday speech is full of other people's words';[24] the speaker has to '[strive] to get a reading on his own word [...] within the alien conceptual system of the understanding receiver'; he 'constructs his own utterance on alien territory'.[25] Language for Bakhtin 'lies on the borderline between oneself and the other. The word in language is half someone else's' (*Dialogic Imagination*, p. 293), and he stresses that 'forcing [language] to submit to one's own intentions and accents is a difficult and complicated process' (p. 294). Bakhtin thus proposes as a general human condition a predicament that has a particularly acute relevance to the postcolonial subject (it has marked similarities with Glissant's formulation of the relation between 'langage' and 'langue', for instance, as discussed in chapter 10), and is therefore a useful supplement to postcolonial theory. More specifically, as I argue in chapter 3, Bakhtin's concept of the 'object-word' is potentially a valuable theorization of the exotic commodification of language in postcolonial novels.

But if these other approaches can offer insights into francophone literature and thought that postcolonial theory is less well equipped to provide, it is also true, conversely, that importing them into the postcolonial arena can reveal some of their own biases and limitations. Structuralist criticism has been attacked by postcolonial theorists for its ahistorical and asocial character, and an example of this is arguably Benveniste's absolute separation of (subjective) *discours* and (objective) *histoire*. But I have shown, in chapter 7, how these two concepts can be recontextualized to reveal the relative, culturally determined nature of conceptions of knowledge: indeed, the very starkness of the opposition highlights the peculiarly ambiguous status of *Le Quatrième Siècle*'s narrative discourse and its historical specificity.

Barthes' *S/Z* is similarly constructed around an opposition, that between the 'texte lisible' and the 'texte scriptible', that is, the realist and the anti-realist text: 'Notre littérature est marquée par le divorce impitoyable que l'institution littéraire maintient entre le fabricant et l'usager du texte [...] En face du texte scriptible s'établit donc sa contre-valeur, sa valeur négative, réactive: ce qui peut être lu, mais non écrit: le *lisible*'.[26] Unlike earlier structuralist literary theory, Barthes' literary codes, and the definition of meaning that results from them (discussed here in relation to Condé's *Traversée de la mangrove* in chapter 5), have implications that go beyond literature: they constitute an ideological encoding of the real. However, Barthes relates them to literature in such a way that the realist text – the 'texte lisible' – can merely enact and so reinforce them; only the anti-realist 'scriptible' can subvert the codes, and therefore, precisely because it is anti-realist, the impact of the subversion does not extend beyond the literary text itself. I argue, however, that *Traversée de la mangrove* exhibits many of the ideologically subversive features of the 'scriptible' in a text that remains realist, that is, 'lisible'. Both of the central oppositions that underpin these theorists' work – Benveniste's *histoire/discours* and Barthes' *lisible/scriptible* – are thus deconstructed by Glissant and Condé's novels.

As the above discussion of Barthes suggests, a major disjunction between (post)structuralist theory and much postcolonial fiction centres on the question of realism. For structuralist theory, the idea that the novel is a fictional representation of reality is an illusion to be dissipated by analysis of the formal structures of the text, which reveal the extent to which the text is determined and motivated, not by the author's attempt to write something which will be as 'true to life' as possible, but by the largely unconscious functioning of formal rules and codes. Equally, Barthes' poststructuralist *S/Z* defines realism as the mere rehearsal and reinforcement of ideological codes. This position is developed rather differently in the Althusserian Marxist strand of poststructuralist literary theory exemplified by Pierre Macherey, Terry Eagleton and Catherine Belsey, in which ideology is not an illusion and the text's relation to it is theorized in a more complex fashion.[27] Here too, however, it is taken for granted that the realist novel's basic claim to be a representation of reality is entirely ideological, albeit in a less pejorative sense than that of Barthes. In both cases, the position is closely linked to the general anti-humanist thrust of poststructuralism's theorization of the subject; for example, the rejection of the humanist notion of 'voice' as an immediate human presence governing the text (see chapter 6) is by the same token the removal of one of its guarantees of realist authenticity. From the (post)structuralist point of view, novels that subscribe to a realist aesthetic are both naïve and reactionary.

On the other hand, however, much postcolonial fiction does subscribe to such an aesthetic, in the sense that it is committed to saying something about the human condition – or indeed the postcolonial condition – in the real world. (Under this definition, the representation of magic is not incompatible with realism.) Of the novels discussed here, Maximin's

*L'Île et une nuit* is furthest away from a conventional realist novel in the instability of its diegesis, the elusiveness of its *sujets d'énonciation*, and the intensely poetic quality of some of its language. Nevertheless, it has an eminently clear and simple time-scale, and it is 'about' both a hurricane and the specific situation of the Guadeloupean community. It is not self-referential in the way that the *nouveaux romans* of Alain Robbe-Grillet or Jean Ricardou are. Nor, as I argue at the end of chapter 9, are Glissant's later, more apparently postmodern novels; he has rejected postcolonial use of what he calls Western realism, certainly, but what he means by this is actually a very narrow and superficial kind of naturalism.[28] Exoticism, most notably in Depestre's *Hadriana dans tous mes rêves*[29] (see chapter 3), departs from realism in a way entirely different from that envisaged by Barthes, since it is non-realist rather than *anti*-realist; and while the intertextual dimension of the novels studied in chapter 4 could be seen as distancing them to some extent from the immediate representation of their authors' real-life experience, they remain overwhelmingly realist in their orientation.

Condé's very straightforward conception of realism – 'Finalement, l'œuvre d'un écrivain c'est quoi sinon présenter la vie autour de lui dans sa complexité et dans son étrangeté?[30] – is in fact central to what she is trying to achieve in her novels. For her, realism is not ideological but, on the contrary, a way of combatting ideological stereotypes: the stereotypes of exoticism, for example, as she makes clear in her interview with me. She says that exoticism is 'a non-realistic vision of a society and its people' (p. 172), and

> When you try to stick closely [...] to the reality of today, the exoticism disappears. There is nothing exotic about Guadeloupe today: when you lock up your house at six in the evening because you are afraid that armed gangs are going to come and burgle you, that's not exotic at all. (p. 173)

So, when Condé, either flagrantly or subtly, breaks the 'rules' that Barthes identifies as the basis of the realist text – as my analysis shows her doing – she is not doing so as a rejection of realist literature, but as a means to construct a text that will be *more* realistic than ideological; the uncertainties of her 'Flaubertian' irony do not serve to subvert the reader's faith in the realism of the text, as in Barthes' analysis, but rather question the apparent comprehensibility of social reality.

For Glissant, both the undermining of omniscient *histoire* in *Le Quatrième Siècle* and the more explicit, elaborate challenging of the boundary between novelist and character in *Mahagony* and *Tout-monde* work against the conventional notion of the text as representation of reality. They do this, however, not by replacing representation with a text that excludes *any* kind of relation with the real, but by setting up a different but equally powerful relation between the text and the world, which Glissant takes from Deleuze and Guattari's *Mille Plateaux*, and which I discuss in chapters 9 and 11.[31] This is the idea that, rather than being a representation *of* reality, the text exists on the same plane of reality as everything else because it is 'rhizomatically' connected to everything else; in *Une Nouvelle Région du monde* Glissant theorizes it more fully in terms of the primacy of generative *differences* that, as I put it in chapter 11, 'jump' the boundary between the work of art and the real.[32]

Sorensen's claim that postcolonial theory suffers from a 'kind of schizophrenia; that is, a textually-based approach to allegedly "experimental" works – and a thematic, content-based approach to so-called "conventional" texts' (*Postcolonial Studies,* p. 10) foregrounds the importance of critical attention to the *formal* characteristics of *realist* texts, in a way that is extremely pertinent to authors such as Condé and Glissant. In these novels – as also in Maximin's *L'Île et une nuit* – realism is not rejected, but reworked and renewed; and one can perhaps argue that this constitutes a significant feature of postcolonial literature in general. To the extent that neither postcolonial nor (post)structuralist theory *per se* can adequately account for them, these new kinds of postcolonial realist text are a strong argument for the need to bring together a variety of different critical approaches in order to develop new types of formal and textual analysis to do them justice. I hope that the essays collected in this volume go some way towards preparing the ground for such developments.

# PART I

# Genre, Intertextuality, Discourse

# How to be Primitive

## *Tropiques*, Surrealism and Ethnography

The review *Tropiques* was produced in Martinique during the years of the Second World War. Its principal aim was to establish the autonomy and specificity of French Caribbean culture on equal terms with that of Europe; although it never had a large readership, it marked an important moment in the intellectual and literary history of the region. Its editors were Aimé and Suzanne Césaire and René Ménil, who were at the time teachers at the Lycée Schoelcher in Fort-de-France; they had recently returned to Martinique from Paris, where Ménil had been active in Marxist and surrealist circles, while Aimé Césaire had, together with the Senegalese Léopold Senghor, founded what was to become the Negritude movement. All of these influences shaped the orientation of *Tropiques*, although the strict political censorship operated until 1943 by the Vichy regime in Martinique meant that Marxism was less overtly prominent than surrealism and Negritude. Negritude's commitment to the promotion of a collective 'black' identity, reconnecting Antilleans with their African roots, came together with surrealism's enthusiasm for *l'art nègre* and primitive cultures to produce an interest in a primitivist literature characterized by the instinctual, the supernatural, the irrational, closeness to nature and the spontaneous expression of untrammeled emotion rather than intellectual subtlety or sophisticated literary form. All of these qualities were attributed to Africa, which for *Tropiques* assumed the role of a figure of unproblematic primitivity.

But after André Breton's famous unscheduled visit to the island in 1941, it was surrealism that was the most obvious influence on the review.[1] Michel Leiris suggests that for Antillean intellectuals such as Ménil at this time, 'Le surréalisme apparut – sur le plan esthétique et, plus largement, psychologique – comme susceptible de les aider à surmonter une complexe d'infériorité' (p. 108);[2] and argues that whereas previously they had felt obliged to conform to European cultural values, surrealism's rejection of these values enabled them to 'retrouver une authenticité' (p. 108) that was inseparable from their racial identity as people of African descent.[3] Thus, Leiris goes on, in *Tropiques*, 'Aimé Césaire et ses amis mettront très fortement l'accent sur l'importance de la composante négro-africaine dans la culture antillaise' (p. 109). But while he is sympathetic to this project, Leiris emphasizes the point that surrealism, like Negritude, was incapable of providing a basis for the political liberation of the Martinican people, which was the most important issue. After the war, therefore, he argues, the intellectuals who had been associated with *Tropiques* turned to communism instead (p. 110). Whereas they 'avaient cru trouver dans le surréalisme un instrument de libération et dans la valorisation de l'Afrique noire un antidote contre le complexe d'infériorité qui affecte la plupart des Antillais' (p. 114), both of these strategies were destined to fail – because surrealism became a mere 'poncif' imported from Europe, a 'mode littéraire, à laquelle on se conforme comme on le fait pour d'autres modes importées de Paris' (p. 114), and Negritude was now merely a 'thème esthétique ou sentimental d'autant plus arbitraire que la distance à tout le moins culturelle est, en fait, considérable entre l'Antillais même le plus foncé et un noir Africain' (p. 114). Thus they now, in the 1950s, renounced surrealism and Negritude in favour of communism:

> Aimé Césaire et ses amis, maintenant communistes, sont les premiers à tenir pour dépassées les positions qu'ils prirent, alors qu'ils s'en remettaient à une sorte de primitivisme littéraire et à l'idée d'une renaissance d'inspiration africaine, pour parvenir à cette ressemblance avec eux-mêmes dont il semblait que le rationalisme occidental les avait détournés. (p. 114)

They have, in other words, progressed from a psychological and identi-tarian problematic, defined in terms of surmounting an inferiority complex, authenticity and 'ressemblance avec eux-mêmes', to a political stance which, in embracing communism, obliges them to renounce not only Negritude – Leiris here echoes Sartre's analysis of Negritude as a necessary but inadequate stage on the way to communism[4] – but also surrealism.

But this account is somewhat oversimplified. In the first place, while Césaire joined the Communist Party only in 1945 (and left it in 1956), Ménil had been a Marxist since at least the 1930s, and his joint adherence to surrealism and Marxism had not seemed to him at all contradictory.[5] It is also inaccurate to imply, as Leiris does, that the *Tropiques* team as a whole rejected surrealism after the war: Ménil certainly did (describing it in 1959, for instance, as merely the latest form of exoticism[6]), but Césaire did not, and in fact Ménil makes a significant exception for Césaire's poetry on the grounds that it combines surrealist techniques with a political commitment to liberation.[7] More generally, although Caribbean surrealism started only in the 1940s – at a time, in other words, when surrealism in Europe had long parted company with communism – in the Caribbean it still appeared a politically revolutionary force. Indeed, Suzanne Césaire argues that the current war-time situation has revived the political importance of surrealism as a demand for freedom: 'lorsqu'en 1943 la liberté elle-même se trouve menacée dans le monde entier, le surréalisme qui n'a pas cessé un seul instant de se tenir au service de la plus grande émancipation de l'homme, se veut résumé en ce seul mot magique: liberté' (8–9, p. 15)[8] – and describes *Tropiques*' engagement with it in the same terms: 'Pas un moment au cours de ces dures années de la domination de Vichy, l'image de la liberté ne s'est ternie totalement ici et c'est au surréalisme que nous le devons' (p. 18). Thus, to claim that surrealism for *Tropiques* meant only primitivist self-representation, in line with Negritude, is clearly reductive.[9]

But, equally, *Tropiques*' attitude to primitivism itself is actually far more ambivalent than Leiris implies. Ménil's claim in the introduction to the 1978 re-edition of *Tropiques* that their literature was *never* primitivist – he attacks 'le contresens qui consiste à prendre la littérature de la revue pour une littérature spontanée et naïve appartenant à une manière d'art primitif considéré a priori comme propre aux pays sous-développés' ('Pour une lecture critique de *Tropiques*', p. xxix) – would seem to have more to do with the subsequent development of his thought than with the reality of *Tropiques* in the 1940s. However, his observation a few pages later that 'les textes de *Tropiques* renvoient, en effet, [...] à diverses philosophies, dont certaines sont apparentées et voisines, et certaines autres opposées et franchement contradictoires' (p. xxxii) is entirely convincing: there were from the start a number of conflicting pulls within the review. Against Leiris' view that *Tropiques* seized on surrealism simply because of the possibilities for reclaiming an authentic identity that its primitivism offered them, therefore, I want to explore the *ambivalence* towards the concept of the primitive that can be found within the pages of the review, and the problems which the recourse to ethnographic knowledge of African culture posed for them.

There are, certainly, some clear expressions of the view that Martinican intellectuals are close to a primitive sensibility in a way which distinguishes them from their French surrealist counterparts. The fifth issue, for instance, opens with Aimé Césaire's poem 'En guise de manifeste littéraire', dedicated to Breton, which defines the people of the Caribbean in opposition to European rationality – 'Parce que nous vous haïssons, vous et votre raison, nous nous réclamons de la démence précoce, de la folie flambante, du cannibalisme tenace' (5, p. 7) – and, among other things, as 'hougans' or *vodou* priests – 'Qui et quels nous sommes? Admirable question! Haïsseurs. Bâtisseurs. Traîtres. Hougans. Hougans surtout. Car nous voulons tous les démons' (5, p. 8).

The European surrealists' attitude towards them was also an important factor in encouraging this line of thinking. The circumstances of Breton's 'discovery' of Aimé Césaire – not in Paris but in Martinique, not through his fellow writers but via the habadashery shop run by Ménil's sister – set the scene for Césaire to be presented to the French surrealists as an authentically primitive genius (rather than as someone who had studied at the Lycée Louis le Grand and the ENS in Paris). In fact Breton's preface to a bilingual edition of 'Cahier d'un retour au pays natal' published in the United States, printed in *Tropiques* no. 11, does not present Césaire as a primitive but as a representative of progressive humanity in general. But others among the French surrealists did put a certain pressure on the *Tropiques* team to 'be primitive'; and they were happy to play along with this. For instance, they reprint Benjamin Péret's introduction to the Cuban edition of the 'Cahier', which in one short paragraph (6–7, p. 60) systematically rehearses all the usual primitivist reference points. Thus Césaire is completely uninfluenced by any other literature: 'Aimé Césaire ne doit rien à personne: son langage n'est qu'à lui [...]'; he is the true voice of nature, '[...] ou plutôt c'est le langage flamboyant des flèches des colibris zébrant un ciel de mercure' – but of a distinctively savage, non-European nature: 'une poésie qui est le cri sauvage d'une nature dominatrice sadique'. The supernatural is also prominent: Péret applauds Césaire's poetry for having 'l'accent obsédant des tambours du vaudou' and for its anti-Christian black magic, which 's'oppose jusqu'à la rébellion aux religions des esclavagistes où toute magie s'est momifiée, toute poésie est morte à jamais'. And, finally, it is guided solely by instinct, rejecting all intellectual constraints: Césaire is 'le premier grand poète nègre qui a rompu toutes les amarres et s'en va sans se soucier d'aucune étoile polaire, d'aucune croix du sud intellectuelle, guidé par son seul désir aveugle'.

It is, however, extremely revealing to place Péret's characterization of Césaire's poetry alongside Césaire's introduction to the African-American poets of the Harlem Renaissance (specifically, James Weldon Johnson, Jean Toomer and Claude MacKay) whose work is published in the second issue of *Tropiques* – and which is written from a viewpoint strikingly similar to that which Péret adopts on Césaire. In other words, Césaire here is very much adopting the position of the *French* intellectual who is critical of his own culture, delightedly discovering something more invigorating, because spontaneous and natural. After an extraordinarily stereotyped evocation of African-American society, he introduces the poetry of this 'peuple inconsciemment artiste' (2, p. 38) as an art characterized by its spontaneity and lack of artifice – 'ce déversement subit du trop plein d'une âme vite remplie' – and so 'comment y trouverions-nous les ruses, les réticences, les abandons étudiés et les départs foudroyants à quoi nous a habitués l'artificieuse poésie de l'Europe?' (p. 41). This poetry, in other words, is good because it is *very simple*: it can only express 'trois états d'âme, toujours les mêmes, les plus élémentaires et les plus simples: le cafard, la joie, l'émotion religieuse' (p. 41). Lacking lyrical colour and 'la magie du son', all it has is rhythm, to which we respond on a very basic somatic level: 'du rythme, mais de primitif, de jazz ou de tam-tam, c'est-à-dire enfonçant la résistance de l'homme en ce point de plus basse humanité qu'est le système nerveux' (p. 41). And, although the Harlem Renaissance poets do not (regrettably, he implies) practice *vodou*, the prominence of Christianity in their literature, compared with that of the French Caribbean, is interpreted in entirely primitivist, corporeal terms: 'Ici c'est la frénésie qui mène à Dieu, c'est l'ancestral et fondamental paganisme du nègre qui l'embrasse. Plus de tam-tam, plus de danses il est vrai, mais par un moyen détourné [...] c'est toujours d'une certaine manière le corps qui, porté à un incroyable degré d'incandescence, révèle le Divin' (p. 39).

Most significantly, far from expressing any commonality of vision with the American writers, Césaire stresses how alien this poetry is, not only to Europeans, but also to him and his Martinican readership: 'Et si nous nous apercevions que ce qui allumait notre curiosité était indigne d'elle! Conclusion tentante pour un esprit strictement lettré' (p. 40) – and warns his readers against missing the point of it: 'Autrement dit, la grandeur d'une telle littérature, nous la cherchions là où nous ne saurions la trouver' (p. 41). His attitude to these poets is one of praise, certainly, for their Negritude, but praise of a very patronizing kind, and which positions Césaire himself as the opposite of primitive: as the sophisticated French intellectual confronted with simple-minded Americans. That is, the role of the African as the emblematic figure of the primitive is here assigned to African-Americans; and this identification is particularly striking in so far as the poets of the Harlem Renaissance might actually be considered to be much closer than the Martinicans to the centre of Western civilization (Johnson, for instance, was at different times both a professor at New York University and an American consul in Venezuela).

It is, in other words, hard to reconcile the Césaire promoted by Péret in issue no. 6 and the Césaire who promotes African-American poetry in issue no. 2. But an attempt to do so is made by Aristide Maugée, a fellow-teacher and also brother-in-law of Césaire, in the course of an article entitled 'Aimé Césaire, poète'. He differentiates between Césaire and the Harlem Renaissance poets: 'Poète nègre, Césaire ne l'est pas à la manière d'un Toomer, d'un Hughes, d'un Johnson dont le lyrisme est plus direct et plus simple' (5, p. 17). Césaire is more formally sophisticated, and has 'plus de variété aussi dans le rythme' (p. 18) – *but* he does not achieve this through conscious 'intellectual' experiment; his poetry is just as spontaneous: 'Ici une autre profondeur, une plus grande richesse dans la forme, expression d'un art qui *jaillit sans effort*' (p. 17, my italics). There is nothing calculated, or indeed conscious, about it; he does not 'choose' his images and sounds, rather 'la décantation se forme ici dans le creuset de l'inconscient', resulting in 'une force prodigieuse d'envoûtement' (p. 17). Césaire, in other words, succeeds in combining formal sophistication and primitive instinct, and so gives his readers the best of both worlds.

Maugée's synthesis represents the positive version of *Tropiques*' ambiguous position as Caribbeans, poised between Europe and Africa. But this position is, from other points of view, distinctly problematic. Primitivism is not merely a literary style; it presupposes a particular relation to 'real' primitive culture – which for the Martinicans primarily means traditional African culture. This relation, central to Negritude, goes beyond mere academic interest: it entails recognizing and reconnecting with the roots of one's own culture; and, given the intensively French acculturation of Martinique, for the Martinican adherents of Negritude it therefore means finding a part of oneself that has been 'lost'.[10] But Negritude was never very precise about the modalities of this relationship, and *Tropiques* reflects this vagueness.

For instance, René Hibran, a Martinican sculptor, argues in his 'Le Problème de l'art à la Martinique: une opinion' (6–7, pp. 39–41) that art in Martinique is sterile because it is split between two opposing aesthetics: 'd'un côté chez l'Européen, le sens de la réalité; de l'autre côté, chez le Noir, le sens du mystique' (p. 39). But it is the European side, he claims, that has triumphed. Hibran makes the same reference as Maugée to African-American writing, but this time the comparison does not involve an appeal to the primitive, and is straightforwardly in the Americans' favour – they have gained a universal reputation and, while this is, certainly, because they have preserved their authentic 'black' identity (p. 40), it is presented by Hibran in terms that stress a dynamic evolution rather than primitivism: 'Il a évolué dans un cadre ethnique. Il a assimilé une civilisation. Il ne s'est pas assimilé à cette civilisation' (p. 40).

The Martinicans, in contrast, have repressed the African part of themselves, and this has resulted in 'une personalité ainsi refoulée, tronquée, contredite, une impuissance à se manifester sur le plan artistique. L'Afrique se venge' (p. 40). One might have expected Hibran, therefore, in line with the tenets of Negritude and the ethnographic interests of surrealism, to have recommended a return to the primitive art of the Martinicans' African and Native American ancestors. But he states flatly that this is impossible: 'Il n'est pas possible de faire revivre l'Art Caraïbe ou l'Art Nègre, ce serait faire parler une langue morte' (p. 41). Instead, the Martinican artist should try to create a new 'local' art; and the way to do this is to 'acquérir le sens de l'ethnique et la couleur locale qui lui fait souvent complètement défaut' (p. 41). This is a commendably modest and sensible suggestion, but it is also somewhat contradictory, in that the problem is defined in psychoanalytic terms, as repression, but Hibran's proposed solution is not. He does not propose a Freudian working through of one's repression, or indeed liberating the unconscious through a surrealist recourse to 'automatic writing' – but simply a quasi-ethnographic procedure of finding out about local customs. The problem with this is that if primitive culture is to be a foundation for the Martinican intellectuals' own collective *identity* as Caribbeans, their relation to it must be in some sense *internal*, not just a question of knowledge that anyone could acquire.

Thus Ménil, for instance, makes a similar reference to the value of local folklore, but, unlike Hibran, insists on this kind of internal identificatory connection with it. He exhorts his readers to abandon European literature in order to 'find themselves' in the surrealist 'merveilleux' of local folk tales:

Nous cherchons notre vrai visage. Nous avons suffisamment condamné la littérature artificielle qui prétend nous en donner l'image [...] Narcisse martiniquais, où donc te reconnaîtras-tu? Plonge tes regards dans le miroir du merveilleux: tes contes, tes légendes, tes chants. Tu y verras s'inscrire, lumineuse, l'image sûre de toi-même. (3, p. 7)

Here, in other words, Martinican folklore is assigned the role elsewhere played by traditional Africa – the oral folk culture of Martinique, insofar as it derives from African and Carib sources, also counts as primitive, and by immersing themselves in it the writers of *Tropiques* can reconnect with their black roots.[11]

And *Tropiques* does indeed devote part of the next issue to local folklore, printing French translations of three Martinican folktales. But the attitude towards them is not in fact that of the intimate, redemptive identification that Ménil's 'tes contes, tes légendes, tes chants' implies; rather, it is remarkably similar to Césaire's presentation of black American poetry in issue no. 2. The introduction (4, pp. 7–11), written by Césaire and Ménil, expresses the same kind of distanced, patronizing praise: 'Ne sourions pas à ces naïvetés. Sous une forme de prime abord puérile, mais, en tout cas, directe, document historique d'une valeur inestimable' (p. 8). The sourcing of the three folktales is also revealing. The second two are 'Recueillis et traduits par Georges Gratiant', who was a fellow communist friend of Ménil and contributor to *Tropiques*, but the first one is taken from the collection of Lafcadio Hearn, the nineteenth-century half-Greek, half-Irish traveller whose collections of Martinican folktales, written in English, were translated into French in 1932, and whose descriptions of them Césaire and Ménil quote several times in their introduction.[12] This strongly suggests that, as Hibran indeed pointed out, they have no first-hand knowledge of them, but are forced to depend to a significant extent on a nineteenth-century European traveller and amateur folklorist. As James Arnold comments: 'The Martinican proponents of Negritude were educated in the humanist mold of metropolitan France and were effectively cut off from direct participation in what remained of the folkloric tradition' (*Modernism and Negritude*, pp. 72–73); and overall, there is little sense of them 'recognizing' their true identity in their native folklore, as Ménil had been urging them to do.

But the difficult question of how far they can rely on external, largely European, sources of information about primitive cultures while still claiming that these form an essential part of their own identity as Caribbeans, becomes even more acute when the primitive culture is defined as *African*, since here they are even more reliant on information supplied by European ethnographers.[13] For *Tropiques*, 'Africa' is the most prominent and unambiguous example of primitivity; but if they are obliged, so to speak, to go through Europe to find Africa, can they claim to be closer to it than the Europeans?[14] Whereas on one level ethnography is just one aspect of the surrealist movement that they adopt along with the aesthetic valorization of *l'art nègre*, it also implies, for them, a rather complex relationship between *self-knowledge* and *knowledge of the Other* – the latter in two senses: both in that ethnography defines the object of its knowledge as essentially 'other', and in that the knowledge it produces, since ethnographers in the 1940s at least were overwhelmingly European, is, from the point of view of Caribbeans, the Other's knowledge. This tension is visible in their attitude towards the late-Romantic German ethnographer Leo Viktor Frobenius, whose work had already had a significant influence on Césaire before the war, and who is the subject of an article by Suzanne Césaire in *Tropiques*' first issue ('Léo Frobenius et le problème des civilisations', 1, pp. 27–36) and also a major reference point in her 'Malaise d'une civilisation' (5, pp. 43–49).[15] This issue also contains an extract from Frobenius' *Histoire de la civilisation africaine* published in French in 1933, entitled 'Que signifie pour nous l'Afrique?' (5, pp. 62–70), and prefaced by a paragraph by Aimé Césaire and Ménil. This short introduction starts by claiming that despite their European education they have, and must recognize and celebrate, a privileged *biological* relationship to Africa:

> il coule dans nos veines un sang qui exige de nous une attitude originale en face de la vie [...] nous devons répondre, le poète plus que tout autre, à la dynamique spéciale de notre complexe réalité biologique. En remontant l'une de nos lignes de force nous rencontrons, cette chose immense, l'Afrique. (5, p. 62)

Africa itself, moreover, is characterized in primitivist terms as 'l'Afrique et son noble abandon à la vie, au mépris des savants brigandages industriels'. But what is most significant is that even here they are conscious of the necessary mediation of this relationship through a European ethnographer, and the tone of their conclusion is extremely defensive:

> Notre tâche n'est-il pas d'atteindre notre humanité totale? Nous ne pouvons l'atteindre, croyons-nous, – que les imbéciles et les lâches n'entendent ici aucune concession de notre part – que par l'expression, *grâce aux précieuses techniques européennes*, de tout ce que notre négritude comporte d'exigences. (p. 62, my italics)

Another important figure for *Tropiques* in this respect was the

Cuban painter Wifredo Lam, of mixed Chinese, African and Spanish parentage. Arriving in Paris in 1938 after studying art in Madrid, Lam became a protégé of Picasso, who introduced him to the art dealer Pierre Loeb, and to the Parisian surrealists. Lam also became a close friend of Césaire, with whom he shared both immersion in high European culture and the desire to reintegrate the African part of his identity in his work.[16] For Picasso and Loeb, Lam's paintings were valuable to the extent that they were primivitist; Picasso's interest in Lam coincided with his own experimentation with incorporating the aesthetics of traditional African sculpture in his work, and Loeb, in a piece reprinted in *Tropiques*, places Lam squarely in the context of the various primitive artefacts that he has already collected: 'Votre art n'était pas nouveau pour moi, cependant, je l'attendais. Depuis longtemps, je vivais entouré de scuptures pahouins, de crânes ornementés de masques de la Côte d'Ivoire [...] de fétiches désolés de l'île de Pâques' (6–7, p. 61). René Ménil, however, argues that Lam's development of a style of painting that rejected European conventions was the very opposite of an unmediated expression of primitive sensibility:

> Assurément, la nouveauté qu'apporte aux hommes son célèbre tableau *La Jungle* [...] est non pas une donnée 'naïve' ou 'naturelle' ou 'spontanée' de sa sensibilité, mais le résultat de réflexions sur les cultures et les civilisations, d'interrogations passionnées sur la 'cosa negra' [...] et peut-être, surtout, de la pratique successive de différents styles d'expression en relation et en contradiction avec les plus grands peintres de l'Occident. ('Pour une lecture critique de *Tropiques*', p. xxix)

A more detailed account of Lam's trajectory, which to some extent reconciles these two opposing views, is given in the French surrealist Pierre Mabille's article on Lam in issue no. 12 (pp. 173–87) of *Tropiques*. When Lam first came to Madrid, Mabille says, he modelled himself conscientiously on the great works of the European tradition; but the deaths of his wife and child precipitated a personal crisis which led to him rejecting his previous work in favour of 'sa realité ancestrale qu'il n'a pas à cacher ou à trahir, qui ne comporte aucune infériorité. Il commence à s'intéresser, de façon d'ailleurs imprécise, à ce qu'il appelle "la cosa negra"' (p. 178). Moreover, this reconnection with his 'ancestral reality' could not have happened had he stayed in Cuba: Lam had to go from Cuba to Madrid in order to see the *art nègre* that would influence his painting (p. 179); and this, Mabille states quite unambiguously, is the situation of all Caribbeans: 'Pour lui comme pour tous les Antillais de couleur, c'est par l'intermédiaire des ethnologues et collectionneurs européens que le contact peut être repris avec l'art ancestral dont d'autres européens les ont brutalement séparés' (p. 179). But this does not, Mabille implies, mean that the Caribbeans' relationship to primitive African art is simply the same as that of their European counterparts. He describes the crucial meeting between Lam and Picasso in 1938 in these terms:

> Le Maître, dans la force de son génie et de sa gloire, encore puissamment marqué par la révélation déclenchée jadis dans sa sensibilité par l'art nègre, voyait se dresser devant lui un noir qui avait connu les valeurs occidentales, s'en était imprégné mais qui, loin d'avoir été absorbé par l'Europe, avait peu à peu repris conscience de sa personne et de ses moyens propres: un homme qui était arrivé a des formes exactement semblables à celles qu'il avait exprimées par un chemin exactement inverse du sien. (p. 183)

That is, Picasso moved away from his own culture towards *art nègre*, whereas for Lam its discovery was a kind of cultural homecoming that enabled him to become conscious of his own authentic creativity. A similar point is made by Madeleine Rousseau in an article in *Présence africaine* in 1948. She describes how Lam would come to her apartment in Paris to look at her African sculptures (and says that he took some of them home with him when he went back to Cuba in 1947): 'Il est certain que Lam, au contact de ces œuvres, ressentit une violente émotion. Il s'attardait devant elles, avec une attention passionnée: "Voyez, me dit-il un jour brusquement, j'ai spontanément retrouvé ces formes! Elles ont ressurgi en moi comme une réminiscence ancestrale!"'[17] Lam is thus claiming to have achieved a position similar to that which Césaire and Ménil, in their introduction to Frobenius in issue 5 of *Tropiques*, cited above, articulated rather in terms of a necessary demand or task.

A possible solution, in other words, to the dilemma of Caribbean writers and artists whose claims to a 'naturally' primitive sensibility might be thought to be vitiated by the fact that they can only access it through European ethnography is provided by the argument that they do indeed need the Europeans to provide them with access to the primitive, but that this initial contact, once made, enables them to recognize *within themselves* some authentic response to it that Europeans by definition cannot have. But the problem is that it is by its very nature largely unverifiable. One can only conclude, therefore, that *Tropiques'* engagement with primitivism is not only often very ambivalent, in that the editors or contributors often seem reluctant to renounce a literary and intellectual sophistication that they associate with Europe, but that even when they do whole-heartedly lay claim to the 'special relationship' with the primitive that has been the central issue of this chapter, it turns out to be extremely difficult to provide any convincing evidence for it.

## 2

# Problems of Cultural Self-Representation

## René Ménil, Patrick Chamoiseau and Raphaël Confiant

In 1959 René Ménil published a short article entitled 'De l'exotisme colonial', in which he claimed that Antillean writers and artists practised an 'abnormal' type of exoticism applied to their *own* society: 'que l'Antillais a de lui-même une vision exotique et qu'il propose de lui-même une expression exotique' (p. 21).[1] Seeing oneself through the eyes of the metropolitan Other results in superficial, picturesque self-representations; and it is a kind of bad faith or 'tricherie': evoking aspects of one's life as though they were 'strange' and as though they belong to 'des "pays lointains"' implies that one is cheating the metropolitan reader, 'puisque le propre pays de l'artiste colonial n'est *ni lointain ni étrange pour lui*' (p. 24, italics original).

It is a form of the all-pervasive colonial alienation that Fanon had analysed seven years earlier in his *Peau noire, masques blancs*. Ménil calls it the 'exotique-pour-moi' complex, and explains it as follows:

> La condition d'une telle aberration n'est pas autre chose que la situation coloniale [...] Je me vois étranger, je me vois exotique, pourquoi? Parce que 'je', c'est la conscience, 'l'autre', c'est moi. Je suis 'exotique-pour-moi', parce que mon regard sur moi c'est le regard du blanc devenu mien après trois siècles de conditionnement colonial. (p. 21)

This phenomenon, in other words, is not so much a literary genre that a writer might or might not choose to adopt, as it is a kind of social-psychological *perversion* – which I am therefore going to designate as *auto-exoticism*. As such, it is not limited to a fixed set of topics or literary styles, but is rather 'un ensemble de déterminations actives et multiples (psychologiques et sociales) tel que, même quand le poète est prémuni contre lui, il n'est pas rare qu'évitant tel ou tel de ses aspects, il tombe cependant dans l'une ou l'autre de ses formes insidieuses' (p. 23).

This implies both that auto-exoticism is an almost inevitable and universal consequence of colonial alienation – indeed, Ménil claims that it will be overcome only by the overthrow of colonialism itself[2] – and also that its literary manifestations are constantly evolving. In this he anticipates more recent definitions of exoticism in general, which have tended to move away from the taxonomic conception exemplified by Régis Antoine, for instance – whose chapter on 'L'exotisme antillais' is divided up into 'Le cadre naturel' (jungle foliage, mountains) and 'Les populations' (the Carib, the 'belle mulâtresse')[3] – and towards an emphasis on exoticism's unpredictability: as Roger Toumson puts it, 'Imprévisible, toujours inattendu, [le discours exotique] s'est prêté [...] depuis la Renaissance jusqu'à nos jours, à des variations déroutantes, inlassablement diversifiées, transformant son thème, l'ornant, quoique sans jamais le rendre méconnaissable'.[4] Auto-exoticism is a *trap*, Ménil implies, that cannot be avoided simply by steering clear of a checklist of traditional stereotypes. Thus Raphaël Confiant's complaint, for instance, that it is no longer possible for an Antillean author to write about palm trees and beaches may be true, but it does not engage with the problem as a whole.[5] Although the history of Antillean literature is, according to Ménil, that of a constant struggle to move away from it, exoticism – 'phénix qui renaît éternellement de ses cendres' ('L'exotisme colonial', p. 22) – always reappears in new forms.

Auto-exoticism, then, is not a conscious choice, but an alienated discourse in which Antillean writers represent themselves and their community from the point of view of the metropolitan Other, without intending to do so and even without being aware that they are doing so. Indeed, it infiltrates even the work of writers who are consciously opposing it.[6] The final part of Ménil's article is devoted to a critique of the literature of Negritude, which he defines as 'l'exotisme contre-exotique' (p. 24). He argues that writers such as Léopold Senghor in fact fail to challenge traditional colonial negative stereotypes of blackness, because they simply reverse the values attached to them, rather than replacing them with new representations:

> Reprendre à notre compte l'image de nous qui résulte de la culture coloniale pour simplement y mettre des couleurs et des qualités opposées

est une erreur. Le fait est que si nous ne sommes pas ce qu'il plaît au Blanc, dans le délire colonial, de penser de nous, nous ne sommes pas davantage le contraire de l'idée qu'il se fait de nous. Nous ne sommes pas 'les opposés' de notre image coloniale, nous sommes *autres* que cette image. (pp. 25–26, italics original)

Thus, while the social-psychological determinants of auto-exoticism are quite clear, its literary manifestations are extremely fluid. Ménil's materialist view of it as an inescapable consequence of colonialism means that it is difficult to pin down exactly what *literary* qualities make a text auto-exotic. And, therefore, it requires an equally fluid conception of exoticism in general. What is it, in other words, that would allow us to determine whether or not a particular text is representing Antillean culture as though through the eyes of an outsider? There has in recent years been a considerable amount of debate on the nature and status of exoticism in general,[7] and it would be impossible to propose a precise and universally accepted definition of it. But certain general character-istics can nevertheless be assumed to feature in most exotic texts. It is an *essentialist* representation of geographical and/or ethnic otherness, in the sense that the otherness is seen as a fundamental, fixed value which cannot accommodate change and whose purity is uncompromised by hybridity or social interaction. It is usually contrasted with *realism*: it appeals to the escapist fantasies of the metropolitan reader; therefore the alien culture is not explicitly denigrated, but presented as attractive (it can arouse fear in the reader, but in the positive sense of awe, or the thrill of an adventure story). A major element of its attraction and escapism lies in its *nostalgic* perspective: looking back to a vanishing world in danger of being destroyed by Western civilization. Finally, it *objectifies* its characters, emphasizing their appearance and activities rather than their thoughts and emotions; in the case of female characters, this above all means presenting them as objects of sexual desire: another major feature of the attractiveness of exotic representations is the ubiquity of desirable and available women.

Exotic representations of the Antilles display most of these charac-teristics, but are also different in significant ways from the exoticism of Asia, Africa or Oceania. The Antilles were among France's earliest colonies, and were from the start a favourite site for exotic writing,[8] but this long period of colonization created in metropolitan readers a feeling of familiarity with the islands which results in far less emphasis, in these texts, on a sense of confrontation with the radical otherness of the totally unknown. Martinique, in particular, became French before either Nice or Savoie, as one of the characters in Confiant's *Le Nègre et l'amiral* proudly points out.[9] Indeed, the island is often referred to as 'la fille aînée de la France': a familiar, then, but also a quasi-*familial* relationship, producing a distinctively 'tame' exoticism.[10] As Antoine puts it:

> on ne repère pas alors cette identité vacillante de l'exote, cette tension vers une autre chose qui se dérobait, cette visée d'un espace inconnu [...] le regard exotique aux Antilles françaises s'est moins nourri de contrastes brutaux que d'une réalité doucement variée [...] Sur le plan humain, ce n'est pas tant l'Antillais dans son 'étrangeté', mais le rapport qu'on entretient avec lui qui a constitué l'axe et le va-et-vient des textes [...] De là, bien visible dans l'écriture, une suite d'effets légèrement contrastés de surprises et de reconnaissances. (*Littérature franco-antillaise*, pp. 331–32)

As well as the islands' much earlier colonization compared to other French colonies, another factor is the absence of any sustained resistance to the settlers on the part of the indigenous Caribs. There was no equivalent to the North American mythology of cowboys and Indians or the confrontations between Native American chiefs and the United States army. In other words, the Antilles were almost never *frightening*. Antoine points out that while in very early exotic texts the Caribs were shown as 'traîtres, horribles, sanglants', later the emphasis was on their dying out (pp. 342–43). But his other ethnic stereotype, the 'belle mulâtresse', continues to dominate the exotic literature of the Antilles, and indeed to encapsulate its particular status: the woman whose seductiveness derives from her being of mixed race rather than completely other. Half black and half white, her whole being holds out the promise that white men can have sex with black women; but in addition to this, she presents the perfect amalgam of the comfortingly familiar and the excitingly, but not challengingly, different.[11]

This relative, ambiguous familiarity of the Antillean exotic cuts both ways: it also means that Antillean writers have a very clear idea of how they are represented in metropolitan exotic texts. Elsewhere in *Antilles déjà jadis*, Ménil quotes Jorge Luis Borges' response to someone who remarked with surprise that there are no camels in the Koran: 'Mahomet en tant qu'arabe n'avait aucune raison de savoir que les chameaux étaient spécialement arabes' (p. 275). But if Arabs had no way of knowing that camels, in Western eyes, were typically Arabic, Martinicans, in contrast, know exactly what is typically Martinican.[12] If they did not, of course, they would not be in a position to write auto-exotic texts; but as well as facilitating the internalization of metropolitan exotic stereotypes, their sophisticated awareness of the latter also in theory helps them to be on their guard against them – and in practice at least enables them to criticize their fellow writers for failing to be so vigilant. A major target of such criticism in recent years has been the novelists of the *créolité* movement, Patrick Chamoiseau and Raphaël Confiant, ever since they became extremely popular and prolific in France in the 1990s.[13]

Among these critics is Ménil, who, while his 'De l'exotisme colonial' focused mainly on Negritude, makes very similar judgements on the *créolité* writers in several of the later essays in *Antilles déjà jadis*. *Créolité*, he argues, is simply a given fact of existence, and so to propose it as a goal or an ideal is pointless and narcissistic: 'Content de soi devant le miroir, c'est bien vite l'applaudissement à son propre pittoresque' (p. 239). Equally, it is a 'philosophie des racines' which looks back to the past and precludes any possibility of dynamism or change (p. 242). Rather than the inauguration of an 'audaciously' new conception of collective subjectivity, it is just the symptomatic reaction of 'une conscience colonisée qui se dégage difficilement, quoi qu'elle dise, de l'emprise coloniale et a du mal à s'autonomiser' (p. 244).

More specifically, he criticizes their appeal to *folklore* in order to 'authenticate' their status as Creole writers despite writing in French, equating this 'dérapage dans le folklorisme' with an 'exotisme paresseux' (p. 275). This leads him into a more general discussion of the place of folklore in literature, which is significantly different from his earlier more straightforward promotion of folklore in the pages of *Tropiques* – to which I have referred in chapter 1 – as a means for Martinican intellectuals to reconnect with the culture of the people. He still believes that this is a valid and praiseworthy project (p. 276), but no longer recommends simply importing folktales, for instance, directly into the literary text. Folklore is an 'object' which must be analysed and integrated into the 'human drama' of the novel (p. 279) rather than merely reproduced for its own sake. He gives a scathing characterization of the *créolité* novels as 'une manière d'inventaire ethnologique tantôt culinaire, tantôt agricole et jardinière, tantôt zoologique avec des colibris et des papillons', which reduces literary language to 'une pédagogie à l'usage des touristes ou bien, dans le meilleur des cas [...] une défense politique de notre identité culturelle' (p. 279).[14] The mistake, he adds, is to 'raconter le folklore de façon folklorique' (p. 279). The crucial distinction is between 'folklore' and 'folklorisme'; what is needed is 'une démarche analytique et dialectique capable de montrer comment, tout en évitant le folklorisme, on peut exprimer le folklore qui est la vie même concrètement perçue dans ses rythmes et la modulation de ses formes' (p. 279).


The rest of this chapter will consider the extent to which the writings of the *créolité* movement could be said to suffer from auto-exoticism. I will look first at the manifesto that brought it to the attention of the French public in 1989 – *Éloge de la créolité*, co-authored by the novelists Chamoiseau and Confiant and the sociolinguist Jean Bernabé – and then at two novels published in the preceding year: Chamoiseau's *Solibo magnifique* and Confiant's *Le Nègre et l'amiral*.

*Éloge de la créolité*, as its title and opening words – 'Ni Européens, ni Africains, ni Asiatiques, nous nous proclamons Créoles' (p. 13) – make clear, is a proud statement of multi-ethnic Creole identity. But it is also a literary manifesto, and as such it takes as its starting point an analysis of Martinican literature that is almost identical to that of Ménil's 'De l'exotisme colonial': 'Nous avons vu le monde à travers le filtre des valeurs occidentales, et notre fondement s'est trouvé "exotisé" par la vision française que nous avons dû adopter' (p. 14). Subject to 'le regard de l'Autre', they have produced 'une écriture pour l'Autre, une écriture empruntée, ancrée dans les valeurs françaises' (p. 14). Unlike Ménil's materialist analysis, however – and also unlike Condé, who sees the necessity of publication in metropolitan France as a major obstacle[15] – they believe that Antillean writing can be transformed solely through a conscious effort of subjective self-liberation. Therefore, the project presented in the *Éloge* consists in eliminating the 'regard de l'Autre' in order to rediscover their own, specifically Creole, vision of themselves and the world. Their alienation is conceived in spatial terms as an opposition between 'outside' and 'inside': from being 'fondamen-talement frappé d'extériorité' (p. 14), they have to work towards 'la vision intérieure' (p. 15). But this is also seen as a temporal progression in which the 'internal' will gradually replace the 'external': more recent novels, such as Glissant's *Malemort* and Frankétienne's *Dézafi*, have shown younger generations that 'l'outil premier de cette démarche de se connaître' is '*la vision intérieure*' (p. 23, italics original), as against 'la vieille fatalité de l'extériorité' (p. 23).

Despite the priority given to interiority, however, they make it clear that they are writing also for an international audience: a section whose title is a quotation from Glissant's *Le Discours antillais*, 'L'irruption dans la modernité' (*Éloge*, pp. 42–43) stresses the importance of writing in a style which keeps up with international modernism: 'Comment se préoccuper d'une expression artistique qui, efficace à l'intérieur de la nation, se révèlerait anachronique ou dépassée une fois pointée à l'extérieur?' (p. 43). Thus it is a question of writing texts that will reveal their authenticity both to themselves and their fellow Antilleans, and to the metropolitan readership that is certainly at least statistically dominant.[16]

A major factor in the alienation of previous Antillean literature, they argue, was its lack of any contact with the spoken language of the islands – in other words, Creole (*Éloge*, p. 35). The centrality of the Creole language to the culture as a whole, and therefore to their identity, is emphasized at length (e.g., pp. 34–35). As an almost wholly spoken language, Creole is closely linked with oral culture and above all the Creole folktale. Thus the opposition between Creole orality and French writing is seen as one of the most urgent problems facing a new Antillean literature.[17] The solution, they claim, is to find ways of integrating Creole oral speech and culture into the written French of their novels; and this – contrary to Ménil's strictures against 'raconter le folklore de façon folklorique' – need not be 'un mode passéiste de nostalgique stagnation' (*Éloge*, p. 36), but a means of enriching and refreshing their literary expression (p. 37), and even creating a whole new literature: 'Bref, *nous fabriquerons une littérature* qui ne déroge en rien aux exigences modernes de l'écrit tout en s'enracinant dans les configurations traditionnelles de notre oralité' (p. 37, italics original).[18] But what is arguably more important for them is that the literary use of Creole re-establishes the continuity that founds their collective identity and helps to guarantee their authenticity.

*Authenticity* is in fact a key term throughout *Éloge*: 'la nervure centrale de notre authenticité' (p. 23), 'les conditions d'une expression authentique' (p. 23), etc. The main thrust of the manifesto is that they must reject the alienated view of themselves in order to rediscover their true reality – in a gesture of purification, 'nous laver les yeux: retourner la vision que nous avions de notre réalité pour en surprendre le vrai' (pp. 23–24). This reliance on an unproblematic concept of authenticity betrays a certain intellectual naivety; however, the basic claim that they are better placed to display the reality of Antillean culture than metropolitan outsiders is perfectly credible, and would seem to imply that they are *not* adopting the Other's gaze in the way that earlier auto-exotic Antillean writers did. But their critique of these writers runs together 'le regard de l'Autre' and 'une écriture pour l'Autre (p. 14) as though the two were exactly synonymous, whereas in fact there is a crucial difference between them. The difference between the earlier writers and those of the *créolité* movement, in other words, may be that while they are not writing *as* outsiders to their own culture, they are writing *for* such outsiders. Their 'authenticity' is therefore limited by the demands that this places on them: while their representations may be more accurate and detailed, less superficial, they are still – in their choice of subject matter and the way in which it is presented – determined by the aim of pleasing the metropolitan reader.[19]

This readership, moreover, has come to accord increasing importance to authenticity. The exotic literature of the nineteenth and early twentieth centuries was not greatly concerned with it, but its contemporary versions are. There is an exact parallel here between tourism and literature: just as tourist advertisements now invite us to 'Découvrez la vraie Martinique', so the quotation from a review in *Le Figaro Magazine* reproduced on the back of *Le Nègre et l'amiral* praises it for offering 'la vraie Martinique' to its French readers. The novel, like the island, is there to be 'discovered': 'Comme je voudrais vous convaincre de découvrir ce livre et de l'aimer!' Authenticity, in other words, has become a commodity; and once this is the case, the difference between conventionally exotic and authentic representations of the culture for outsiders is not so much an opposition as a relative difference in the value of the product. The more authentic it appears, the more sophisticated is its exoticism. Condé points to precisely this commodification of authenticity when in 1995 she writes of Chamoiseau and Confiant that: 'Paradoxalement, pour se convaincre de "l'authenticité" de l'image de leur pays natal contenue dans leurs écrits, ils s'enorgueillissent de faire recette dans les milieux littéraires de l'Hexagone, toujours à la recherche de nouveaux exotismes'.[20] Therefore, while it is true that the *créolité* writers are not alienated in the Fanonian sense of internalizing the metropolitan Other's negative view of their culture, they do – as I shall try to show – suffer from the different type of alienation upon which all tourist economies are based, which consists in exploiting their status as 'insiders' to serve up an attractive and authentic – attractively authentic – version of their culture for the pleasure of outsiders.[21]

*Créolité* is seen in *Éloge* as the third and final stage in the process of moving away from 'le regard de l'Autre' and rediscovering an authentic identity. The first stage was Negritude, and here again they follow the trajectory of Ménil's 'De l'exotisme colonial'. But the reason they give for the inadequacy of the Negritude movement is different from his: for them, it lies in Negritude's attachment to Africa, which, they argue, is ultimately as alienating as the imitation of metropolitan exotic literature. Both Europe and Africa are 'external': 'l'Européanité et l'Africanité, toutes extériorités procédant de deux logiques adverses' (p. 18). Thus although Negritude was a necessary first step, and far less damaging to black identity than the imitation of Europe, it remains an 'illusion': 'Thérapeutique violente et paradoxale, la Négritude fit, à celle d'Europe, succéder l'illusion africaine' (p. 20).

The authors of *Éloge*, therefore, do not reiterate Ménil's critique of Negritude, that it does nothing more than mechanically reverse the values attributed to the stereotypical image of black people, while leaving the image itself intact (so, for example, black people are still seen as emotional rather than rational, but that is now an asset rather than a disadvantage). This is significant, because one could argue that *Éloge*'s own revalorization of Creole culture is open to the same criticism. It is, of course, a programme for fighting back against colonial alienation. The text as a whole is dedicated to the project of rescuing *créolité* from its entrapment in the metropolitan Other's view of it. But the actual content of that 'external vision' is, in *Éloge*'s account, rather simplistically negative, in so far as it is always a question of Creole culture being 'denigrated' by the metropolitan French: for example, 'La francisation nous a forcés à l'auto-dénigrement' (p. 24), 'la vieille carapace du dénigrement de nous-mêmes' (p. 41). The Antillean people and their popular culture are considered 'vulgar' by metropolitan literature (p. 40); *Éloge* does not criticize that literature or, more broadly, that sensibility for representing them as picturesque, or charmingly nostalgic, or as seductive commodities packaged for the pleasure of metropolitan audiences. And yet, to the extent that exotic literature is an aesthetic commodity, these types of representation are far more typical of it than is 'denigration'.[22]

As a result, *Éloge*'s strategy for countering 'le regard de l'Autre' is simply to give a positive value to all the most typical features of Creole life – which, as they list them, replicate many of the favourite *topoi* of exotic literature: vegetable markets, folktales, multi-ethnic origins, cockfights, games of dice, magic beliefs and practices, folk music and cuisine (pp. 40–41).[23] And this programme of rehabilitation consists simply in stressing that all these things are 'beautiful': 'Nous voulons, en vraie créolité, y nommer chaque chose et dire qu'elle est belle' (p. 40). Indeed, establishing their beauty is ultimately a more important goal than analysing the alienation of the people: 'Notre vision intérieure exercée, notre créolité mise comme centre de créativité, nous permet de réexaminer notre existence, d'y voir les mécanismes d'aliénation, d'en percevoir *surtout* les beautés' (p. 39, my italics). One could well argue, therefore, that in limiting themselves to 'positivizing'[24] the pre-existing stereotypes of Creole culture, the authors of *Éloge* are repeating exactly the same inadequate gesture that Ménil attributes to Negritude. Their strategy does nothing to challenge the folkloristic stereotypes that are in fact staples of exotic representations of the Antilles, and to that extent they are, at least in this text, unable to move beyond auto-exoticism.

*Solibo magnifique* revolves around the mysterious death of the 'conteur' Solibo, one of the last surviving tellers of folktales; the police assume he has been murdered but in fact he has been magically killed by an 'égorgette de la parole' – that is, he has been strangled by the fact that very few people now listen to his words. The tone of the novel thus combines the comedy of police ineptitude with the tragedy of the disappearance of traditional oral culture (and moves from comic to tragic as police brutality results in one of the suspects, Congo, committing suicide by throwing himself out of the window of the police station).

The treatment of time in the novel is exactly that of exoticism: the modernization of Martinique consists in the imposition of metropolitan French economic and social practices on traditional Creole society. Modernity is equated with the Europeanization of a once distinctive culture.[25] While middle-class Martinicans have successfully adapted to this, the poor of Fort-de-France are disorientated and disenfranchised; even their sense of time, which was based on the rhythms of their daily work, has become confused as they are now unemployed (pp. 145–46). Congo, for instance, is now reduced to a 'silhouette anachronique, courbée sous un sac de guano, qui longeait les vitrines et les embouteillages' and 'symbolisa vainement ces époques durant lesquelles nous avions été autres mais dont chacun se détournait' (p. 204). But the central focus of this nostalgic perspective is the storyteller, whose death symbolizes the death of folklore and hence, in Chamoiseau's view, of Creole culture as a whole: 'En mourant, Solibo nous a plongés là où il n'y a plus de parole qui vaille, plus de sens à rien' (p. 155). Significantly, only the traditional *quimboiseur* understands how and why he has died (pp. 218–19); after talking to him the police eventually acknowledge the futility of their investigation, and the novel ends on a powerfully elegiac note with their realization 'que cet homme était la vibration d'un monde finissant, pleine de douleur, qui n'aura pour réceptacle que les vents et les mémoires indifférentes, et dont tout cela n'avait bordé que la simple onde du souffle ultime' (p. 227).

The figure of Solibo also provides the basis for Chamoiseau's glorification of the folktale and the traditional storyteller. The novel includes many evocations of the eloquence and mastery of Solibo's speech. But it also insists that his power does not reside in the bare words alone, so that reproducing them in writing (as Chamoiseau does in the appendix entitled 'Dits de Solibo' at the end of the text) is only an impoverished substitute for a living performance irretrievably lost with the death of its performer; thus one of the witnesses describes to the police how 'C'est une question d'oreille, inspectère, la parole du conteur, c'est le son de sa gorge, mais c'est aussi sa sueur, les roulades de ses yeux, son ventre, les dessins de ses mains, son odeur, celle de la compagnie, le son du ka et tous les silences' (pp. 147–48).

Solibo's fidelity to the dying tradition of the 'conteurs' also means that he refuses the attempts to reify him as a cultural artefact which would have helped him to survive in modern Martinique (pp. 222–23); as Maeve McCusker points out, 'the storyteller-hero has resisted recuperation by the commodifying forces of official memory-making: he operates outside the decrees of the "autorité folklorique" and the "action culturelle"' (*Patrick Chamoiseau*, p. 80). This critique of the presentation of folklore as an exotic object for the consumption of outsiders allows Chamoiseau to distance his own novel from any such practices (as does the ironic incident in which a crowd of tourists assume, wrongly, that Congo has dressed up in historical costume for their amusement, p. 205); but in fact it does nothing to exclude the possibility that he himself is representing Solibo and Congo in a more sophisticated – that is, 'authentic' – but still exotic fashion. Indeed, it may even draw attention to this possibility, as McCusker goes on to argue: 'Inevitably, these explicit references to the production and corruption of memory cannot fail to raise questions around Chamoiseau's own implication in the very practices which he is critiquing' (p. 81).

In keeping with the stress in *Éloge de la créolité* on the mixed nature of Creole society, the characters in *Solibo magnifique* cover a number of different ethnicities. The group of witnesses/suspects includes a 'Syrian' (as all those of Middle Eastern origin are termed in Martinique and Guadeloupe), an Indian and a Columbian prostitute, as well as those of African slave descent; Congo differs from the others in that he is descended from the group of Africans who were brought to Martinique after the abolition of slavery; and La Fièvre is 'à l'interstice de quatorze métissages' (p. 155). There is, however, no discussion or comment in the text on the multi-ethnic nature of this community; it is taken for granted, seen neither as a problem nor an enrichment of collective life.[26] In particular, there are no examples of the cultural *change through exchange* that is the basis of the anthropological concept of creolization: of, for example, Indian cultural practices spreading to the rest of the community (and this reflects the social reality of Martinique, which is in this sense not as typically Creole as *Éloge* claims).

In contrast, the clash between this homogenized Creole culture and the norms of French society is the central theme of the novel. Thus Inspector Pilon tries, and fails, to impose a Cartesian rationalist approach on his investigation:

> l'inspecteur principal n'appréciait guère le côté irrationnel des 'affaires' d'ici-là [...] comme l'inspecteur, malgré son long séjour au pays de Descartes, avait levé ici-dans comme nous-mêmes dans la même intelligence de zombis et de soucougnans divers, ses efforts scientifiques et de logique glaciale dérapaient bien souvent. (pp. 117–18)

Although 'ici-dans' and 'nous-mêmes' refer here to Martinique and the Martinicans, for the French reader the effect of the opposition of the two cultures is to reinforce the otherness of the Creole side. The ineffectiveness of the rational approach to police work is echoed in sarcastic allusions to Western social scientific knowledge, implying that only the insider's intuitive understanding of Creole culture has any validity: anthropology ('le douteux Malinowski, Morgan, Radcliffe-Brown', p. 44); psychology ('le psychologue scolaire [...] passa le restant de son séjour à bâtir des passerelles théoriques au-dessus des impasses du complexe d'Œdipe', pp. 54–55) and sociolinguistics ('Solibo Magnifique utilisait les quatre facettes de notre diglossie: le basilecte et l'acrolecte créole, le basilecte et l'acrolecte français, vibrionnant enracinement dans un espace interlectal que je pensais être notre plus exacte réalité sociolinguistique', p. 45).

As this last quotation suggests, one major dimension of the conflict between French and Creole cultures is linguistic, and in its treatment of this theme the novel puts into practice the project expressed in *Éloge de la créolité* both to revalorize the Creole language and to integrate it into literary texts written in French. The superiority of Creole (or the creolized French known as 'français banane') is shown to lie in its inventiveness and creativity – not just in the speech of the storyteller, but more broadly, in the nicknames given to some of the characters, for instance: Doudou-Ménar, Diab-Anba-Feuilles and Nono Bec-en-Or (p. 87); Chamoiseau even rechristens himself 'Oiseau de Cham' and 'Ti-Zibié' (pp. 75–76). It is also life-giving and restorative;[27] the Creole speech of the market women has the power to rescue Solibo from his period of depression: 'Ô paroles de survie, paroles de débrouillarde, paroles où le charbon du désespoir se voyait terrassé par de minuscules flammes, paroles de résistance, toutes ces qualités de paroles que les esclaves avaient forgées aux chaleurs des veillées afin d'accorer l'effondrement du ciel' (p. 78).

This leads to a valorization of oral over written narrative, summed up in the relation between Solibo as 'Maître de la parole créole' and Chamoiseau as he appears as a character in his novel trying to capture these spoken words in writing. Solibo is scornful of these attempts (p. 52), and Chamoiseau himself laments the impossibility of his project – but decides that it is worth preserving even a very inadequate record of this endangered oral culture. The novel contains many long passages of distinctively oral narration by the characters, both in their interrogation by the police and in the memories of Solibo's life that they recount to each other, and the narrator carefully notes the different varieties of Creole that they use (pp. 72, 74, 80). Positioning himself as a 'marqueur de paroles' recording the speech of others, rather than the author of a work of fiction, is a further way in which Chamoiseau gives his text greater authenticity. So too is his role as a character, one of the group of witnesses interrogated by the police – a participant rather than a spectator in the drama. Thus although he cannot do Solibo justice – 'J'aurais voulu pour lui d'une parole à sa mesure [...]' – he can bear witness to his life and death, and in doing so he invokes an equivalent to the face-to-face immediacy of the story-telling situation: '[...] Frappé d'un blanc à l'âme, il ne me reste plus qu'à en témoigner, dressé là parmi vous' (p. 27).

His own narrative also adopts some of the stylistic features of the storyteller: direct address to the audience, for instance ('O amis, qui est à l'aise par-ici quand la police est là?', p. 83), and a colloquial, oral style ('Le car de la Loi approche du tamarinier. Vlap-vlap! La portière avant droite et les deux de l'arrière s'ouvrent au vol', p. 83), but he does not use this style consistently. In fact, his narration moves with great agility between a number of different registers: it is a self-conscious and highly wrought linguistic construction, and as such is completely at odds with his declared status as merely a humble 'marqueur de paroles'. It does, however, demonstrate the extent to which Chamoiseau fulfils the ambition set out in *Éloge de la créolité* to create a new literary language that will be sophisticated and modern, 'tout en s'enracinant dans les configurations traditionnelles de notre oralité' (*Éloge*, p. 37). Allusions to other highly literary writers – 'Tout semblait en désastre Césairien, étonnements et douleurs réveillaient la Savane' (p. 38) – assume a well-educated readership rather than a storyteller's audience. The mock-heroic description of the fight between Doudou-Ménar and the police (pp. 50–52) is a very skilful comic set piece; and, more generally, the text frequently mixes its down-to-earth, colloquial narration with ironically high-flown literary formulations: 'La scène s'éternisa ainsi – et aurait pu s'éterniser encore: un auditoire tafiaté [that is, drunk on cheap rum], assis en rond dans un petit matin, ne s'inscrit pas dans l'éphémère' (p. 37); 'La réalité s'imposa pour certains avant même d'être clairement formulée: ils s'enfuyaient [...] tant il est notoire qu'avec un mort la loi s'en mêle, et qu'alors-hector ta vie devient une manière de la danse haute-taille' (p. 39).

While exotic literature does not exclude humour *per se*, and the comic description of Doudou-Ménar as a typical 'femme-matador' arguably falls into the category of the objectifying stereotype, the significance of the kind of verbal wit exemplified above is that its effectiveness does not depend on cultural otherness: it will be interpreted and appreciated in exactly the same way by metropolitan and Antillean readers. Moreover, it is often self-deprecating, particularly in the context of the auto-exoticism that elsewhere characterizes Chamoiseau's text. For instance, he includes several footnotes explaining Creole terms to his French readers, but also, as a joke, footnotes explaining French words to supposedly uneducated Creole readers (pp. 85, 100) – whose patent superfluity, given his likely readership, serves to point up his awareness of potential accusations that he is writing for a solely French audience.[28] At one point he also gives an ironic description of Pilon's contradictory and hypocritical attitude to Creole language and Antillean customs – but the paragraph finishes with the admission that this is the inevitable condition of 'all of us': 'final, vit comme nous tous, à deux vitesses [...]' (pp. 118–19). More than anything else, the knowing wit and comic verve of his writing go a long way towards redeeming Chamoiseau from the charge of auto-exoticism.


Raphaël Confiant's *Le Nègre et l'amiral* is a much longer and in many ways more substantial novel than *Solibo magnifique*. Set in the period of the Vichy rule of Martinique during the Second World War, its main theme is the islanders' resistance to the regime; but it also uses this theme to showcase a range of aspects of Creole society. In this historical context, *créolité* is presented as in and of itself a mode of resistance, not just to French culture but specifically to an oppressive political domination.[29] The novel's principal characters are Rigobert, the 'nègre' of the title, who represents the authentically Creole lifestyle of the urban poor of Fort-de-France, and also suffers from the self-denigration analysed in *Éloge de la créolité*, cursing God on the first page for having made him a negro (p. 9); Alcide, also black but educated, a schoolteacher; and Amédée, a middle-class mulatto fascinated by a Creole culture that he does not understand (exemplified here by the Morne Pichevin district of the city), who takes as his mistress the prostitute Philomène, and, as he is gradually initiated into the mysteries of the 'quartier', acts as a point of identification for the reader. Through the counterpoint between Rigobert and Amédée, Confiant provides both an 'internal' and an 'external' perspective on the culture.

Like *Solibo magnifique*, the novel mocks traditional exoticism, thus implicitly asserting its own contrasting authenticity: the *béké* family of Salin du Bercy stage a play written by the mayor of Fort-de-France entitled 'Le Caraïbe amoureux', whose plot, 'd'une ennuyeuse platitude', involves the capture of a white woman by a Carib chief and his son (pp. 243–44) – a typical exotic scenario. Moreover, it also contains an explicit critique of *auto*-exoticism: a locally written novel about the love between a Martinican *mulâtresse* and a white captain provokes this reaction on the part of Amédée: 'Cela [...] le confirmait dans l'idée que ce qui tenait lieu de littérature aux îles dépassait rarement le doux balancement des palmes sur l'eau et les frétillements langoureux entre indigènes et beaux Européens' (p. 84). Amédée's friend Dalmeida plays a particularly important role in this critique, extending it to surrealism and Negritude: he argues that Césaire is guilty of imitating the literature of Europe ('Même Césaire et les autres sont embrigadés dans la théorie surréaliste qui est d'extraction purement européenne si je ne m'abuse', p. 130) and accuses *Tropiques* of an excessive 'valorisation [...] du nègre et de l'Afrique mère' (p. 132). He goes on to claim that the only true solution to this alienation is *créolité*: 'La négritude ne saurait être qu'une brève étape vers la créolité' (p. 137); and – closely echoing the opening pages of *Éloge* – that Martinicans are 'des gens qui ne sont ni Africains, ni Européens, ni Indiens, ni Syriens, ni Chinois [...] d'où surgira une nouvelle race, la race créole' (p. 137). The inclusion of this analysis and its conclusion serves to demonstrate the novel's awareness of the

dangers of auto-exoticism and hence to imply that its own representations, because they adopt the standpoint of *créolité*, are not alienated
or exotic.[30]

This does not, however, prevent it from taking the reader on a
guided tour of a number of 'typical' Creole scenes, particularly in the
first part of the text, which lacks any continuous narrative thread or
plot, and consists simply of a series of encounters between Rigobert
and various other characters, the main function of which appears
to be to implement the programme set out in *Éloge de la créolité* of
'systematically' revalorizing the Creole way of life.[31] Thus we are
shown the vegetable market, with its women stall-holders and their
attendant 'djobeurs' (pp. 14–16); the *quimboiseur* who turned himself
into a dog (pp. 36–38); a Creole dance, with an explanation of the
sign-language of the women's 'madras' (different ways of tying one's
headscarf signify varying degrees of sexual availability) (pp. 41–42); 'La
Cour Fruit-à-Pain' where the prostitutes hang out (pp. 62–63); carnival
(pp. 95–98); riddles (pp. 100–02); gambling with dice – 'ce jeu de dés
spécial, appelé "serbi"' – and habitual ways of cheating (pp. 203–04);
and a folktale (pp. 312–16). Rigobert also has a ritualized dance-fight
with Barbe-Sale, with the traditional accompaniment of drumming
(pp. 218–22), in the course of which he reflects that failing to kill his
adversary will result in 'la transformation de cette danse-combat en
macaquerie pour voyageurs métropolitains' (p. 221), signalling, in other
words, the novel's awareness that its 'vision intérieure' is constantly on
the brink of slipping into auto-exoticism (especially since he does not in
fact kill Barbe-Sale).

As in *Solibo magnifique*, the eloquence and creativity of the Creole
language are stressed: Rigobert's use of Creole is admired by his
neighbours because of his gift for inventing new words and creating 'des
images fulgurantes qui vous clouaient sur place nettement et proprement'
(p. 13). Also as in *Solibo*, the black characters have colourful comic
nicknames, which appear in the text as translations from Creole ('Lapin
Échaudé', 'Siméon Tête-Coton' (p. 18), 'Marcellin Gueule-de-Raie'
(p. 23), etc.). Moreover, the novel enhances its authenticity by adopting,
in the first few chapters, an oral style. It refers to Rigobert as 'notre
bougre' (p. 9) and 'notre compère' (p. 10), and introduces an incident
with: 'Voici comment la chose advint: [...]' (p. 14). Similarly, while
not explicitly defining himself as a 'marqueur de paroles', Confiant
implies that his narrative is based on local gossip, and so there are
several possible versions of the same event ('Mais une seconde version

circule, aussi répandue quoique moins plausible' (p. 19); 'De ce jour, ils devinrent inséparables, raconte-t-on, même si parfois il se transmet un autre dit tout aussi écoutable' (pp. 26–27); 'Selon une autre version, moins répandue il est vraie [...]' (p. 55). But these characteristics fade out as the momentum of the narrative gathers with the more serious plot of resistance to the Admiral Robert's rule.

It is, however, in its portrayal of sexuality – a topic not touched on in *Éloge de la créolité* – that *Le Nègre et l'amiral* is most deeply implicated in auto-exoticism, despite its obvious attempts to demarcate itself from it. There are an enormous number of sexual encounters and expressions of sexual desire throughout the novel, and they are all recounted from the 'masculinist' perspective that James Arnold has argued is characteristic of the *créolité* writers, which objectifies women as mere objects of male desire.[32] In contrast to the romanticism of traditional exotic representations of sex, these encounters are described in earthy, would-be Rabelaisian physical detail, with an emphasis on their animality which in fact objectifies both the man and the woman involved. Thus Confiant contrasts his exaggeratedly lyrical French translation of the expression 'faire une coulée' – 'ce qui veut dire, dans notre langue, une descente dans la douceur vertigineuse des préludes amoureux' (p. 146) – with, in the next sentence, a far cruder version of its conclusion: 'l'étreinte des corps et le coq qui grimpe sur la poule avec une sauvagerie muette' (p. 146). Amédée, similarly, prizes Philomène's ability to 'susciter de telles étreintes dont la seule règle est l'animalité pure' (p. 164). Women are generally presented as being easily available, but their promiscuity is less a consequence of their own sexual desire than a tactic for gaining money or social advancement: Carmélise, for instance, 'songeait qu'il lui faudrait se fatiguer à trouver un nouvel amant, elle que onze grossesses [...] provoquées par onze verges différentes avaient rendue quelque peu blasée à l'endroit de l'amour' (p. 33).

The representation of sexuality throughout the novel is also racially coded: all the black (and Indian) women are sexy, and none of the white women. Thus Amédée, for example, likes his prostitutes to be as black as possible, 'par contraste avec sa propre épouse, une créature pâlote' (p. 61). Black women are so desirable, in fact, that Helmut, the wounded German naval officer (technically a prisoner of war but treated as a guest by Salin du Bercy) who expresses his disgust at his host's habit of sleeping with black women (p. 233), finds that even his fascist belief in racial purity cannot prevent him from succumbing to the charms of the maid Noëllise (pp. 245–46). As a typical *béké*, Salin du Bercy is an 'amateur d'orgies avec ses négresses' (p. 325), and these orgies are further evidence, if such were needed, of the greater attractiveness of black women. But they are also the object of great resentment on the part of the black men of the island: Rigobert refers bitterly to the 'amour-nègre que les Blancs-pays avaient su découvrir avant tout le monde et dont ils voulaient se garder le privilège' (p. 279), and the idea that the white masters have for centuries been stealing their women allows us to interpret their own sexual hyperactivity as an attempt to reclaim the women for themselves. Dalmeida, in his role as the analyst of alienation, tries to persuade Alcide that the Martinicans' attitude to sexuality is merely an internalization of the colonizers' fantasies:

> Ce petit pays [...] a été tout entier construit sur la fornication. La relation esclavagiste a été fondamentalement axée sur le viol permanent des négresses et des mulâtresses par les maîtres blancs. Rien n'a changé aujourd'hui, mon vieux, à part que nous, les hommes de couleur, nous avons intériorisé les phantasmes des békés [...] le phantasme du colon a toujours consisté à transformer la femme de couleur en un matador, une sorte de créature lubrique essentiellement vouée à la séduction. (p. 119)

But, as with Dalmeida's other explanations, this position does not inform the novel as a whole. Indeed, when Rigobert later falls in love with the black woman he meets in the countryside, who is referred to only as 'Celle-qui-n'a-pas-son pareil', he cannot believe that he used to masturbate every day in front of photographs of white film stars (p. 278): 'Ce corps ferme et noir, ces seins plantureux [...] cette coucoune chaude aux lèvres d'un rose violent dont la languette sentait bon le vétiver' (p. 279) all prove to him the superiority of 'l'amour nègre' – and this in turn undermines Dalmeida's claim that this is merely a white fantasy, and reinstates the exotic stereotype of the uniquely beautiful sexy black woman.

Like *Solibo magnifique*, *Le Nègre et l'amiral* emphasizes the multi-ethnicity of the community. It introduces us to 'Syrians', Indians and Chinese, as well as to the different racially-based social classes: mulattoes, 'petits blancs' and 'békés', and to the differences between urban and rural black people. But while 'nègres, mulâtres, chabins, Indiens, Syriens, bâtards-Chinois et même quelques Blancs-pays' all come together to celebrate the end of the war (p. 367), this is an exceptional occurrence, and in general the ideal of Creole harmony is far from being achieved since considerable hostility is shown to exist between the various groups: the 'nègres' think that the 'syriens' are 'une race de sacrés malpropres' (p. 28); the Indians are described as 'tous ces coolies malpropres qui envahissaient Fort-de-France depuis quelques temps' (p. 205), and so on. One could read this as a critique of the alienation that Creole society has to overcome; in any case, it is certainly a more realistic portrait of Martinican society in the 1930s and 1940s than one would expect from a novel trying simply to promote the virtues of Creole 'diversalité'.[33]

The historical setting of the novel sidesteps the issue of nostalgia that is such a central feature of Chamoiseau's auto-exoticism: the society that Confiant depicts is not on the verge of disappearance. But nor is it presented as completely timeless. The portrayal of the relationships between the *békés* and the mulattoes shows the latter in the process of struggling, with considerable success, against their 'ennemis héréditaires, les békés créoles' (p. 75) to gain wealth and professional advancement; and the *békés* readjust to this new situation by falling back on their core power base as landowners. As Salin du Bercy explains to Helmut,

> Ces mulâtres sont de bons médecins, croyez-moi [...] D'ailleurs, nous leur avons tout laissé, la médecine, le droit, la littérature, les arts et, ma foi, ils se débrouillent à merveille. Quel besoin aurions-nous d'aller user nos culottes sur les bancs de la Sorbonne, puisque toute les terres et toutes les usines nous appartiennent? (pp. 230–31)

This portrayal of an ethnic group taking over the roles and functions of another group illustrates the changes and exchanges essential to the anthropological definition of Creole society. Strikingly, however, the novel's representation of a dynamically evolving society does not extend to the lower-class black community which embodies its ideal of Creole culture. It is true that Alcide, who comes from a poor black family, succeeds through intelligence and education in becoming a school teacher; but this social elevation is seen in purely negative terms as a kind of exile from his 'true' culture: 'Il comprenait peu à peu à quel point son éducation petite-bourgeoise et française l'avait tenu à l'écart de son peuple et de sa véritable culture' (p. 59). Conversely, it is the authentic, timeless culture of *créolité* that Amédée seeks out in preference to the 'hypocrisy' of his 'pseudo-French' bourgeois lifestyle (pp. 132, 170). It is in this sense that Creole culture is essentialized and as such acts as the fundamental value of the novel.

If Confiant and Chamoiseau ultimately remain at least partially trapped in auto-exoticism, at least in these two novels, it is above all because of their essentialist conception of *créolité*. Their claim, in *Éloge de la créolité* and the later *Lettres créoles*,[34] that this is not the case, rests basically on two arguments: that *créolité* is open-ended and constantly in movement, and that it is a hybrid phenomenon rather than the glorification of one particular race. Thus the conclusion to *Lettres créoles* describes it as 'un mélange mouvant, toujours mouvant, dont le point de départ est un abîme et dont l'évolution demeure imprévisible' (p. 204). But this is far from borne out in the two novels I have discussed; the notion of cultural change through exchange between the different component groups is, within the community that the authors consider truly Creole, entirely absent.[35] Equally, *Éloge* defines *créolité* as 'une spécificité ouverte [...] non une synthèse, pas simplement un métissage, ou n'importe quelle autre unicité' (pp. 27–28) and emphasizes that 'le principe même de notre identité est la complexité' (p. 28). In his interview with Dominique Chancé, moreover, Chamoiseau dismisses quite aggressively Glissant's contention that *créolité* is an essence, on the same grounds:

> Il nous a accusé de vouloir créer une nouvelle essence identitaire [...] C'est son petit conflit théorique qui l'anime, mais ça n'a pas de fondement [...] [Les créolités] ne sont pas des essences identitaires, puisqu'elles sont des diversités. Je ne vois pas comment on pourrait recréer une essence identitaire comme la négritude, ou je ne sais quoi [...]. (*L'Auteur en souffrance*, p. 209)

Hybridity is indeed often seen as incompatible with, almost as the opposite of, essentialism – in the work of Bhabha, for instance[36] – and equally as the opposite of exoticism. Forsdick writes: 'It [colonial hybridity] may even be represented as exoticism's other, for whereas hybridity refers to uneven syntheses and the emergence of new, transcultural forms, colonial exoticism tends to accentuate the polarities of difference and to deny the implications of contact' ('Travelling Concepts', p. 13). But hybridity in this sense involves far more than the simple existence side by side of mixed ethnicities that it signifies for the *créolité* writers. Moreover, as I have argued earlier, the type of exoticism particular to the Antilles is based on precisely the co-existence of the strange and the familiar, and its central figure is the racially mixed 'belle mulâtresse'. It is not only individual races, in other words, that can be essentialized as Chamoiseau seems to think. In according such a privileged status to the 'authentic' Creole mixed-race community, he and Confiant effectively present it as an essence.[37] Its positioning as the culmination of a whole historical trajectory in which Negritude and Glissant's *Antillanité* (*Éloge*, pp. 17–22) are merely imperfect stages on the way to achieving authenticity very much reinforces this. Also, the authors' stress on 'originality' is highly significant: several of their formulations of *créolité* present it as a mixture of races, *but* out of which will emerge a single new entity. Thus in *Éloge* we read: 'La Créolité est donc le fait d'appartenir à une entité humaine originale qui à terme se dégage de ces processus' (p. 31). Indeed, in Dalmeida's version this entity – in a passage I have already quoted – is even presented as a new *race*: 'des gens qui ne sont ni Africains, ni Européens, ni Indiens, ni Syriens, ni Chinois [...] d'où surgira une nouvelle race, la race créole' (*Le Nègre et l'amiral*, p. 137). Thus while neither of the novels discussed above is wholly or simply auto-exotic – both are marked by complex ambiguities and contradictions, as I have tried to show – in the final analysis, and despite the acute consciousness which they exhibit of the mechanisms of alienation and of the exotic stereotypes that they should avoid, it is this essentialism that above all prevents the writing of Chamoiseau and Confiant from completely escaping the trap of auto-exoticism.

# 3

# Eating their Words

## The Consumption
## of French Caribbean Literature

Postcolonial studies, in its concentration on culture and subjectivity, has sometimes seemed to lose sight of the fact that colonialism was largely motivated by economic concerns. The colonies provided both a cheap labour force and a supply of raw materials to be exported to Europe. From cotton to gold to tea, colonial economies were driven by the export of a range of commodities; among these, a major subcategory has always been food and drink, and this is especially true of the Caribbean. Originally the 'spice islands', the Caribbean soon devoted itself to the production of cane sugar for the European market; the decline of this market resulting from the expansion of European sugar beet in the late nineteenth century meant that the region subsequently had to diversify, but the diversification remained within a range of products for *oral* consumption: rum, coffee, tobacco, bananas, pineapples, mangoes, avocadoes. On most of the islands this agricultural sector has now been overtaken by tourism as the major source of revenue; but in the European imagination, the Caribbean, it would seem, is still associated with eating and drinking.

More recently, one of the French Caribbean's main exports to metropolitan France has been novels. These have to be so exported because the islands are too small to sustain a viable independent publishing industry; but it is equally true that the global publishing industry has over the past twenty to thirty years become far keener than previously to publish novels from Third World writers, creating a market in what Graham Huggan terms 'the postcolonial exotic'. And in the case of novels from Martinique, Guadeloupe and Haiti, what is most striking about their marketing is the extent to which it presents them as *edible*:

as though the association between the Caribbean and food products is so powerful that the most obvious mode of consumption of its literary products is also oral.[1] There is, in other words, a correlation between the real export of food products and the construction of an imagination in which representations of the Caribbean landscape and society have become objects of consumption in the most basic sense.

Nor is this phenomenon restricted to the more openly commercial discourses of publishers' blurbs or reviews in the mainstream press; it occurs also in the work of academic critics. The veteran specialist and author of a six-volume history of French Caribbean literature Jack Corzani writes in his introduction to Haitian Jacques Roumain's novel *Gouverneurs de la rosée*:

> Mais surtout, surtout, humez ce roman comme vous humeriez le grillade de cochon, le maïs à la morue, le riz-soleil et les pois rouges au petit-salé de Rosanne [...] Vous y reviendrez, vous en reprendrez et, à chaque fois, vous sentirez votre gorge se nouer.[2]

– a description that might be considered to verge on the 'tasteless', since the characters of the novel are all faced with the prospect of imminent starvation. Even Alain Rouch and Gérard Clavreuil's *Littératures nationales d'écriture française*, which presents itself as a neutral, informative reference work, describes Guadeloupean Simone Schwarz-Bart's *Pluie et vent sur Télumée Miracle* in these terms: 'Simone Schwarz-Bart nous dévoile dans ce roman tout l'univers coloré des Antilles; la langue, riche en expressions imagées et truculentes, nous offre, en français, la saveur du parler créole'.[3] This invitation to 'eat' the text amounts to a crude literalization of the 'consumption' of literature. Everything in the novel is *offered* to the reader – and there is a clear parallel here with the workings of the tourist industry, in which the characteristic ingredients of the Caribbean landscape and people are made easily accessible, packaged for the consumption of the outsider.[4] The edible novel thus eliminates the *mystery* that is a traditional component of much exotic literature; but, as I have argued in chapter 2, the exoticism of the Caribbean has always been distinguished by its relative familiarity and its lack of radical otherness.

The predominance of oral consumption is also evident in the texts of many of the novels themselves.[5] The vegetable market has become a staple ingredient of French Caribbean popular culture as represented in novels – throughout Chamoiseau's work, especially in *Chronique des sept misères*, but also in Pépin's *L'Envers du décor*, for example.[6] Here food appears explicitly as a commercial commodity: the paratextual marketing of the novel as food is mimicked by the market selling food within the novel. But oral consumption is also prominent in the representation of sexuality – another standard ingredient of the exotic novel. The advantage of the sexually desirable 'native' woman, from the point of view of the European male, lies not only in her exotic beauty but also in her supposed freedom from repressive European sexual morality: with her, sex becomes as innocent a pleasure as eating and drinking. It is thus not surprising that the pleasures of both merge together, and the woman is described in terms of *fruit*. Léon-François Hoffmann, for example, criticizes the Haitian poets in whose work 'on ne sait vraiment plus si la femme est décrite en fonction de fruits tropicaux, ou si au contraire c'est un catalogue de produits fruitiers qui prend forme de femme'.[7] In René Depestre's *Hadriana dans tous mes rêves*, equally, Hadriana's mouth is 'un fruit éclatant de fraîcheur auquel toute bouche assoiffée aurait voulu mordre jusqu'à l'extase' (p. 83); her breasts are 'Fruits frais et superbes!' (p. 161); and she refers throughout to her private parts as 'mon amande'.[8] Less lyrically, the three respectable matrons who have been sexually penetrated by a magic butterfly assimilate this novel experience to their more usual occupation as hostesses: 'elles voyaient, à la fin du coït, leur sexe disposé avec grâce sur une table d'apparat au milieu d'autres plats aussi somptueusement garnis. Elles entendaient leur propre voix crier: "Monseigneur, à table! C'est servi chaud"' (p. 30). And, finally, the conjunction of sex, fruit and oral consumption is taken to a logical conclusion when Hadriana has oral sex with another girl: 'J'étais ravie d'avoir dans sa bouche mon amande mieux aoûtée que n'importe quel fruit de la saison, mangue Madan-Francis ou royal melon de France' (p. 172).

In general terms, the association between Caribbean culture and the pleasures of eating goes back a long way.[9] However, the more specific phenomenon of the production by writers and marketing by publishers of 'edible' French Caribbean novels dates mostly from the late 1980s – in other words, the period in which globalized marketing began its enhanced commodification of non-Western cultural products. Huggan has analysed in detail this construction of 'postcolonial/Third World texts as exotic objects, circulating within a metropolitan-regulated economy of commodity exchange' (*Postcolonial Exotic*, p. 19). As far as the French Caribbean is concerned, one major change that this commodification of novels brings about is that it is no longer just the content of the exotic representation ('fruity' women, for example) that is presented as an object of oral consumption, but also, and especially, the language in which the novels are written. Thus in the text of Simone Schwarz-Bart's *Pluie et vent sur Télumée Miracle*, published in 1972, the reader's attention is not explicitly drawn to the quality of its language – but in 1987, the reference to it in *Littératures nationales d'écriture française* quoted above highlights its language, which 'nous offre, en français, la saveur du parler créole'. The 'saveur' of the language depends on its exotic difference from standard literary French.

The two novels published in 1988 that I have analysed in chapter 2 receive the same treatment: the blurb on the back cover of Chamoiseau's *Solibo magnifique* concludes with an italicized reference to '*le goût du mot, du discours sans virgule*'; and that on the back cover of Confiant's *Le Nègre et l'amiral* describes it as evoking 'Un petit monde avec ses clans, ses rêves, ses souffrances, sa gaieté, *ses mots savoureux*' (my italics). In very similar fashion, the blurb preceding the 1996 Folio edition of *Hadriana dans tous mes rêves* (first published in 1988) links it with the author's previous works *Alléluia pour une femme-jardin* (1981) and *Le Mât de cocagne* (1979) to comment: 'La joie de vivre caraïbe, la sensualité, l'érotisme solaire, le surréalisme vaudou, *une langue qu'on savoure comme un fruit exotique* caractérisent ces œuvres que le prix Renaudot a récompensées en 1988' (my italics).

Contrary to the impression given by the blurb, these three novels by Depestre in fact show a marked trajectory from the savage and despairing political satire of *Le Mât de cocagne* in 1979 to the whimsical exoticism of *Hadriana* in 1988, the only one to be awarded a French literary prize. Another difference between them is that *Hadriana* is the first to contain a glossary at the end, giving translations of Creole words used in the text. This seems to suggest that exotic sex and magic go together with elements of Creole language, as long as these do not present any problem of comprehension for the metropolitan reader. Creole words and their translation are not necessarily exotic elements; they are used by a large number of Caribbean writers, with differing effects. But in the context of a novel such as *Hadriana*, whose main – indeed, only – themes are sex and magic, the Creole language does seem to function above all as a further exotic ingredient, offering the reader oral *pleasure* rather than insight into the society depicted. This is reinforced by the exoticism of the semantic fields covered: almost half of the items in the glossary refer to aspects of *vodou* and magic, and a substantial further number to sexuality and to dancing. More generally, the language of the novel seems designed above all to give pleasure to the reader, and the equation of speech with oral pleasure is imaged at one point when the narrator, now a lecturer at the University of the West Indies, describes his female students as 'drinking in' his words, and brings this dead metaphor back to life by having them licking their lips while listening to his lecture: 'Les belles étudiantes [...] buvaient mes paroles en laissant leur langue également rose errer sensuellement sur leurs lèvres humides' (p. 145).

There is some evidence that the Creole language has long been considered by Europeans visiting the Caribbean to be inherently attractive and sensual. Lafcadio Hearn, for instance, writing in the nineteenth century, describes it as 'the most liquid, mellow, languid language in the world, especially a language for love-making', but also as possessing a child-like innocence: it 'sounds like pretty baby-talk'.[10] But with the *créolité* movement its status not only as a guarantee of authenticity but also a source of pleasure becomes even more prominent. I have already outlined, in the previous chapter, how the authors of *Éloge de la créolité* aim to reinvigorate literary French by incorporating into it elements of Creole, and how the novels of Chamoiseau and Confiant thematize and to some extent mimic the procedures of the Creole *conteur*. In *Le Nègre et l'amiral* the Creole language is *exhibited* to the reader, particularly in its effect on foreigners: the novel shows a fictionalized André Breton, for instance, 's'émerveillant des sonorités cajoleuses de la langue créole dans la bouche des gamins de rue à qui il tapotait les joues' (p. 124). These authors also occasionally make an explicit connection between Creole language and food; for instance, in an article written in 1991, Confiant describes oral creole culture as a 'vivier stylistique dans lequel il n'y aura aucune honte à plonger' – the French term for the tank in which fish are kept alive before being eaten conveniently echoing the 'living', reviving qualities of Creole as opposed to French.[11] Or it becomes indistinguishable from physical sexuality – as for Amédée in *Le Nègre et l'amiral*:

> C'est Philomène qui m'apprend à aimer, dans un même balan, et son corps et le créole car elle fait l'amour dans cette langue, déployant des paroles d'une doucine inouïe, incomparable, qui ébranle mon être tout entier. Aussi, dans nos babils post-coïtaux, je ressens un bien-être physique à habiter chaque mot, même le plus banal, et à être habité par lui [...] Je m'avise avec incrédulité que la langue de nos tuteurs blancs n'a pas de mot aussi beau que 'coucoune' pour désigner le sexe de la femme [...]. (pp. 167–68)

In order to produce these effects, it is of course necessary that the novels should not actually be written in Creole (as Confiant's earlier novels were); not only because they would be inaccessible to the metropolitan readership to whom they are marketed, but also because it would be somewhat risky for a novel written in Creole to simultaneously proclaim the stylistic richness and creativity supposedly inherent in the language *per se*; and above all because a novel wholly and simply written in Creole would be unable to thematize and display fragments of Creole to the reader.[12] Therefore, Chamoiseau and Confiant either have to provide translations of the Creole words in their texts, or invent a variety of French that evokes or connotes Creole while remaining comprehensible to the non-creolophone reader. They do both, in fact, but it is the second strategy that perhaps most effectively fulfils their ambition of creating a new literary language. It takes advantage of the existence of intermediate or interlectal forms of creolized French ('français banane') to produce a 'language' which is perceptibly different from standard French, and which as it were gestures towards creole without actually compromising the text's intelligibility to its French readers. The early pages of *Le Nègre et l'amiral*, for example, are studded with such words, which are easy for the metropolitan reader to understand while at the same time creating an exotic difference in the language: 'tout-à-faitement' (p. 14); 'la belleté de son dire' (p. 15); 'la maudition' (p. 16); 'méprisation' (p. 17); 'la sérieusité' (p. 19); 'la haïssance' (p. 20), 'la foultitude' (p. 20), etc. Further, this interlect is expanded by *inventing* words which do not exist in Creole but sound as though they might: thus Marie-José N'Zengou-Tayo refers to what she calls Chamoiseau's 'effet-de-créole',[13] and in relation to Confiant Jean Bernabé explains the procedure as follows: 'Chez Confiant, au créolisme objectif est associé un créolisme fictif fondé sur une reconstruction, grâce aux ressources de l'ancien français, d'un créole donné comme authentique, mais puisant en fait son sève dans le seul artifice de l'écriture'.[14] Confiant's aim is to create in the reader the *illusion* that s/he is reading Creole: he limits this to the creolophone reader, claiming to 'donner au lecteur antillais l'illusion de lire du créole'.[15] But, as Gauvin comments, it has the same effect on the French reader (*Écrire, pour qui?*, p. 123), with the difference that rather than a pseudo-recognition of one's own language, it becomes a source of exotic pleasure.[16]

What links this to the notion of 'eating' language is that the illusion of reading Creole is compounded by another illusion: that of orality. The fact that Creole is a predominantly oral language, and the *créolité* writers' repeated emphasis on the virtues of spoken rather than written language, extensively influence their novels. I have already discussed

*Solibo magnifique*'s insistence on the superiority of Solibo's oral storytelling over Chamoiseau's written narrative; but both this text and Chamoiseau's and Confiant's other novels make extensive use of spoken narrative and the *mise en scène* of storytelling: characters recount their stories face-to-face with their audiences. Marie-Sophie's *telling* of the story of Chamoiseau's *Texaco* to the urban planner, for instance, makes up the main part of this novel.[17] As the examples I have already quoted make clear, edible language is also to a significant extent oral language – 'la saveur du parler créole', etc. – but an oral language that is in reality written down in a published text, and is different and striking by virtue of its ostentatiously promoted relationship to the islanders' speech. Thus while the 'taste' of the novels' language can be defined objectively as its stylistic deviation from metropolitan literary French, a deviation resulting from the reproduction of the features of spoken quasi-Creole discourse, on another level it is rather a question of a fantasy of edible language that relies on the reader imagining it as spoken. This imaginary orality merges all the more easily with the fantasy of eating the texts: the two senses of orality – speech, and eating or tasting – are fused together: 'la langue' as language, in other words, but also as tongue.[18]

The general principle of a novelistic discourse which incorporates into itself words belonging to a perceptibly different discourse has been most thoroughly theorized not within postcolonial theory but in the work of Mikhail Bakhtin.[19] His *Problems of Dostoevsky's Poetics* and *The Dialogic Imagination*, although addressing a very different type of novel, shed an interesting light on the effects of Creole edible language. Bakhtin's central concern is with what he calls the dialogic or polyphonic novel, that is, a novel in which the representation as a whole is not under the control of a single or 'monologic' authorial voice, but results from the interplay of a number of different voices or perspectives, each of which is accorded a degree of autonomy within the text. To this end he distinguishes three types of discourse: direct authorial discourse, objectified discourse, and double-voiced discourse. It is the last of these that characterizes the dialogic novel and is therefore, as he puts it, 'the chief subject of our investigation, one could even say its chief hero' (*Dostoevsky*, p. 185). In double-voiced discourse, 'two voices collide' (p. 184); it 'has a twofold direction – it is directed both toward the referential object of speech, as in ordinary discourse, and toward *another's discourse*, toward *someone else's speech*' (p. 185, italics original).[20] In it, the author is still concerned to express his own meanings and intentions, but does so *through* 'someone else's voice'.

It is, however, the second type, objectified discourse, that is most relevant to the phenomena I have identified above. It does not enter into dialogue with the author's voice, and the latter regards it not as another consciousness, but as an object.[21] It has meaning, of course, but this meaning 'does not lie in the same plane with the author's speech [… it] is itself, as characteristic, typical, colorful discourse, a referential object toward which something is directed […] it is treated as an object of authorial understanding, and not from the point of view of its own referential intention' (pp. 186–87). It is language seen from the outside, valued for its typicality – or cultural authenticity – rather than its meaning, with the focus on its social determinations (as non-standard French, for example) and perhaps also on its exotic sound. The word can be eaten only as an object, not a 'referential intention'. In *The Dialogic Imagination* Bakhtin introduces the further idea of 'display', equating objectified discourse with 'the word on display' (p. 322); the translator explains that 'A word "displayed as a thing", [is] reified, a word maximally deprived of authorial intention. It involves a manipulation of context in such a way that the word is stripped of those overtones that enable it to be perceived as natural' (p. 427). This captures exactly the techniques of Chamoiseau and Confiant that I have described above, drawing the reader's attention to a creole (or pseudo-creole) expression as an exotic object.

Moreover, Bakhtin also links objectified discourse with objectified characters, as opposed to the open-ended characterization of the autonomous subjects of the dialogic novel: 'But the fact is that language differentiation and the clear-cut "speech characterizations" of characters have the greatest artistic significance precisely in the creation of objectified and finalized images of people. The more objectified a character, the more sharply his speech physiognomy stands out' (*Dostoevsky*, p. 182). If double-voiced discourse is the 'hero' of Bakhtin's analysis, objectified discourse is surely its villain. Its role in his own work is ultimately less as an object of interest in its own right than as a counter-example to the dialogic novel. If the latter is dedicated to the manifestation of a plurality of different subjective discourses, each expressing its own semantic intentions in 'a continuous and open-ended dialogue' (*Dostoevsky*, p. 251) – as he goes on to say: 'Authorial discourse cannot encompass the hero and his word on all sides, cannot lock him in and finalize him from without. It can only address itself to him' (p. 251) – then it follows that a novel dominated by objectified discourse, in contrast, positions its characters as objects defined from the outside: even their speech, which in principle expresses their own subjective intentions, is reduced to a tangible, 'displayed' example of sociocultural peculiarities. This reification correlates exactly with the emphasis in many critiques of exotic literature on its external, 'superficial' character: as René Ménil, for example, writes in 'De l'exotisme colonial': 'la tendance naturelle, dans l'exotisme, est de rater le "sérieux" et l'authenticité du drame (de l'autre) pour s'en tenir à une vision idyllique, superficielle [...] s'attacher au décor, au pittoresque extérieur, à l'homme dans le décor, à l'homme comme objet et comme décor (paysages, costumes)' (p. 20) – but with the difference that in the case of the novels I am concerned with here, the external focus on the picturesque goes beyond the representation of 'décor' to encompass also the supposedly 'inner' phenomenon of language.

This in turn raises the question of how the reader responds to the 'referential intention' of edible language. I have discussed above the ways in which the authors deal with the problem of making creole phrases accessible to a non-creolophone reader. But in a more general sense, the consumption of literature as food problematizes the whole question of understanding. Products of different cultures always pose this question in a different way from products of our own culture; and they also raise the problem of the *ethics* of understanding. The 'alien' object, whether it is a text, as in this case, or some other artefact, offers a resistance to our attempts to understand it.

Glissant, for instance, analysing the situation of his own Martinican society, talks in visual terms of 'opacity' and 'transparency', and treats the question of the West's understanding of the Caribbean in an explicitly ethical perspective. He argues that the value which Western humanism places on transparency is complicit with an imperialist drive to constitute the Other as object of knowledge: 'quelle que soit l'opacité de l'autre pour soi, la question sera toujours de ramener cet autre à la transparence vécue par soi: ou bien on l'assimile ou bien on l'annihile' (*PR*, p. 62). Therefore opacity becomes a prime positive value, signifying the resistance that the oppressed put up against being understood, which is equated with being objectified and appropriated. In this system of visual metaphors, therefore, understanding, as transparency, is far from unambiguously positive. But at least the perception of the text's opacity is interpreted as a resistance to our understanding; at least understanding is posed as a problem. The gustatory metaphor, on the other hand, has the effect of short-circuiting the whole issue. In everyday speech, seeing equates with understanding: we say 'I see' when we mean 'I understand'. Taste, however, has no relationship at all with understanding or failing to understand: how can one *not understand* a taste? The metropolitan reader, it would appear, is no longer concerned to understand and therefore control, but simply to consume.

I have already described the way in which creole words in *Hadriana dans tous mes rêves* are both 'displayed' in the text and translated in the glossary at the end. But the importance of understanding to which such a glossary would seem to attest is in fact doubtful. The explanations of the terms relating to *vodou* do little more than demonstrate that they do in fact relate to *vodou*, which is usually obvious from their context in the main text anyway. (They are also often defined with another creole term, which is then in its turn explained, thus allowing Depestre to include yet another creole term, and so on: for example the definition of *bokor* is: '*houngan* (prêtre) du vaudou qui pratique la magie noire' (p. 211); that of *houngan* is: 'prêtre du vaudou, qui officie dans un *houmfort* (temple)', p. 212.) Or, the description of a woman dancing includes the sentence: 'Son yanvalou-dos-bas* était empreint d'une époustouflante sensualité: sous le voile transparent les forme nues imitaient à la perfection la course chaloupée d'un bateau de rêve' (p. 80). The asterisked term is then defined in the glossary as follows: '*Yanvalou-dos-bas*: danse vive et gaie exécutée le corps penché en avant, les mains sur les genoux pliés, accompagnée d'ondulations des épaules' (p. 214), which arguably does not add much of interest to what the reader has already picked up from the main text. Sometimes, indeed, the translation is completely superfluous: in a reference to 'des séances de contes fantastiques tirés* tard le soir durant les longues vacances d'été' (p. 101), the sense of 'tirés' is already perfectly clear, and the glossary entry – '*Tirer conte*: raconter une histoire, un conte, le soir' (p. 214) – merely draws the reader's attention to this non-standard use of the verb 'tirer'.

If what we are invited to do to the text is in effect to eat it, then its resistance – its alien or even incomprehensible quality – is simply reduced to its exotic, picturesque 'saveur'. Thus what in a metropolitan novel might be condemned as 'indigestible' is transformed by exoticism into something much more positive and palatable. Its strangeness has something in common with what we more generally think of as *poetic* language, as indeed does the focus on the material qualities – the 'saveur' – of the words. But it is crucially different from poetic language in so far as the latter produces meanings that are subtle, implicit and elusive, and cannot be reduced to simple translations in a glossary or a footnote; the interpretation of a poem is a very different process from the consumption of the 'object-word' of edible language.

The extract I have already quoted from *Littératures nationales d'écriture française* in fact uses both visual and gustatory metaphors in the same sentence: 'Simone Schwarz-Bart nous *dévoile* dans ce roman tout l'univers *coloré* des Antilles; la langue, riche en expressions imagées et truculentes, nous *offre*, en français, la *saveur* du parler créole' (p. 192, my italics). Significantly, the difference between the two verbs – Schwarz-Bart *reveals* the colourful universe and *offers* us the taste of creole speech – aligns the visual metaphor with discovery, hence knowledge and understanding, while the 'taste' of the language is 'offered' to us as though we were guests at a dinner party. The gustatory metaphor, then, implies that cultural difference exists to be consumed. One might almost say that the more the text 'resists', the more enjoyable is its consumption; one could return here to Leiris' contrast between the insipid 'pain quotidien' of his own culture and the Caribbean 'nourriture plus savoureuse et plus stimulante', which he is so eager to consume (see note 7).

In this context, the notion of *assimilation* acquires interesting connotations. The doctrine of assimilation was an official French policy in the nineteenth and twentieth centuries; its aim was to impose the norms of French civilization on the colonies, largely through education, and so to create the greatest possible cultural uniformity across the empire. But from the point of view of the imaging of cultural resistance as unfamiliar, 'stimulating' food, it is highly relevant that assimilation is also a digestive metaphor; according to the *Oxford Dictionary*, it means not only to 'make similar' but also to 'absorb and incorporate; to absorb into the system'. Assimilation, therefore, assumes an initial resistance, in the form of cultural difference, because otherwise it would have nothing to work on. That is, the Other is posed as different precisely in order to legitimate the process of assimilation. And cultural assimilation, to follow the logic of this metaphor, works as infallibly as the robust European digestive tract breaking down the alien ingredients of the curry or couscous or *court bouillon de poisson* that its owner has consumed. As a result, the alien culture ceases to exist: in a kind of reverse cannibalism, the European cultural missionaries 'devour' and annihilate the Caribbean savage. Confiant expresses precisely this fear of being devoured when he refers to 'l'acceptation au sein de nos élites locales du processus de phagocytage de nos sociétés par l'Europe'.[22]

But where the goal of assimilation was uniformity, that of the 'marketing of the margins', to borrow Huggan's phrase, is the opposite: to cultivate difference in order to exploit it commercially. The activity of eating includes both taste and digestion, but these two aspects have opposite implications; the sensation of taste requires the continuing presence of the food in the mouth, not its elimination. And as the principle of assimilation has increasingly been rejected by the people of France's former colonies, so too the metropolitan population has replaced the metaphor of digestion with an emphasis on taste, which links oral consumption more directly with pleasure and variety, rather than simple sustenance. In this context it is worth noting that the food and drink exports of the Caribbean have never been staples such as rice, for instance, but items valued for the luxurious pleasure of their taste: sugar, fruit, rum, etc., and of course spices, whose function is precisely to enhance the taste of more ordinary types of food. Caribbean exoticism is 'spicy': it is revealing that when, in the interview published in this volume, Maryse Condé wants to convey the difficulties of avoiding exoticism in her novels, she chooses the metaphor of cooking without spices: 'It's like a cook who doesn't add any salt, who doesn't add any spices or pepper, it's so much more difficult' (p. 173).

One may conclude from all this that the predominance of metaphors of taste in the marketing and production of French Caribbean novels in the era of globalization illustrates a specifically Caribbean version of a major shift in the attitude of the metropolitan population towards the postcolonial Other. Current forms of neo-colonialism are no longer concerned either to control the Other via a body of knowledge, as in the visual metaphor of opacity/transparency, or to reduce the Other to being the same as oneself via the policy of assimilation, but simply to consume the Other as a commodity which is valued precisely for its difference, and in the Caribbean case for its special 'saveur'.

In the opening paragraph of this chapter I suggested that it was the parallel with the export of real food products from the Caribbean that motivated the presentation of its literary exports as 'edible'. This can be formulated as a relationship between the economic and the ideological levels of society: the French metropolitan subject's economic consumption of food exports from the Caribbean leads to the ideological represen-tation of its literary products also as a kind of exotic food – which serves to literalize the notion of consumption itself, so that the economic status of the subject as consumer is over-determined by the imaginary level of oral pleasure. Reading is experienced as eating. This is of course a fantasy, produced by the historical association of the Caribbean with food, and reinforced by the way in which the literature is marketed by the publishing industry and associated critical writing: the French reader *imagines*, subconsciously, that s/he is eating the Caribbean novel.

But a rather different sense of the term 'imaginary' is also relevant here. When Louis Althusser defines ideology as the imaginary relation to the relations of production, he is referring to the specifically Lacanian sense of the imaginary as the mode of the individual's conscious experience of him/herself, based on the mirror stage, in which the infant identifies with his/her image in the mirror.[23] This 'imaginary' is not an illusion; Althusser insists that ideology is not an illusion either, but a *practice* which transforms men's consciousness, and therefore has real effects.[24] Ideology is produced by 'appareils idéologiques d'état' – such as the Catholic Church, the family or the secular French education system – whose mode of functioning, like the mirror stage, is specular: the individual recognizes him/herself in the image which the ideological apparatus reflects back to him/her. Althusser's term for this process is 'interpellation': the individual is interpellated by the apparatus as an ideological subject.[25]

For Althusser, the main purpose of ideology is to reproduce a labour force ideologically conditioned to fulfil the demands of economic production as efficiently as possible. But there is no reason in principle why an ideological apparatus should not also be directed towards the subject as consumer – the advertising industry, for example, could be considered to be an ideological apparatus. And in the case under discussion here, that part of the publishing industry that specializes in producing postcolonial novels for the international market is also an ideological apparatus. Seen in this Althusserian perspective, the ideological nature of its activity lies not in selling illusions – that is, illusory, because exotic, representations of postcolonial culture – but in interpellating its audience as consumers. Whereas most marketing operations try to disguise the fact that they are actually trying to persuade the public to buy something, the publishing industry here, by promoting the fantasy that its products are to be eaten, indirectly and ironically highlights the reality that it is promoting the *consumption* of a commodity. Equally, whereas the earlier institutions of imperialism interpellated the French ideological subject as guardian of the values of French civilization and propagator of such values to the unenlightened colonized masses, in the globalized postcolonial world s/he is interpellated as first and foremost a consumer: more specifically, the consumer of a commodified exotic culture. And in the case of the French Caribbean, the process is given particular impetus by what one might term the '*oralization*' of consumption: eating their words.

# 4

# Intertextual Connections

## The Jewish Holocaust
## in French Caribbean Novels

From Desmond Dekker's 'The Israelites' to Bob Marley's *Exodus*, the Caribbean story of exile and struggle for freedom has frequently compared itself to the Old Testament account of the Jewish people. In the early twentieth century, Jamaican Marcus Garvey's Black Zionism movement used Jewish Zionism as a template for the Caribbean aspiration to return to Africa; and some Rastafarians consider themselves to be 'the Twelfth Tribe of Judah'. In 'Deux figures du destin', his introduction to 'Mémoire juive, mémoire nègre: deux figures du destin', Roger Toumson points out that this parallelism extends to the whole of the Americas: 'Le récit exilique de l'Ancien Testament est devenu, depuis les premières chroniques de la traite, une référence obligée du destin nègre aux Amériques' (p. 11).[1] On the narrower issue of France's attitude towards its Caribbean colonies, Toumson shows how Jews and black people, these two exemplary manifestations of the Other, have long been closely interconnected: the 'Code noir' of 1615 is mainly concerned with regulating the treatment of African slaves in the French Caribbean, but its first article '[enjoint] à tous nos officiers de chasser hors de nos Isles tous les juifs qui y ont établi leurs résidences' (p. 11); conversely, the Abbé Grégoire became famous in the eighteenth century as much for his castigation of anti-Semitism as for his defence of Negro slaves, and, as Toumson describes it, for 'raisonnant par analogie, posant et résolvant dans les mêmes termes le problème de la condition civile des Juifs et celui de la condition servile des Nègres' (p. 12).

In the aftermath of the Second World War, however, these parallels assume a rather different form. In the 1950s and 1960s, Europe was both coming to terms with the Jewish holocaust and witnessing the beginnings of large-scale immigration from the Caribbean. Now, in other words, the focus is less on Jewish exile in Egypt and more on Jewish incarceration in concentration camps; and the Caribbean experience of diaspora is less that of the original exile from Africa than the new migrations from the Caribbean to Europe. In France, the racism encountered by Caribbean immigrants has obvious similarities with – as well as important differences from – the older anti-Semitism. Frantz Fanon's analysis of the anti-black racism of the French in *Peau noire, masques blancs* makes frequent use of Sartre's *Réflexions sur la question juive* – and Sartre himself followed this text, published in 1947, with 'Orphée noir' in 1948.[2] For Fanon, despite the difference in racial stereotypes[3] and the distinctiveness caused by the inescapable visibility of the black man's blackness, as opposed to the Jew, who can pass for Gentile (p. 95), the mechanisms of racism are identical in both cases; the identity of the racists is the same, and this creates a necessary solidarity between their victims: 'un anti-sémite est forcément négrophobe [...] Je rejoignais le Juif, frères de malheur' (p. 100).

This does not of course mean that black and Jewish communities have in reality always co-existed harmoniously, either in France or elsewhere; in particular, the equation of the holocaust with slavery has recently, in the general context of Islamic anti-Zionism, been vehemently rejected by right-wing Jewish writers such as Alain Finkielkraut.[4] But from the Caribbean point of view, the long-standing familiarity with Old Testament narratives of the exile of the Jews formed a natural basis for the appropriation, in the post-war years, of the imagery of the Jewish holocaust as a means of representing the Caribbean diaspora in France. The intertextual relations with which I am concerned here interrogate the way in which the French Caribbean *imaginaire* turns to the situation of another diasporic people in order to construct a representation of its own situation and, perhaps, to claim recognition of its own suffering through an appeal to the exemplary image of suffering offered by the holocaust. In their ambivalent status, as both a gesture of solidarity with the Jews and a possibly rather presumptuous imaginary appropriation of their situation, these intertexts illustrate the interconnectedness of different diasporic cultures, and show how these connections are actively put to use in the structuring of individual and collective experience.

The concept of intertextuality, first theorized by Julia Kristeva and developed out of Bakhtin's notion of heteroglossia, includes a text's explicit quotations of or allusions to specific other texts, but also, and more importantly, the much broader and more diffuse sense in which a text is inhabited by a plurality of cultural discourses – is, in Kristeva's reading of Bakhtin, 'un *croisement de surfaces* textuelles, un dialogue de plusieurs écritures: de l'écrivain, du destinataire (ou du personnage), du contexte culturel actuel ou antérieur'.[5] The intertextual relations that I discuss here range from the explicit and particular to the implicit and general (and the former, of course, owe much of their resonance to the latter). Thus, for instance, the way in which French Caribbean immigration to France is experienced as a kind of *incarceration* echoes the incarceration of that other ethnic group, the Jews, in Europe. It is sometimes compared to the confinement of animals in cages: in Vincent Placoly's *La Vie et la mort de Marcel Gonstran*, for instance, Marcel, living a miserable and isolated life in Paris, is introduced to us as 'cet homme qui vécut comme un ours en cage' (p. 11). While this is of course a common metaphor for imprisonment, the history of slavery and the racial connotations of animality reinforce its relevance to the Caribbeans.[6] The racist reactions of the French to their presence create a further kind of psychological imprisonment within the self: in *Peau noire, masques blancs* Fanon – just a few pages before the expressions of solidarity with the Jews quoted above – repeatedly describes the refusal of the white French to recognize him as a fellow human being in these terms: 'l'autre, le Blanc, qui, impitoyable, m'*emprisonnait*' (p. 93); '*Enfermé* dans cette objectivité écrasante, j'implorai autrui' (p. 90); 'Je hélais le monde et le monde m'amputait de mon enthousiasme. On me demandait de me *confiner*, de me *rétrécir*' (p. 94, my italics).

These texts contrast strikingly with more recent and better known representations of Caribbean migration, which tend rather to emphasize its mobility, and see diaspora as a dispersal of people in a series of centrifugal movements. Glissant, for example, writes 'Les Antillais [...] éparpillent partout comme un poudre, sans insister nulle part' – and goes on to compare them with the Jewish diaspora: 'et nous ne savions pas non plus que ceux-ci, les Juifs, dont nous n'avions aucune connaissance directe et distinctive, avaient multiplié plus à large que tout ce que nous pouvions imaginer, dans le monde' (*TM*, pp. 385, 386). For Caribbean immigrants to Europe there is in fact a causal connection between the movement of migration and the resulting enforced immobility or imprisonment of 'exile' in Europe, which echoes the Jewish diaspora: the movement that brings the 'wandering' Jews to Europe results, ultimately, in the confinement of the Jews in ghettoes and then in the Nazi concentration camps. Thus in representations of the early period of Caribbean migration to Europe in the 1950s and 1960s, the dominant emphasis is not on movement so much as on an enforced immobility; having reached France (or England: Samuel Selvon's *The Lonely Londoners*[7] is a classic early example of this), the immigrants gradually realize that they will never be able to save enough money to go home, and life in Europe therefore becomes a kind of exile. So too the impossibility of returning home, combined often with an unfamiliarity with French society which makes it difficult to move around freely within it, is experienced as a form of imprisonment; and in certain texts this is compared to the Jewish experience of the concentration camps.

But there are, of course, also many historical and cultural differences in the two peoples' situations. One particularly significant contrast is in their attitude towards the country that they regard as the 'homeland'. In an article entitled 'L'identité et le désastre (origine et fondation)', Daniel Maragnes stresses the implications of the Jews' rootedness in tradition and in the sacred texts of Judaism, with their concomitant certainty that Israel is indeed the true homeland of the Jewish people, and goes on:

> Rien de semblable aux Antilles. Tout se passe véritablement comme si s'effectuait un mouvement parfaitement inverse, posant la mémoire dans les marges même de l'existence, comme son exclue [...] entre l'individu et l'événement aucune symbolique ne s'institue, aucune communauté ne se rassemble, aucun sens ne se forme et ne s'accomplit.[8] (p. 276)

With this in mind, I want now to examine two texts by Guadeloupean writers: Gisèle Pineau's *L'Exil selon Julia* and Simone and André Schwarz-Bart's *Un Plat de porc aux bananes vertes*. In both, the theme of exile as incarceration is explicitly linked to the Jewish holocaust, while the Caribbean homeland is evoked in a markedly ambivalent manner. *L'Exil selon Julia* is an autobiographical text recounting Gisèle Pineau's childhood and adolescence, but revolving around the figure of her paternal grandmother Julia, familiarly known as Man Ya. Maréchal, Gisèle's father, brings Man Ya from Guadeloupe to live with the family in France in order to rescue her from her violent husband Asdrubal; Man Ya, however, has no desire to leave Guadeloupe and is extremely unhappy at what the text's title makes clear is her enforced 'exile' in France. There are frequent references to her 'melancholy', with which Gisèle gradually comes to empathize ('Alors, je comprends mieux la mélancolie de Man Ya, sa peur de mourir ici', p. 117) and which she eventually defines as a 'maladie de l'exil' (p. 129).[9] Man Ya spends long periods indoors, while 'son esprit voyage sans fatiguer entre la France et son pays de Guadeloupe où chaque jour elle espère retourner' (p. 16); and she sees the family apartment and the immediate surroundings as a kind of prison: the door always has to be kept locked against dangerous intruders (p. 81) (as opposed to her house in Guadeloupe, which is 'ouverte sur les quatre bords [...] Sans demander, sans frapper, la vie entre là', p. 139); the children have to grow up in 'la geôle de ces maisons' (p. 128); even the trees are 'emprisonnés dans le béton des trottoirs' (p. 129). Her excursions beyond the immediate neighbourhood are fraught with danger: when she goes to collect the children from school in her son's army greatcoat, she is arrested for illegally wearing French army uniform; when she sets out to walk across Paris to the Sacré Cœur, she has no conception of how far away it is, and gets lost.

But if Man Ya is the most obvious example of the immigrant 'incarcerated' by her depression and her unfamiliarity with Paris, the careful wording of the autobiography's title (not 'L'Exil de Julia', but '*selon* Julia') alerts us to the possibility that the narrator herself also suffers from being in exile from the Caribbean, despite having spent only a few months of her childhood there. Gisèle's 'exile' is the result of the racism of her teachers and fellow pupils at school in France, and it is in connection with this that the explicit comparison with the persecution of the Jews is made. This comparison concerns only a single, albeit repeated, incident, but takes on added resonance against the background of the determining influence of the Second World War upon the family's life. Maréchal was one of the young 'dissidents' who left Guadeloupe in order to join De Gaulle's Free French forces. He becomes an enthusiastic supporter of De Gaulle, and this leads to his decision to emigrate from Guadeloupe with his wife, and to become a professional soldier in the French army.[10] As his daughter explains:

> Qui peut dire que nos destins ne sont pas liés à celui du Général? Il est là au commencement de la vie militaire de papa [...] Si papa n'était pas entré en dissidence pour le rejoindre, où serions-nous à l'heure qu'il est? Si papa n'avait pas porté l'uniforme de l'armée française, ma manman Daisy lui aurait-elle dit oui pour la vie? Voilà comment des Antillais naissent en France. (p. 161)

Conversely, the French people's rejection of De Gaulle in 1968 precipitates Maréchal into a serious depression and makes him decide to take his family back to the Caribbean (p. 163).

But if 1968 is traumatic for Maréchal, it also marks the date of the single most traumatic experience of the text; and it is this that draws together the theme of incarceration, now in relation to Gisèle rather than Man Ya, and the theme of the holocaust. One long chapter consists entirely of letters that Gisèle, aged eleven, sends to Man Ya, who has by then returned home to Guadeloupe. In one of these, she tells her grandmother how she is the only black girl in her class at school, and how one of her teachers persecutes her simply because 'Elle n'aime pas voir ma figure de négresse, ma peau noire' (p. 152). This teacher gives her punishments for no reason: primarily, making Gisèle crouch on all fours beneath her desk. As Gisèle recounts it:

> Alors, elle m'a punie en m'obligeant à entrer sous son bureau. Maintenant, j'y vais presque à tous ses cours. Comme un chien à la niche. J'obéis. Je respire l'odeur de ses pieds. Je vois les poils de ses grosses jambes écrasés sous ses bas. Je serre les dents pour ne pas pleurer. J'entends les voix des élèves. J'ai honte. J'ai peur. Accroupie sous le bureau. Personne ne proteste. Personne ne prend ma défense. (p. 152)

The comparison with a dog in its kennel echoes the imagery of imprisoned animals mentioned above. Gisèle reacts with such a paranoid fear of confinement that she cannot bear to be in a room with a closed door: 'dès que je suis enfermée dans une pièce, je sens que j'étouffe' (p. 152). What is particularly significant, however, is that this description of confinement is followed immediately by a reference to the diary of Anne Frank:

> Les vacances de Pâques arrivent bientôt. Je ne verrai pas Madame Baron pendant quinze jours. Je vais essayer d'écrire l'histoire de ma vie, comme Anne Franck. C'est Manman qui m'a offert le livre. Elle vivait en Hollande avec sa famille. Comme ils étaient juifs, pendant la guerre, ils sont restés cachés dans un réduit jusqu'à ce que les nazis de Hitler les trouvent et les arrêtent en 1944. Ils ont été conduits dans un camp de la mort. Son histoire m'a donné à réfléchir. Je crois qu'après les vacances, je supporterai un peu mieux d'aller sous le bureau. Je penserai à Anne Franck qui est restée serrée dans la noirceur pendant deux années de guerre et puis qui est morte sans pouvoir réaliser son rêve: devenir actrice à Hollywood. Comment vivre dans un pays qui vous rejette à cause de la race, de la religion ou de la couleur de peau? Enfermée, toujours enfermée! Porter une étoile jaune sur son manteau. Porter sa peau noire matin, midi et soir sous les regards des Blancs. (pp. 152–53)

The parallelism between the Jewish and the black situations is emphasized by the parallel syntax of the last two sentences.[11] But it is Anne Frank's *confinement* in the attic, prefiguring her incarceration in the camp, that forms the basis for the comparison between her and Gisèle ('Enfermée, toujours enfermée!'), although Gisèle takes from it also the realization that her own situation is much less serious, which in turn gives her the strength to endure it. Above all, the fact that she explicitly intends to model her autobiography (that is, the text that we are now reading) on Anne Frank's diary – 'Je vais essayer d'écrire l'histoire de ma vie, comme Anne Franck' – shows how representations of the holocaust provide a template for representations of the early period of Caribbean exile.

*Un Plat de porc aux bananes vertes* is the story of a Martinican woman called Mariotte who has ended up, alone and penniless, in an old people's home in Paris in 1952. The narrative is in the form of her diary, which she has to hide from the other residents, and which ends abruptly with her death; the parallels with Anne Frank's diary are evident, and are made more explicit by Mariotte (who is in her eighties) imagining herself when she is writing as a child: she writes in a 'cahier d'écolier' and her words are 'pareils à des bulles de savon qu'envoie au ciel un enfant solitaire' (p. 56).

The novel is striking in the first place for its dual authorship; Simone Schwarz-Bart is Guadeloupean while her husband André was the son, born in France in 1928, of Polish Jewish refugees who were deported from France by the Nazis and died in Auschwitz in 1941; André himself escaped capture and joined the French Resistance. In 1959 he published his first novel, *Le Dernier des Justes*, recounting the story of the Jewish people from the Middle Ages to the holocaust, which was awarded the Prix Goncourt.[12] There are several intertextual references to it in *Un Plat de porc aux bananes vertes*, and *Le Dernier des Justes* also contains its own allusions to the parallels between Jewish victims and Caribbean slaves: in the final scene in the crematorium, Ernie, the hero, reflects that the Jews 'depuis deux mille ans [...] n'eurent jamais ni royaumes de mission ni esclaves de couleur' (p. 423). Both *Le Dernier des Justes* and *Un Plat de porc* draw on previous textual sources, which are listed at the end of both novels: non-fictional accounts of experiences in the concentration camps in the first case, and the works of Césaire and Leiris, among others, in the second. French documentary sources are cited for the representation of life in the old people's home; but it also seems clear, as I shall show, that the latter is informed by the accounts of the camps that underpin *Le Dernier des Justes*. All of this contributes to the extent to which both novels are, rather than direct expressions of lived experience, 'un croisement de surfaces textuelles', in Kristeva's words.

*Un Plat de porc* makes an extended comparison between the Caribbean subject exiled in France and the Jewish subject incarcerated in the concentration camp, as is clearly stated in the book's blurb: 'ce livre [...]

porte témoignage d'une mémoire collective: celle de la servitude, du sort réservé au peuple noir – sort qui, aux yeux d'André Schwarz-Bart [...] apparenterait les descendants d'esclaves aux juifs d'hier et d'aujourd'hui'. Moreover, the book's double dedication to Aimé Césaire and Élie Wiesel, two of the most canonical chroniclers of, respectively, Caribbean and Jewish oppression, adds an explicitly intertextual dimension to the parallel. (Césaire's *Discours sur le colonialisme* itself in fact makes the connection, seeing Nazism not as an aberration but as the logical culmination of colonialism.)[13] The text of *Un Plat de porc* contains specific allusions to Césaire's poems (p. 151), pointed out in the authors' notes at the end of the volume. But there is also a much more general connection between Wiesel's *Night*, about his experiences in Auschwitz and Buchenwald – which was published in French as *La Nuit* in 1958 before finding an American publisher – and the representation of the old people's home in *Un Plat de porc*.

In other words, the parallels that are constructed within the novel are not between Jewish persecution and slavery in the Caribbean, but between the world of the camps and the world of the old people's home, in which Mariotte is the only black resident. She, in other words, compares her exile in Paris and her incarceration in the home with the concentration camps. The anti-Semitism expressed by many of the home's inhabitants is paralleled by their racism towards Mariotte. There are some explicit references to the holocaust: for instance, during one of the residents' frequent conversations about death, an old man suggests that the nurses ought to give them all a fatal injection: '"comme pour les youpins; une piqûre et hop!"' (p. 76). In particular there is an episode describing a woman nicknamed 'Biquette', who has been transferred to the home from long-term residence in Charenton psychiatric hospital. The initial emphasis in this passage is on her isolation, which Mariotte describes in terms echoing Fanon's images of imprisonment in oneself: 'elle me regarderait d'un air effrayé, sans que nul mot ne traverse la carapace invisible dont elle s'entoure' (p. 77) – and this description is also true of Mariotte herself, equally isolated from the other residents of the home. Another link between Mariotte and Biquette is Mariotte's reference to herself as a 'vieille bique' (p. 26). Biquette's nickname (a 'biquette' is a young female goat), although it is sarcastically affectionate, also evokes, together with her 'petits yeux cristallins de cobaye' (p. 77), the metaphors of caged animals that we find elsewhere in descriptions of Caribbeans exiled in Paris – and that we also find in *Le Dernier des Justes* in several descriptions of Jews as animals: rats caught in traps, for instance (pp. 159, 179). In fact, Biquette's most striking characteristic is that she claims to be Jewish, although there is no evidence that she really is. She reacts violently to the anti-Semitic remarks of the other residents, hurling herself headfirst against the walls whenever 'le mot de Juif est prononcé d'une manière qui heurte en elle quelque souvenir enfoui dans la démence, ou quelque fantasme à jamais prisonnier de ses doux petits yeux ronds de cobaye mélancolique' (pp. 77–78). On one occasion the comment that precipitated this reaction was 'considérant le nombre de "juéfs" qui sont encore en vie, quelqu'un se demande: "A ce qu'il semble, leurs crématoires c'étaient des couveuses?"' (p. 77) – and in fact Biquette, who has a number written in ink on her forearm, claims that she herself has been in a concentration camp. This, however, is definitely untrue, given the number of years she has been in the Charenton hospital; in fact, it is presumably this incarceration, followed by that in the old people's home, that has produced the fantasy of imprisonment in a Nazi camp.[14] In other words, although she is white and in all probability Gentile, Biquette serves to create a link between Jews and Caribbeans: she is described with the same images that are often used to characterize Caribbean exiles, and she identifies with the Jews, and with their suffering in the holocaust. At the same time, her conviction that she is in a concentration camp also illustrates the phantasmatic power of the holocaust in the years following the war, showing the extent to which it became an exemplary instance of oppression with which other oppressed groups or individuals identified.

Biquette's equating of the old people's home with a concentration camp is just one example of the parallels between the two places. The home, like the camps, is suffused with an atmosphere of imminent death: Mariotte laments 'N'est-ce donc pas assez de la mort et nous faut-il agoniser dent à dent, membre à membre, et jusque dans chacun des organes de l'intelligence et du cœur?' (p. 71). The similarity to the Nazi death camps is particularly evident in the rumour going round the female ward that, in order to relieve the overcrowding on the male ward, the nurses 'auraient maintenant la consigne secrète de nous *expédier* le plus discrètement possible' (p. 79). Whether this is true or not, the inmates have in any case been left there to die, and oscillate between a determination to survive and the constant temptation of suicide: at the bottom of the main staircase of the home is 'une grande dalle usée [...] qui accueille les maladroites et celles qui ne le sont qu'à demi – et que nous appelons, aussi haut qu'on remonte dans l'histoire de l'hospice: Consolation' (p. 30). The link with Jewish concentration camps here takes the precise form of an intertextual link to *Le Dernier des Justes*, where the description of the camp at Drancy includes a reference to prisoners who similarly kill themselves by jumping out of a sixth-floor window onto 'une certaine plaque de ciment qui devint tristement célèbre au camp' (p. 398). The principal reason for the suicidal desires in the old people's home is the level of physical abjection and pain that virtually all of them suffer; life in the home is reduced to a pure question of physical existence that is also reminiscent of accounts of concentration camp prisoners: there is never enough to eat; they have debilitating and humiliating illnesses; and there is a relentless emphasis on urine and bowel movements. Also, Biquette's concentration camp number may be fake, but it is still the case that all the inmates of the home are, like prisoners, dehumanized by being referred to not by name but by the number of their bed: Sister Marie des Anges, though she is kind to Mariotte, always calls her 'le Quatorze': 'Sérieusement, le Quatorze, j'estime que ça vous fera du bien' (p. 24). And, as in the camps, this is a world without money; like prisoners, the inmates create their own currency of cigarette ends, which they collect on the rare occasions that they are allowed to go outside, and barter for glasses of wine, extra food or other favours.

We learn very little of Mariotte's life after leaving Martinique and before entering the old people's home; but towards the end of the novel there are three brief and cryptic references to a certain Moritz Lévy (pp. 149, 180, 205), who appears to have been Mariotte's lover and who died two years previously, at the point at which she entered the home. The suggestion that Mariotte has had a Jewish lover forms another kind of parallel between Caribbean and Jewish communities in France and, more specifically, another intertextual link with *Le Dernier des Justes*, in which Ernie's brother is called Moritz Lévy.

In these two novels, then, the Jewish holocaust provides a framework within which to situate and represent the Caribbean experience of exile-as-incarceration. But the allusions and parallels that I have described exist alongside a number of equally important differences, which relate in particular to the way in which the lost *homeland* is conceptualized. For Pineau's and the Schwarz-Barts' characters, in other words, the Caribbean plays a more complex and ambiguous role than Zion does for the Jewish diaspora. In the latter case, exile is from the Holy Land: the ancestral home of the Jewish people for thousands of years, sanctioned by biblical authority. The Caribbean diaspora, however, if taken in the sense of the migration from the Caribbean to Europe, is a secondary consequence of the other, original diaspora that was effected by transportation from Africa; and Caribbean literature, especially in the poetry of the Negritude movement, is full of references to the loss of the *original* homeland, which is Africa. Thus, while Césaire's 'Cahier d'un retour au pays natal' (one of the two epigraphs at the beginning of *Un Plat de porc*) designates Martinique as the land of his birth, much of his other poetry is dedicated to the evocation of Africa as the lost motherland of the Caribbean people.[15] While Caribbean literature of course often celebrates the natural beauty and the culture of the islands, there is no real equivalent to the idealization of Africa that we find in the poetry of Negritude. From this point of view, it is Africa that most closely replicates the status of Zion as the *ideal* of origin, that is, the idealized homeland that Israel was for European Jews in the 1940s: in *Le Dernier des Justes*, for instance, Ernie comforts the children being transported to Auschwitz with a vision of the 'royaume d'Israël':

> Là-bas, les enfants y retrouvent leurs parents, et tout le monde se réjouit. Car le pays où nous allons est notre royaume, sachez-le bien. Là-bas, le soleil ne s'y couche jamais, et on peut y manger toutes les choses qui vous viennent à l'esprit. Là-bas, une joie éternelle couronnera vos têtes; l'allégresse et la joie s'approcheront, et la douleur et les gémissements s'enfuiront. (p. 413)

The Caribbean islands, in contrast, are a *real* home and, for Caribbeans in France, a source of real and hence often ambivalent memories. The sense of exile in Europe that results from their disillusionment, from having to give up their original hopes of a better life, produces a bitterness towards Europe and, certainly, a longing for home – but it is not a simple longing.[16] 'Exile' versus 'home' in other words, is not a straightforward opposition in which 'home' figures as a fully positive term, different in all possible ways from exile in Europe. What we find instead in the novels of both Pineau and the Schwarz-Barts is a deeply ambiguous evocation of Martinique and Guadeloupe, in which the sense of alienation that blights the characters' lives in Europe also affects their memories of home.

In *L'Exil selon Julia* Man Ya's longing to return to Guadeloupe is entirely wholehearted, and her eventual return is described as a 'délivrance' (p. 135). But Guadeloupe is inextricably tied up with her husband Asdrubal – had it not been for his mistreatment of her, Maréchal would never have forced her to leave the island – and her relationship with him is an overtly ambivalent one in which her hatred of his cruelty coexists with the pity she feels for him and her dutiful sense that a wife should remain loyal to the husband whom God has given her. The other characters feel strongly that this attachment to Asdrubal is perverse and destructive, and there is a sense in which Asdrubal functions as a displaced symbol of a suppressed love-hate relation to the island itself. Thus Man Ya's attachment to Guadeloupe is presented as entirely visceral and, literally, *unreasonable* – almost as though she is deluding herself:

> Elle veut une seule chose, retourner sur sa terre de Guadeloupe [...] même s'il est vrai que cette terre maudite ensorcelle, amarre les destinées. Elle ne philosophe pas sur le pourquoi et le comment de l'attachement à sa terre. La raison s'affaisse devant les sauts du cœur. Il n'y a pas de mots, seulement le manque qui aveugle et étourdit. Il n'y a pas de grandes théories, seulement de candides souvenirs que la mémoire travestit, des broutilles agaçantes, une pantomime extatique. (p. 137)

All the other adult Guadeloupeans in France, as Gisèle notices, express contradictory, consciously ambivalent attitudes towards the island, fluctuating between 'l'ivresse qui éclôt de chaque retour et la renaissance qui dit accompagner l'exil'; they speak about it with 'amour, nostalgie et dépit' and Gisèle concludes that 'Ils l'aimaient, oui, mais d'une manière équivoque, comme un amour de jeunesse qu'on n'arrive pas à oublier même s'il n'a pas donné de fruits' (p. 29). She herself has only lived in Guadeloupe for a few months, when she was very young; nevertheless she too regards it as her homeland, wishes that her parents had never emigrated (p. 28) and, particularly after Man Ya's departure, dreams of going to live there permanently (p. 140).

Yet when the family do finally leave France and return to the Caribbean, the experience for Gisèle and her siblings is not exactly that of a homecoming. The fact that Maréchal is first posted not to Guadeloupe but to Martinique can in itself be read as indicating a slight disjunction: that this is a return to somewhere that is nearly, but not quite, home. Fort-de-France greets them on their arrival with a disconcerting mixture of the familiar and the strange; when the children decide to walk to the sea, they set off confidently, sure that they will not get lost in this place that miraculously combines novelty and familiarity: 'Tout ici-là est inconnu et pourtant reconnu' (p. 177). At first, they experience a euphoric sense of belonging that they never attained in France: 'Chaque pas nous ramène en nous-mêmes. Toute la misère des lieux nous parle et nous console, nous dit: "Vous êtes d'ici!"' (p. 178). But the sea turns out to be much further away than it had seemed, and as they traverse almost the whole of Fort-de-France their surroundings cease to appear welcoming; they realize that they are completely lost, and their euphoria turns to fear (p. 180). The busyness of the streets around them creates a kind of sensory overload in which crowds, bright colours and loud noises become so overwhelming that they begin to appear not only unfamiliar but actively hostile. Most strikingly, these three black children find themselves – as in the stereotypical reaction of the white visitor to the colonies – seized with panic at being surrounded by black people: 'Non, nous ne sommes pas acclimatés à ces débordements, à ces visages parlants, à cette fièvre qui habite la rue. Et puis, il y a tous ces Noirs autour de nous. Tellement de Noirs, plus ou moins noirs' (p. 181). They wish they had never left the security of the fort – in other words, the French army – and realize that 'Nous ne connaissons rien d'ici' (p. 182).

Thus, a journey which had started as a euphoric expression of self-realization through an almost spiritual homecoming, ends as a panic-stricken admission that they do not belong here: Fort-de-France is in no sense their home. But while this emphasizes the cultural and emotional distance between France and the Antilles, the journey is given a further significance that paradoxically brings the two places together – but with equally negative connotations. In the course of this section of the narrative, the children's attempt to walk to the sea is explicitly paralleled (pp. 177, 179, 182) with Man Ya's attempt, recounted much earlier in the novel, to walk with Gisèle's brother Élie to the Sacré Cœur. In both cases, the journey's destination recedes as they walk towards it and initial confidence gives way to confusion and fear, in a hostile environment. Man Ya did in fact eventually reach the Sacré Cœur and return triumphantly to the family's apartment. Nevertheless, her long walk across Paris was a desperate attempt to alleviate her misery at living there, and merely served to emphasize her isolation and the hostility of her environment: there was no sense of recognition or of homecoming involved. As a result, bringing these two incidents together in the text inevitably minimizes the joyful elements of the children's journey, and suggests that Fort-de-France may pose the same kinds of problems for them as Paris did for Man Ya – problems perhaps symbolized by the cockroaches, mosquitoes and other pests that constitute the 'cinq plaies du retour au pays pas natal', as one of the chapters is tellingly entitled (p. 193): the ironic reference to Césaire's *Cahier d'un retour au pays natal* underlines further their sense of alienation. This disillusionment does not mean that the novel has an unhappy ending. However, Gisèle's successful adaptation to life in the Caribbean is made possible by her realization that it is *not* home but a new place with strange ways of behaving that she will have to learn (p. 184). Her mother expresses the ambiguity of the children's position, but also their determination to make a new life here: 'Ils sont d'ici sans en être vraiment mais ils s'y essaient, chaque jour, passionnément, avec la volonté de ces gens de la ville qui font un retour à la terre' (pp. 210–11).

In *Un Plat de porc aux bananes vertes*, in contrast, Mariotte's old age continues in unrelieved despair until her death in the old people's home: she never returns to Martinique. But the two novels do nevertheless share a very similar questioning of the ideal of the homeland. For instance, *Un Plat de porc* also creates parallels as well as contrasts between the Caribbean past and the present in Paris: Mariotte's memories start from and frequently return to her dying grandmother, who is described in similar terms to the residents of the old people's home; and a key remembered scene takes place in a prison cell, echoing the theme of incarceration that dominates the representation of the home.

But a more pervasive undermining of the ideal of the homeland in this novel occurs through its exploration of the disjunction between memory and fantasy. Since Simone Schwarz-Bart is a native of Guadeloupe, and the couple lived there, one might have expected them to choose Guadeloupe as the homeland of their heroine.[17] The reason for the choice of Martinique, I think, lies in the circumstances of Mariotte's departure from the island: she left in 1903, after the eruption of the Mont Pelée volcano which destroyed the town of St Pierre, killed her mother and obliterated her village. In other words, it would seem to be important to the novel that Mariotte migrates from a place that has been destroyed: in the narrow sense, she has no home to return to. She is longing for something which is not only spatially out of reach, but also belongs to the past. Although she knows this, she still longs to return to Martinique as it was before the eruption. This creates a tension between her memory of what happened and the fantasy of return that depends upon repressing the memory – a tension that is perceptible in the way in which the text moves from a sudden involuntary memory of seeing the island for the last time to an idyllic image of St Pierre as she *wishes* to remember it:

> [...] Subitement elle m'apparut, comme la dernière fois, en 1903, lorsque le vapeur qui amenait vers la Guyane son chargement de rescapés de Saint-Pierre [...] eut gagné la haute mer: un court morceau de terre verte entouré d'eaux multicolores avec, sur les hauteurs de la Montagne Pelée,

la gueule béante du cratère encore empanachée de cette cendre bleuâtre qui avait recouvert ma vie, quelques centaines de mètres plus bas [...]

Mais le St Pierre de mon imagination n'offrait pas un spectacle de fin du monde. (p. 84)

– and this last sentence leads into a detailed description of peaceful boats in the harbour, churches, the theatre, hills which are not covered in lava but still green and fertile, and the evocation of her village and her mother's house (p. 84). The break between the two paragraphs signals the transition from an actual memory to imaginary wish fulfilment.[18]

Mariotte's evocation of Martinique is mainly devoted to much earlier memories, in particular an incident in which her mother visits her lover Raymoninque (who may or may not be Mariotte's father) in prison, accompanied by Mariotte, and brings him the 'dish of pork with green bananas'. The central image of the novel provides another powerful example of the ironic disjunction between her longing to go home and her memories of it, which problematizes the evocation of home as a straightforward opposition to exile. Mariotte and her mother take the dish to give to Raymoninque in his prison cell; Mariotte, of course, is not allowed to eat any of it, and it smells so wonderful that she can hardly stop herself from crying (p. 117). This is the image that gradually comes to sum up for her all her memories of Martinique; everything else fades away:

Brusquement tout a disparu, la Martinique, l'asile, tout cela s'est évanoui dans l'air et il ne restait plus devant mes yeux éblouis [...] que la ration de porc tendu à Raymoninque, l'autre siècle, avec regret [...] car je savais que c'était le dernier morceau et qu'il n'y en avait plus à la maison: plus du tout! (p. 131)

That is, the whole novel is structured around Mariotte's longing for Martinique: but the whole of Martinique itself is concentrated in the memory of this dish of pork *that she was not allowed to eat*. Her symbol of Martinique is not one of fulfilment, but of desire and lack.

It is therefore entirely appropriate that the end of the novel replays the scene in the same register of non-fulfilment. Mariotte decides that she wants to eat Caribbean food one more time before she dies, and manages, with great difficulty, to walk out of the old people's home to the Creole restaurant in the rue Gît-le-Cœur that she used to frequent. Standing outside its door, she imagines a scene in which she is recognized and welcomed by its owner and sits down to eat a 'dish of pork with green bananas'. This imaginary scene is evoked in vivid and lengthy detail (pp. 201–09), but then she realizes that she cannot face entering the restaurant because she would not be able to stop herself from crying (as in Raymoninque's prison cell). So she sets off back to the home, but suffers a stroke on the way and is brought back by ambulance. She writes her notebooks in the two weeks that follow this incident, and, since the text ends abruptly in mid-sentence, we assume that she dies at that point.

Thus the *object* of the exiled subject's longing is itself a longing for something precious that was always out of reach. This double structure – a longing for a longing – echoes the double structure of diaspora in the Caribbean in which migration to Europe is superimposed on the original African diaspora, with the result that the Caribbean home always figures as a less than ideal homeland, and can never wholly fulfil the fantasy of return from exile. For Gisèle Pineau, Guadeloupe is not, ultimately, 'home' but a new country; for Mariotte, Martinique is a lost home that in reality never fulfilled her desires. Thus, whereas the Jewish holocaust acts as a powerful image and reference point for these evocations of the French Caribbean situation in post-war Europe, the Caribbean experience of diaspora in these years is also more emotionally ambivalent: not in its relation to France, but in its complicated attitude towards a 'home' that is itself characterized by lack and longing.

# Breaking the Rules

## Irrelevance/Irreverence in Maryse Condé's
## *Traversée de la mangrove*

'Je suis une personne très moqueuse, heureusement'.[1] Maryse Condé's antipathy to pious clichés and reassuring stereotypes is well known. Régis Antoine, for instance, writes: 'Travaillant dans la dérision, la satire et la dénonciation de l'intolérable, elle vise à déplaire intellectuellement, pour éveiller'; and Leah Hewitt describes her as 'an iconoclast who picks apart the clichés of the communities she has lived in'.[2] Condé's sardonic humour forms, in her own view, the basis of her realism: 'La réalité du monde noir est tellement triste que si on n'en rit pas un peu, on devient complètement désespéré et négatif. Pour moi, me moquer est une façon de regarder les choses en face'.[3] Realism, in this sense of writing against the stereotypical, is achieved through vigilant attention to reality, which Condé presents as a conceptually simple matter of unbiased observation: 'Finalement, l'oeuvre d'un écrivain c'est quoi sinon présenter la vie autour de lui dans sa complexité et dans son étrangeté?'[4]

Much has already been written on Condé's ironic realism and her refusal to conform to literary or cultural conventions;[5] much has also been written specifically on *Traversée de la mangrove*.[6] But there is one aspect of this novel which demands a rather different theorization of Condé's treatment of the stereotype, and which therefore allows us to see more precisely how multi-level and all-pervasive her 'irreverence' is. The transgressive force of her work compared to other Antillean writers is not in fact restricted to its clearer, more hard-headed vision of reality, involving narrative events, themes and characters. Its irreverence also operates on the level of the very small structures of the text: the structures of paragraphs and, most strikingly, of individual sentences. It attacks the stereotype also through purely discursive manoeuvres.

This implies that the stereotype has its own discourse; or, as Barthes would put it, its own code. In *S/Z* he imagines a new radical stylistics that would:

> s'attache[r] essentiellement à dégager et à classer des modèles (des patterns) de phrases, des clausules, des cadences, des armatures, des structures profondes [...] dépassant l'opposition du fond et de la forme, [la stylistique] deviendrait un instrument de classement idéologique; car, ces modèles trouvés, on pourrait à chaque fois, le long de la plage du texte, mettre chaque code *ventre en l'air*. (p. 107, italics original)

To return to the semiological criticism of the 1960s and 1970s may seem an odd move to make, when postcolonial theory has developed so far in such different directions. It is worth remembering, however, that Barthes was one of the first to focus attention on the 'cultural code' of colonialism and cultural difference in post-war France. *Mythologies* is famous for its analysis of the photograph of the black soldier saluting the French flag on the cover of *Paris Match*, and the volume contains a number of other equally acerbic dissections of colonial mythologies: 'Bichon chez les nègres', 'Le "Guide bleu"', 'Grammaire africaine', '"Continent perdu"', 'La grande famille des hommes'.[7] *Mythologies* also provides a basis for further analysis: its key insight, the 'naturalization' of cultural and social phenomena, would apply in exemplary fashion to the Antilles, whose 'natural paradise' is in fact an almost wholly man-made phenomenon. Most of the vegetation that we think of as typically Caribbean was, as Condé points out, imported by Europeans from Africa and the Indian Ocean, so that 'On a l'impression que le paysage entier a été totalement fabriqué. Finalement, les Antilles sont des créations totalement artificielles du système capitaliste'.[8] *Traversée de la mangrove* itself, as part of its undermining of exotic stereotypes, stresses the commercial cultivation of plants and animals: the orchids in the Lameaulnes' 'pépinière', Carmélien's computerized crayfish farming.

It is not, however, Barthes' critique of colonialism and exoticism but a far more general feature of his intellectual sensibility that seems to me to offer the most illuminating perspective on *Traversée de la mangrove*: namely, his acute awareness of the coercive but covert *rules* that underlie all social behaviour. The concept of the rule, as Barthes formulates it, brings together ideological content and formal structure; hence his insistence on what is *politically* at stake in the *stylistic* analysis of social and literary discourses. (He himself demonstrates this in a colonial context in 'Grammaire africaine'.) This in turn leads him to be very sensitive to the disproportionately far-reaching effects of breaking these 'little' discursive rules. 'Écriture', in his radical sense of the word, is ideologically transgressive *through* its formal transgressions; its function is to 'rendre dérisoire, annuler le pouvoir (l'intimidation) d'un langage sur un autre' (*S/Z*, p. 105).

This double transgression is, I hope to demonstrate, responsible for the peculiarly unsettling effect of *Traversée de la mangrove*. Condé's iconoclastic stance, in other words, does not involve only the substantive representations of characters and their opinions; it also derives from her predilection for breaking the formal rules of literary discourse. I want to focus on one particular type of sentence that recurs throughout *Traversée de la mangrove*. Its structure is deliberately inelegant – rambling, clumsy and unbalanced – and it occurs in two different forms, which I shall (also somewhat inelegantly) designate as the 'skid' and the 'loop'. The skid moves by free association through a number of topics, ending up somewhere completely unrelated to its starting point. For instance, Man Sonson's disorganized train of thought:

> J'aurais aimé qu'on m'enterre ici même derrière la case en bois du Nord que Siméon, mon défunt, a mise debout tout seul de ses deux mains, car c'était un vaillant Nègre, de l'espèce qui a disparu de la surface de la planète et on peut chercher son pareil à ses quatre coins, on n'en trouvera pas, sous le manguier greffé que j'ai planté un matin de septembre à la lune montante, dans cet endroit que je n'ai jamais quitté, même pas quand mon fils Robert le deuxième s'est marié en métropole avec une femme blanche qu'il a connue dans le bureau de poste où il travaille. (p. 81)

The loop, in contrast, has a circular structure; it starts and ends with a short main clause, but in between has a much longer digressive series of subordinate clauses – for instance:

> Du jour au lendemain, Carmélien – garçon qui ne manquait de rien, 'Ti-Mal' de son papa qui, après l'avoir longtemps juché sur son guidon de bicyclette, lui avait offert sa propre Motobécane, toute chromée, constamment réprimandé par sa maman, mais il ne s'occupait pas, ne prêtant pas plus d'attention à ce babier qu'au bourdonnement des mouches à la saison de mangue – changea. (p. 177)

In the first place, both types break the formal requirement that good literary style should possess a streamlined coherence that reads smoothly and unambiguously; in Man Sonson's sentence, for instance, the transition from 'on n'en trouvera pas' to 'sous le manguier greffé' confuses the reader into wondering momentarily whether she is looking for her dead husband under the mango tree, rather than wanting to be buried there herself. The loop in particular produces a characteristic disjunction where the reader as it were stumbles on returning to the main clause; this point is marked in the above example by the second dash, but in other cases, as we shall see, there is no punctuation to clarify the transition.

At the same time, since their syntax tends towards infinite expansion through the addition of yet more clauses, these sentences also allow – in fact, require – the inclusion of *irrelevant information*. They therefore also break the rule that requires good narrative prose to eliminate non-essential distractions, keeping the reader's attention focused on what is relevant to the central theme of the novel as a whole (in the above examples: death, and Carmélien's sexual awakening). Their precise syntactic structure is particularly important since, as the text consists largely of interior monologues, they might be thought to have a different kind of significance: as a psychologically realistic representation of inner speech and a means of characterizing their subjects (Man Sonson as a dotty old woman, Carmélien as a confused adolescent). Interpreted in this way, they would be far less transgressive. But, in fact, the syntax of these long sentences with numerous embedded subordinate clauses is usually too carefully constructed for an explanation in terms of psychological verisimilitude to be credible. Thus Delphine Perret refers to 'les nombreuses phrases complexes, au rythme cadencé, dont la syntaxe peut illustrer une certaine liberté [...] mais est rarement brisée comme dans la langue parlée familière ou populaire'.[9] (One can, it is true, also find 'skidding' and 'looping' paragraphs, which are readable according to this kind of realist alibi, while performing most of the other characteristic functions of the sentences.) Scattered through the novel, they occur in a variety of contexts and produce a variety of different effects. But the feature that they have in common is simply their conspicuous irrelevance, and it is this, first and foremost, that constitutes their irreverence.

The clearest theoretical justification for this claim that irrelevance *per se* is subversive is provided by Barthes' 1966 article 'Introduction à l'analyse structurale des récits', with its central insistence on the total intelligibility of the classic narrative structure in which everything is meaningful because it is all, down to the smallest detail, integrated into the overall structure: 'un récit n'est jamais fait que de fonctions:

tout, à des degrés divers, y signifie [...] c'est une question de structure: dans l'ordre du discours, *ce qui est noté est, par définition, notable'* (my italics).[10] In Barthes' analysis, the narrative structure is made up of different levels and the units of the lower levels are entirely, without leaving any residue, subsumed into the larger units of the higher levels. Each element is meaningful because it forms one term of a relation with others and is integrated into a vertical hierarchy of levels.[11] In the classic narrative text 'meaning' thus becomes virtually synonymous with relevance, integration and hierarchy; and all three of these terms are signally alien to the skidding and looping sentences of Condé's novel. *Traversée de la mangrove*, in other words, does not integrate its wayward fragments of irrelevant meaning into any kind of hierarchy; by breaking a low-level rule of sentence structure it simultaneously refuses to conform to the much higher-level order of the intelligible whole.

Four years later, in *S/Z*, Barthes introduced a fundamental distinction between the classic realist text, now called the 'texte lisible', and the radical 'texte scriptible', which breaks all the structural rules that govern the 'lisible'. This latter is now seen as determined by a number of 'codes' rather than rules, which, however, work according to the same principle of integrating particular instances into a larger unit of meaning. These codes provide an equally illuminating basis for an analysis of *Traversée de la mangrove* – despite the fact that Condé's novel does not fit straightforwardly into Barthes' framework: its realism disqualifies it as a 'texte scriptible', but it also transgresses the codes of the 'lisible' as Barthes defines them. Precisely because of this, however, *S/Z*'s theoretical framework reveals what is at stake in Condé's ironic manipulation of the codes that it establishes.

The clearest example is the 'hermeneutic code': the setting up and gradual unravelling of a mystery. The opening of *Traversée de la mangrove*, the discovery of Sancher's body, is a strong indication that the hermeneutic code is going to dominate the rest of the novel: how has Sancher died? And we very quickly realize that there is also another, related but larger, mystery: who was Sancher, where was he from and why did he come to Rivière au Sel? But although the text mimics the sequential stages and operations of the hermeneutic code, neither mystery is ever solved with any certainty. There are hints, but no more; it is, as Condé herself describes it, 'un puzzle dont beaucoup de pièces manquent'.[12] Yet the text never draws attention to its defeat of the hermeneutic code; it is not until the reader has reached the end that s/he realizes there is going to be no dramatic discovery or dénouement.

This creates a retroactive effect which is all the more powerful for being delayed; on the scale of the narrative as a whole, the status of the hermeneutic code as an organizing principle of the text is fundamentally undermined.

The fact that the illusion of a hermeneutic code is sustained until the end of the text also means that on a smaller, local scale, the reader goes on attempting to assess each piece of information in terms of its possible status as a clue; in other words, is it *relevant* to the mystery or not?[13] A typical pattern is for the skidding or looping sentence to start from a memory of the speaker's first, or last, or only meeting with Francis Sancher – one of the standard conventions of the discourse of mourning – and then to move surreptitiously but relentlessly away from him. Thus Léocadie, for instance, tells us:

> Je n'ai plus jamais revu Francis Sancher. J'ai entendu qu'il avait continué ses méfaits et jeté cette fois son dévolu sur l'innocente Vilma que j'ai vue gonfler mois après mois le ventre de Rosa qui n'arrêtait pas, malgré tout ce qu'on lui disait, de pleurer sa petite Shireen, décédée quelques mois auparavant, avant d'entrer dans notre monde sans joie, un matin de juin alors que Sylvestre était allé acheter des boeufs au Moule, ce qui fait qu'il n'a vu sa fille que vieille de deux jours. (p. 151)

The text thus progresses in a series of centrifugal movements away from its ostensible main theme, which is the life and death of Francis Sancher, and towards a whole range of disparate and apparently far less important concerns; Sancher himself at times seems to be less the focus of the novel than a mere pretext for its random trajectories. Whereas the hermeneutic code, if operating successfully, would establish a powerful criterion of relevance and hence organization, there is here nothing to *hold the text together*; the reader, left with a series of uncoordinated fragments of meaning – which may be relevant to the central mystery, but seem increasingly unlikely to be so – does not know what to do with them.[14] In other words, it is impossible to establish a hierarchy of importance of meanings; the sentences enact their own version of the 'paratactic structure of the novel' that Mireille Rosello finds in *Les Derniers Rois mages*.[15]

This refusal to attach more importance to some meanings than others is in itself a radical form of irreverence to the rule that structures a literary text in terms of its overall unity, composed of a central theme, a build-up, a climax and a dénouement. But there is a more concrete kind of irreverence as well, insofar as the irrelevance is in itself comical, producing an effect of bathos. It is particularly noticeable in the cases of a centrifugal movement away from a memory of Francis Sancher, as in this further example from Léocadie's chapter:

> Et pourtant, de son vivant, je ne le portais pas dans mon coeur, cet homme-là, et j'étais bien de l'avis de ceux qui s'apprêtaient à envoyer une lettre recommandée au maire pour qu'on l'expulse comme les Haïtiens et les Dominicains qui transforment les terrains de football de Petit Bourg en terrains de cricket. (p. 139)

Or in Moïse's skid from mourning his friend to his modest pride in his garage:

> Il s'en souvenait du midi lumineux où il l'avait vu pour la première fois. Il terminait la tournée qui le menait chaque matin de la poste de Petit Bourg au Trou au Chien, puis à Mombin, Dillon, Petite Savane, Rousses, Bois l'Étang et qui se terminait à Rivière au Sel où il avait son chez-lui et même un garage en planches pour abriter la camionnette jaune de la poste. (p. 30)

But all the irrelevant sentences have this characteristic irony. Used in both first-person monologue and free indirect discourse, the juxtaposition of solemn and trivial, or the sheer amount of unnecessary detail, result in an ironic deflation of the characters – their pretentiousness but also their suffering – and the themes that the novel elsewhere presents with complete seriousness. The most striking example is Sancher's death itself, which right at the beginning of the novel, even before we enter the characters' interior monologues, is treated in an extremely casual manner:

> Vers neuf heures et la lune se reposait derrière un nuage couleur d'encre qui bientôt, on le sentait, allait crever en eau, alors que Monsieur Démocrite, le directeur de l'école, avait donné permission d'aller chercher la bâche qui servait à abriter le terrain de football, le docteur Martin arriva de Petit Bourg au volant de sa luxueuse B.M.W. et s'enferma un long moment seul à seul avec le mort. (p. 23)

Here the solemnity of death is mocked by its being tacked onto the end of a sentence which encompasses other very prosaic details, implying that the villagers were more concerned with ensuring that the mourners did not get wet, and with envying the doctor's car.

Because irony of this sort is associated with satire and parody, and hence with irreverence, it is normally considered to be subversive: attacking social convention, cultural codes and the power of ideological discourse. It may therefore seem surprising that Barthes makes it very clear in *S/Z* that he does not regard irony as subversive, but as 'une parole *classique*' (p. 52, italics original), squarely on the side of the 'lisible' – the conventional and the authoritative. Irony, in his view, is itself a code ('Le code Ironique', p. 145) which, far from sapping the strength of the other codes, merely adds to their hierarchical organization by forming one more layer on top of all the others. Moreover, it is an expression of the author's dominance, asserting his or her superior intelligence by ridiculing the more naïve codes upon which the irony nevertheless depends (p. 52). Barthes does, however, make an exception for a particular kind of 'Flaubertian' irony that does not proclaim the author's controlling presence and introduces indeterminacy rather than certainty: 'Flaubert cependant [...] en maniant une ironie frappée d'incertitude, opère un malaise salutaire de l'écriture: il n'arrête pas le jeu des codes (ou l'arrête mal) en sorte que [...] *on ne sait jamais s'il est responsable de ce qu'il écrit*' (p. 146, italics original).

The irony that pervades *Traversée de la mangrove* fluctuates between these two types, and in doing so makes Barthes' opposition appear less clear cut. Some of it is definitely 'classical'; Condé's straightforward, vigorous satire of, for instance, the writers of the *créolité* group ('As-tu comme le talentueux Martiniquais, Patrick Chamoiseau, déconstruit le français-français?', p. 228) quite unashamedly asserts her own point of view and has no problem with the idea that she is right and others are wrong. It is significant that for Condé irony or mockery is closely linked to the fictional text's ability to engage with the real and hence to speak the 'truth', as in the remark I have already quoted: 'Pour moi, me moquer est une façon de regarder les choses en face'. This classic, assertive irony is particularly in evidence where it serves to condemn cruelty; the racial cruelty of the light-skinned Mira to the Indian boy Carmélien is a good example of a looping sentence used in accordance with Barthes' classic ironic code. The love-struck Carmélien has bought her a doll:

> Elle parut surprise, regarda la poupée, puis le regarda depuis ses pieds chaussés d'escarpins que Rosa [his mother] avait achetés chez Bata jusqu'à la raie qu'elle avait tracée à coups de brillantine Vitapointe avant de l'asperger d'eau de Cologne Bien-Être et dit simplement: – Kouli malabar! (p. 179)

But it also occurs as a less serious ridicule – for instance, skidding along Emmanuel's consumerist pretensions: 'Emmanuel allait chercher deux verres et une bouteille de whisky Glenfiddich, puis mettait en marche la chaîne hifi qu'il avait achetée lors d'une réunion d'experts en forêts à Manaus et à laquelle personne n'avait le droit de toucher' (p. 114). It is very clear in both these examples that the ironic layer of code completes rather than undermines the work of what Barthes variously calls the 'semic code', or 'Voix de la personne'. This is the code responsible for characterization (I shall refer to it as the 'character code'), which operates by a process of accumulation, building up the illusion of a whole unified individual from a collection of 'semes' scattered through the text ('la personne n'est qu'une collection de sèmes', *S/Z*, p. 196). Here, the evidence of Mira's arrogance and Emmanuel's smugness accords with and consolidates the overall representation of their characters.

On the other hand, some of the novel's irrelevant sentences create a more diffuse, subtle and indeed Flaubertian ironic effect. Barthes criticizes classic irony for working against the 'multivalence' and 'duplicité' of the 'scriptible',[16] but in this second type of sentence the irony acts to introduce, precisely, multivalence and duplicity into the text, and thus also to counteract the character code by preventing the semes from cohering into a unified whole. For instance, it presents Loulou's moment of suicidal depression as follows:

> Pour la première fois, lui, le lutteur, dur à la peine, qui en trente-cinq ans s'était offert deux fois dix jours de congé, d'abord pour conduire Aurore Dugazon à la Nouvelle-Orléans, tout cela pour la voir s'aliter dans une chambre d'hôtel à cause d'un café-crème, ensuite pour conduire Dinah à Amsterdam, ville pluvieuse, où, beau choix pour une bigote de son espèce, les putains s'exhibaient demi-nues dans des loggias éclairées de rouge, souhaita en finir pour de bon. Allonger ses vieux os dans la prison de marbre du caveau des Lameaulnes sous les filaos compatissants. (p. 128)

Here, not only does this evidence of Loulou's vulnerability conflict with the dominant emphasis on his bullying cruelty, and hence evoke our sympathy rather than our disapproval, but it is juxtaposed within the same sentence with his callousness to both his wives. This in turn creates a disjunctive ambivalence of tone, the pathos of his despair and exhaustion combining with the rather brutal trivializing humour of the 'café-crème' and the Amsterdam prostitutes. Equally, in the course of the sentence's loop, the meaning of the two honeymoons skids 'duplici-tously' from constituting proof of his capacity for hard work (only two holidays in 35 years) to demonstrating instead the pointlessness of both his marriages. The resulting uncertainty of tone makes it difficult to assign the sentence as a whole to an authorial point of view.

*S/Z*'s model of classical irony as the top layer of a vertical superimposition of one code on another echoes the vertical hierarchy of levels of meaning that Barthes put forward in his earlier 'Introduction à l'analyse structurale des récits'. Therefore, irony that deflates the hierarchical principle itself must surely count as subversive of the codes as a whole. Significantly, an example of this occurs on the very last page of the text, where a skidding paragraph serves in the first place to deflate Sancher's death:

> Certains, comme Loulou ou Sylvestre, songeant que justice avait été faite, se sentaient purifiés. Ils pourraient à nouveau aller la tête haute et regarder le monde dans les yeux. Loulou se demandait s'il n'allait pas parler à Sylvestre de cette pièce de terre qu'il convoitait en bordure de la rivière Moustique, non pas pour y planter des serres d'orchidées cette fois, mais une variété de pamplemousses venus de la Dominique, la chair plus rose et plus juteuse que ceux de la Californie. Sylvestre madré voyait bien où l'autre voulait en venir et préparait dans sa tête une offre qui saurait le décourager. (pp. 250–51)

However, this downward spiral from the quasi-sacred feeling of catharsis that death inspires to Loulou's mundane preoccupation with varieties of grapefruit also attacks the very idea of a hierarchy of meanings. It starts from the uplifting notion that death reconciles conflicts among the living. This, the cliché that 'it all seems so unimportant now', invokes just such a hierarchy, in which the supreme importance of death relegates petty quarrels to irrelevance. But the paragraph then skids into, precisely, another petty conflict between Loulou and his business rival Sylvestre, and so collapses the levels of meaning into one another; the verticality of hierarchy is replaced by the paratactic structures of irrelevance.

For Barthes, the ironic code in fact operates mainly in relation to the cultural code rather than to the character code.[17] In *Traversée de la mangrove*, however, where irrelevant sentences involve cultural stereotypes these are usually not treated with classical irony but more subtly dissipated with an excess of paratactic detail – as in this looping sentence, where the picturesque stereotype of the old-fashioned embroidered pillowslips is expanded to the point of meaninglessness:

> De même, ce qu'elle faisait la nuit avec Sylvestre dans le grand lit soigneusement recouvert d'un drap blanc, avec à sa tête deux coussins rose saumon décorés de poissons verts, jaunes, rouges, aux nageoires bleues qu'elle avait brodés au point de croix l'année précédente quand elle attendait Alix et que le docteur lui avait recommandé le repos ne le tracassait pas du tout. (p. 177)

Alternatively, when the cultural stereotype depends upon hierarchized values, the irrelevant loop in the paragraph serves to position the two differentiated groups on the same level. For instance, Haitian immigrants are stereotypically stupid and ignorant and, therefore, inferior to their employers. But a representation of Aristide's emotional turmoil is interrupted by four sentences from the point of view of his despised workers, showing them to be following the Haitian elections with intelligent and well-informed interest, and the simple juxtaposition of sentences at the end of this paragraph equates him paratactically with them: 'D'autres gardaient la tête plus froide, tant de fois échaudés auparavant. Aristide, lui, épuisait ses journées et ses nuits dans cette interrogation: que faire?' (p. 76).[18]

The cultural code is, however, less central to *Traversée de la mangrove* than one might expect of a postcolonial novel. There are some prominent examples, but overall it is in relation to the character code that one finds the most pervasive and far-reaching transgressivity. It is here, in other words, that hierarchy and coherence are most profoundly exposed to the corrosive effects of irrelevance. One can of course argue that in any case the whole structure of the novel works against the character code in so far as this depends upon collecting together compatible semes which can be integrated to form a unified individual personality, whereas in *Traversée de la mangrove* the semes come from the various narrators' different, often contradictory, but equally weighted opinions of others, with no authorial overview. But the narrators are also characterized by their own thoughts and memories. These express their often intense feelings of loneliness, love, hatred, fear and so on; but at the same time the skidding and looping sentences create the more disturbing impression of an inability or a refusal to prioritize. Ultimately, it is the repeated, incongruous juxtaposition of the serious and the trivial that most effectively prevents the characters cohering into stereotypes. Condé's remark that *Traversée de la mangrove* is about 'people who are not heroes, who are ordinary men and women, and whose life seems totally meaningless'[19] is thus open to a more positive interpretation than she perhaps intended: that their 'meaninglessness', in the sense of their disinclination to codify or hierarchize the meanings they produce, to attach differential values to them, allows them to escape the stereotyping of the character code.

More generally, this strangely obstinate promotion of irrelevance also impacts on literary codes, as we have seen, and ultimately transgresses wider cultural and ideological codes. From Barthes' point of view, such transgression is necessarily anti-realist, since for him realism, as a literary genre, is *per se* an ideological construct. Condé, in contrast, sees realism as the writer's means of combatting ideology through the dismantling of stereotypes, via a range of strategies including the type of sentences I have been analysing here; although this is no doubt a more naïve position than that of Barthes (and of structuralist and poststructuralist theory as a whole), it is also indicative of a much broader re-evaluation and rehabilitation of realism in the postcolonial novel in general; and by resituating 'scriptible' tactics of fragmentation, 'duplicity' and de-hierarchization in a determinedly realist context, it can perhaps even extend the scope of the transgressivity beyond the purely literary (i.e., challenging the reader's expectation of a realist diegesis) to the ideological codes that structure our view of reality. *Traversée de la mangrove* has been described as 'a writing on the edge of failure',[20] in various senses; I would like to extend this to include its ambiguous failure to prioritize, to edit out what is unimportant, or to obey conventional codes of seriousness. Irrelevance is not just the failure to make sense out of one's experience (although it is that) but, by signifying the refusal to think that some things are more important than others, it is also a subtle and profound kind of irreverence and a radical breaking of the rules.

# Discursive Agency and the (De)Construction of Subjectivity in Daniel Maximin's *L'Île et une nuit*

Issues of gender have long been an important topic in Third World literature, and, at the intersection of postcolonial and feminist theory, a substantial body of critical texts now exists on literary representations of the subjectivity of postcolonial women.[1] These representations may be fictional or autobiographical, and in any case the difference between the two genres is minimized: the novels are often based closely on the real-life experiences of their authors, and they also often adopt the textual conventions of the autobiography or *journal intime*. Betty Wilson, referring to French Caribbean women's novels, comments that 'the structure of the fictional autobiography, journal, diary, letter or other relatively "intimate" genres seems to be the preferred vehicle for expressing feminine/feminist/female consciousness'.[2] The fact that both the authors and the protagonists of these novels are female in itself encourages critics to assume some kind of biographical continuity between the two – what Carole Boyce Davies and Elaine Savory Fido in their introduction to *Out of the Kumbla* call 'a doubled female voice of woman-poet-author and woman-speaking-subject' (p. 5).

The specifically female *voice* is in fact a central concept of this critical discourse; the concern is with (de)colonized women as silenced subjects finding a voice, being 'authorized' to 'speak'. The theorization of subjectivity in autobiography is underpinned by the notion of 'coming to voice', as Sidonie Smith and Julia Watson point out in their introduction to *Women, Autobiography, Theory*: 'Attention to "the colonized subject" and to what has been termed marginal or minoritized discourse has spurred rethinking of the paradigms of subjectivity. And a central site in that revisionary struggle has been autobiographical discourse, the coming to voice of previously silenced subjects' (p. 27). But it is equally prominent in the analysis of fictional texts, as for instance in the opening sentences of the introduction to *Out of the Kumbla*:

> The concept of voicelessness necessarily informs any discussion of Caribbean women and literature [...] By voicelessness, we mean the historical absence of the woman writer's text [...] By voicelessness we also mean silence: the inability to express a position in the language of the "master" as well as the textual construction of women as silent'. (p. 1)

However, 'Out of this voicelessness and silence, contemporary Caribbean women writers are beginning some bold steps to creative expression' (p. 2).

The assumption of unmediated expressivity that underlies both these features – the biographical continuity of female author and protagonist, and the centrality of the female 'voice' producing the text – has been contested elsewhere in both postcolonial and feminist theory. But the concept of 'coming to voice' remains an influential one, offering as it does a very straightforward conception of agency. It therefore provides a useful starting point for my investigation here, that is, of a novel that is centrally concerned with postcolonial female subjectivity but that clearly, almost provocatively, fails to conform to the humanist model of 'voice'; and also, as I shall go on to argue, diverges significantly from later feminist and postcolonial theorizations of the subject.

*L'Île et une nuit* is a novel by the Guadeloupean writer Daniel Maximin, whose central character is a Guadeloupean woman called Marie-Gabriel. This, then, is a text with a male author and a female protagonist. Despite the slightly androgynous name ('Gabriel' rather than 'Gabrielle'), the latter's femininity and feminism are emphasized throughout the text; but the biographical link between author and character is absent. The narrative covers one night, as the title implies: a night during which a hurricane passes over the island. It is divided into seven chapters, each narrating one hour of the hurricane's passage. But the title also alludes to *Les Mille et Une Nuits*, the French translation of the *Arabian Nights*: Marie-Gabriel is an 'Antillaise Shéhérezade' (p. 163), trying to ward off disaster and ensure her survival by telling stories. This might seem an obvious example of the female voice asserting itself through narrative. However, unlike the original Scheherezade, Marie-Gabriel is actually the narrator of only the first and the third chapter; in all five others, she is spoken to, or spoken about in the third person. Moreover, she is usually referred to simply by a pronoun, and this pronoun therefore changes from chapter to chapter according to her relationship to its narrating subject. The effect of these pronominal shifts is both to undermine any sense of her as a solid character with a consistent identity, and to obscure the identity of the narrative voice, also unnamed and varying.[3] Even in the third chapter, she is speaking, apparently to her lover in France, down a telephone line that we eventually discover has been cut off by the storm: a nice image for the voicelessness of the postcolonial woman, rather than evidence of the effectiveness of her speech.

This placing of Marie-Gabriel as the *object* of address and of representation in speech would seem to suggest that she is suffering from voicelessness; in terms of the temporal dynamic that Boyce Davies and Savory Fido invoke, she has not yet 'come to voice'. Insofar as voicelessness is also a metaphor for lack of selfhood, it is certainly true that a progression from voicelessness to voice has been reflected in the evolution of French Caribbean fiction over the past 30 years. The novels of the 1960s and 1970s are dominated by the pain of existential emptiness – in Glissant, for instance, or Placoly, or in the 'folie antillaise' of Schwarz-Bart's characters.[4] This group of novels has mainly been discussed within a modernist framework in which postcolonial subjectivity is characterized by alienation and lack of selfhood. Simon Gikandi's *Writing in Limbo: Modernism and Caribbean Literature*, for instance, considers a wide range of Caribbean novels and reads them all as portraying a painful struggle to achieve subjective wholeness and authenticity.[5] His 'Introduction' generalizes this perspective: 'An integrated discourse of self is surely the ultimate or possibly utopian desire of Caribbean writing, but it can only be reached after the negotiation of a historically engendered split between the self and its world, between this self and the language it uses' (p. 18) – and emphasizes 'the despair of Caribbean modernist literature' (p. 18) that this causes.

But these congruent paradigms of voicelessness coming to voice, and alienation motivating the quest for a whole, authentic self, were superseded in later critical theory by a postmodern, antihumanist version of subjectivity. Once the humanist concept of the unitary, autonomous, self-present, 'full' subject has been abandoned, the problem for feminism and postcolonialism, insofar as they need to retain their commitment to political struggle, has been to find a way of reinstating agency within the new framework. Smith and Watson formulate the position of feminist theory in the aftermath of Althusser and Foucault as follows:

> Dissatisfied with a problematic scientific objectivity, on the one hand, or total subjection on the other, critics began to pose questions aimed at probing the agency of the subject. How can the subject come to know itself differently? Under what conditions can the subject exercise any kind of freedom, find the means to change? [...] Questions of agency became central to discussions of women's autobiography. (*Women*, p. 23)

They go on to point out that, within a specifically postcolonial context, the same problem is raised by Spivak's work:

> Spivak's provocative question about the unspeakability of the subaltern has elicited countertheories that intend to account for possibilities of resistance and agency. Theorists of postcolonial agency ask the following kinds of questions: [...] How might subjects come to voice outside, or despite, the constraints of Western models of identity? What alternative possibilities of identity have been overwritten by Western models? (p. 28)

Teresa de Lauretis, in one of the most influential attempts to combine a discursively constructed subject with an emphasis on conscious strategy and resistance, outlines the possibility of a 'subject in the two senses of the term: both subject-ed to social constraint and yet subject in the active sense of maker as well as user of culture, intent on self-definition and self-determination'.[6] She thus differs from Foucault – and, more explicitly, from Lacan – in reasserting the active self-determination that had characterized the humanist subject, but without returning to essentialism: 'this feminist concept of identity is not at all the statement of an essential nature of Woman, whether defined biologically or philosophically, but rather a political-personal strategy of survival and resistance that is also, at the same time, a critical practice *and* a mode of knowledge' (p. 9).

This may look as though it is simply trying to have the best of both worlds. But what makes the combination possible is the crucial lack of homogeneity of the discursive systems within which the subject is constructed/constructs herself. Their contradictions provide the subject with some room to manoeuvre. The notion of *plurality* is crucial.[7] Foucault's own view of the plural, conflicting sites of discursive power (rather than Lacan's monolithic Symbolic Order) gives a basis for a conception of the subject as exploiting the contradictions and playing off one discursive system against another. Thus Joan W. Scott moves directly from reiterating the stress on agency to the notion of contradictory plurality:

> Treating the emergence of a new identity as a discursive event is not to introduce a new form of linguistic determinism, nor to deprive subjects

of agency [...] Subjects are constituted discursively, but there are conflicts among discursive systems, contradictions within any one of them, multiple meanings possible for the concepts they deploy. And subjects have agency. They are not unified, autonomous individuals exercising free will, but rather subjects whose agency is created through situations and statuses conferred on them [...] These conditions enable choices, although they are not unlimited. Subjects are constituted discursively, experience is a linguistic event (it doesn't happen outside established meanings), but neither is confined to a fixed order of meaning.[8]

The link between multiplicity/contradiction and agency is also evident in De Lauretis:

> the concept of a *multiple, shifting*, and often *self-contradictory* identity, a subject that is not divided in, but rather at odds with, language; an identity made up of heterogeneous and heteronomous representations of gender, race and class, and often indeed across languages and cultures; an identity that one *decided to reclaim* from a history of multiple assimilations, and that one *insists on as a strategy*' ('Feminist Studies', p. 9, my italics).

De Lauretis in fact distinguishes clearly between it and the poststructuralist formulation of the subject: 'It seems to me that this notion of identity points to a more useful conception of the subject than the one proposed by [...] poststructuralist theories' (p. 9). In other words, it is an alternative – antihumanist but not poststructuralist – solution to the problem of agency posed by the collapse of the humanist subject.

Françoise Lionnet's *Postcolonial Representations* adopts this solution of a 'multiplicity of subject-positions' (p. 58). The postcolonial texts with which she is most concerned are those that effect 'a radical and subversive *appropriation* of the cultural codes by a subject who constructs herself through her discourse' (p. 175, italics original).[9] Agency comes from a flexible, strategic 'braiding' of different identities, with the emphasis on active, and indeed skilful, self-positioning: 'The postcolonial subject thus becomes quite adept at braiding all the traditions at its disposal, using the fragments that constitute it in order to participate fully in a dynamic process of transformation' (p. 5). The notion of a subject negotiating within a plurality of disjunctive cultural systems is especially persuasive in a multicultural situation. It therefore has a particular resonance for postcoloniality (and, perhaps, particularly for the Caribbean) where the phenomena of *métissage* and creolization have long informed all debates about identity. Lionnet's earlier *Autobiographical Voices* bases its theoretical stance on a concept of *métissage* which she sees as the only adequate response to the hegemonic universalism of the West.[10] Thus the general emphasis placed by De Lauretis and others on multiplicity chimes with, and is given added impetus by, the specifically postcolonial promotion of *métissage* – and Lionnet brings the two explicitly together: 'If, as Teresa de Lauretis has pointed out, identity is a strategy, then *métissage* is the fertile ground of our heterogeneous and heteronomous identities as postcolonial subjects' (p. 326).

There is also an obvious sense in which both postcolonial *métissage* and plurality *per se*, in their common rejection of unicity, hegemony and hierarchy, are typically postmodern. Several critics have defined the postcolonial novel's transition from a problematic of alienation and marginality to one of creolization as a shift from modernity to postmodernity.[11] *Métissage* thus acts as a point of overlap between the postcolonial and the postmodern, as Lionnet argues: 'the postcolonial novel exhibits the mixture of cultures and the *métissage* of forms that also defines the "postmodern condition"' (*Postcolonial Representations*, p. 174). Thus the theoretical move from the humanist full subject to the postpoststructuralist subject of De Lauretis and Lionnet (among others) is paralleled on the level of postcolonial fiction by a move from a modernist experience of lack of self to a postmodernist plurality of self. On this level the transition is made via the concept of *fragmentation*, which shares connotations with both. In the modernist context, fragmentation is part of the negative experience of lack of wholeness; but it is also a positive starting point for multiplicity, and one can see how, in the critical discourse, it migrates from one framework to the other, facilitating the transition between them. Thus Simon Gikandi describes how Michelle Cliff 'finds discursive value in the very fragmentation that other commentators have seen as the curse of West Indian history. According to Cliff, fragmentation can indeed function as a strategy of identity since the colonized writer struggles "to get wholeness from fragmentation while working within fragmentation"' (*Writing in Limbo*, p. 234). For Lionnet, similarly, in a sentence I have already quoted, 'fragments' are recuperated as *transformation*: 'The postcolonial subject thus becomes quite adept at braiding all the traditions at its disposal, using the fragments that constitute it in order to participate fully in a dynamic process of transformation' (*Postcolonial Representations*, p. 5). A similar operation is evident in the comment of the editors of *Out of the Kumbla*, that women's texts privilege 'the quilted narrative, braided or woven' (p. 6), which they define explicitly as the positive version of 'fragmented': 'the "quilted" use of form (quilted here posited as a revision of "fragmented")' (p. 6).

At this point the crucial notion of contradiction, which was the necessary starting point for this posthumanist construction of the subject, begins to disappear. In its place comes a more free-floating, carnivalesque version of plurality which is no longer based in the fragmentation of a posited whole, but itself constitutes a kind of *abundance*. This is evident in the work of Chamoiseau and Confiant – in the final words of *Lettres créoles*, for instance:

> ce processus que nous vivons depuis plus de trois siècles se répand, s'accélère: peuples, langues, histoires, cultures, nations se touchent et se traversent par une infinité de réseaux [...] Il nous faut désormais tenter d'appréhender [le monde], loin du risque appauvrissant de l'Universalité, dans la richesse éclatée, mais harmonieuse, d'une Diversalité. (p. 204)

*Creolité* here is promoted by a whole rhetoric of enrichment that stands in deliberate contrast to the modernist anguish of earlier Caribbean writers. But these new connotations of abundance and harmony inevitably lead to it being seen as a kind of *plenitude* that is ultimately not very different from the plenitude of the original humanist subject. There is still a difference in principle, in that the plenitude is located on the level of collective identity rather than the individual of classic humanism; in practice, however, the individual too in this context benefits from the overall abundance of selfhood. Thus Jeanne Perrault, for instance, can write that: 'Recent discussions of multiplicity of "selves", or the deconstruction of the figure of the indivisible "self ", have not so much undermined the valorizing of selfhood as extended it, giving the "selves" a share in the belief of the rights of the individual'.[12]

I have retraced here a sequence of theoretical shifts in which what started as an antihumanist reworking of agency based on contradiction, division and fragmentation slides into a celebration of *métissage* as plenitude that ends up surreptitiously reinstating some of the assumptions of the 'full' humanist subject. One could describe it as a move from plurality as division to plurality as multiplication. And it does figure in many recent Caribbean novels, as Lionnet demonstrates.

But what is striking about *L'Île et une nuit* is that its central character, Marie-Gabriel, is not at all like this. In this novel there is no emphasis on *métissage*; rather, it presents a subjectivity that is *empty* – but in a completely different way from the anguished emptiness of the characters in modernist Caribbean novels. The interest and originality of *L'Île et une nuit* lie in its construction of a subject marked by lack rather than multiplicity, but which does not experience its emptiness as alienation. Nor does it struggle to achieve selfhood through the 'braiding' of different discursively constructed identities. Instead, it develops the positive dimensions of lack itself, reworking emptiness as lightness, openness and mobility. This is a similar tactic to the reworking of fragmentation into positive multiplicity that I have described above; both situate themselves initially within a poststructuralist framework and modify it to produce a conception of the subject that allows for agency. But Maximin's version does not revert back to the humanist 'full' unitary subject, and is different in other ways as well. Taking lack rather than fragmentation as the starting point foregrounds the Lacanian dimension of poststructuralism from which De Lauretis distances herself most explicitly: 'It is neither, in short, the imaginary identity of the individualist, bourgeois subject, which is male and white; nor the "flickering" of the posthumanist Lacanian subject, which is too nearly white and at best (fe)male' ('Feminist Studies', p. 9). But the black female subject that is Marie-Gabriel does 'flicker' – while being at the same time the site of a new conception of agency.

That is, the text of *L'Île et une nuit* constructs a subject that is in some ways extremely Lacanian.[13] It not only slips, as I have shown, from one anonymous pronominal form to another, but also repeatedly disappears into various metaphors of itself: the island, the house, the child heroine of a folk-tale in the sixth chapter. It is thus a vacillating – indeed, 'flickering' – presence, exactly the 'temporal pulsation' and 'movement of disappearance' of Lacan's *aphanisis*.[14] Therefore, unlike the 'coming to voice' model, the subject is never in conscious possession of his/her voice. Above all, Maximin's subject is based on lack and division: 'Tout vous échappe, vous divise, en tous sens' (p. 42). Marie-Gabriel has been hollowed out by the wind – or more precisely, by the 'eye' of the hurricane boring into her: 'Le vent a pénétré par le couloir profond de votre gorge [...] Dans la calebasse pleine qui oscille sur vos épaules, il tourbillonne, et *l'axe de son œil invisible* creuse un puits au centre de votre vie' (p. 38, my italics). The eye of the hurricane, in relation to which Marie-Gabriel is placed (there are many references to it 'looking' at her), is like the Lacanian gaze which reveals the lack at the heart of being. Since the seeing 'eye' itself is of course nothing but the empty hole at the centre of the hurricane, it is a very appropriate metaphor for 'le regard [qui] ne se présente à nous que sous la forme d'une étrange contingence, symbolique de ce que nous trouvons à l'horizon et comme butée de notre expérience, à savoir le manque constitutif de l'angoisse de la castration' (*Les Quatre Concepts*, p. 85). Marie-Gabriel's house becomes an important metaphor ('Suivre l'exemple de la maison', p. 29) for the empty self, as in this juxtaposition, which initially echoes the despairing tonality of Glissant or Placoly: 'Dans la maison, tout sera pour toujours déplacé, racines déchaussées. Au milieu de votre maison: le trou. Au milieu de votre mémoire: le trou. Au milieu du cœur de votre vie: un trou de la taille d'un cratère refroidi' (p. 39) – but is immediately transformed into a far more positive emphasis on freedom of movement: 'Puis une nécessité de portes et de fenêtres ouvertes croîtra en vous jusqu'à édifier les murs qui pourront les soutenir et vous laisser sortir' (p. 39). If the walls do not serve to contain the people inside the house, but to make possible the doors and windows that let them out, then the opposition between secure containment on the one hand, and openness and mobility on the other, is deconstructed.

The hurricane thus provides a context for elaborating a conception of resistance that depends on non-containment, non-enclosure; the houses that will survive are those that let the wind blow through them, that are not too heavy or solid. Whereas 'les villas riches' have to be evacuated because their hermetically sealed glass windows are liable to shatter (p. 16), the 'HLMs' where the poor live do not, because they are draughty enough not to oppose the wind's force – Marie-Gabriel adds, 'A cause de l'eau, on va peut-être tout perdre dans la maison. Mais on aura préservé la maison' (p. 16). In other words, what matters is the open, empty structure of the house itself, not its contents. Marie-Gabriel's own house has the same quality of non-containment:

> Case antillaise tout en portes, en fenêtres et en persiennes, jamais hermétiquement fermée aux jalousies de la lumière, des cœurs et des yeux. Notre maison bien commune, case sans chacun pour soi, construite juste pour la pudeur, mais pas l'intimité ni la solitude, avec ses palissades ajourées qui laissent passer l'air des querelles, les rires du jour et les cris d'enfants, et obligent à chuchoter la musique des chambres d'amour.
> (p. 28)

Not only is it not closed against the outside world, but it also lacks any secure internal boundaries separating and enclosing the individuals living in it. Its strength – 'un refuge depuis si longtemps si fragile et si sûr' (p. 29) – is its very instability, the apparent lack of any protection that it can offer: 'Une maison qui ne saurait trahir puisqu'elle n'a rien promis de sûr, juste un refuge composé de sorties provisoirement barricadées' (p. 29). It will survive because it is light and flexible, and can afford to lose parts of itself: it 'saura plier pour nous survivre, nous replier de pièce en pièce vers son dernier poteau-mitan' (p. 29).[15]

Emptiness is transformed into the positive strength of having nothing to lose.[16] The victims of the hurricane reassure their relatives: 'on a tout perdu, mais tout n'est pas grand-chose et on va bien' (p. 56). The destructive force of the hurricane is undercut by the lack of anything – any content – to destroy. This then opens the way to revealing its positive connotations as a *levelling* force that punishes the rich but not the poor: 'il disperse les cartes [...] pour une donne nouvelle et plus égale: qui a le moins perdra le moins, qui a plus aura plus perdu' (p. 98). Emptiness thus mutates into lightness and flexibility; the way to resist the hurricane is *not* to resist it – but to bend to its force and let it blow through you. The opposition between strength and fragility as these are usually understood no longer operates: 'Comme l'île, cette nuit, mon corps va apprendre à résister, c'est-à-dire lutter avec sa fragilité pour arme' (p. 62).

One particularly prominent aspect of Marie-Gabriel's emptiness, shared by the island as a whole, is the absence of *origin*. It is 'un pays [...] d'enfants sans origine par manque d'espace pour trier les couleurs' (p. 154). In this it is closer to the multiple subject of *métissage*, whose racially disoriginated status is one of the prime motivations for constructing an alternative subjectivity on the basis of plurality. Maximin, however, does not move towards a celebration of plurality, but simply stresses the advantages of lack of origin *per se*. It is seen, for instance, as a *release* from the past; one of the benefits of the hurricane is that it acts as 'un vrai déluge de vents qui détachaient l'île de ses passés trop ancrés, pour [...] une séparation d'avec le trop ancien, le trop lourd à porter, les maisons et les arbres trop ancestraux' (p. 81).

Marie-Gabriel herself is disoriginated in the specific sense of being an orphan; her father's death has deprived her of a solid foundation in life: 'Pères tombés. Sans avoir eu le temps de vous assurer ni sol ni ciel' (p. 39). Even this personal tragedy, however, is seen as another version of the freedom of having nothing to lose: 'Père et mère, elle avait déjà tout perdu de son passé. Qu'avait-elle donc à perdre d'essentiel encore à l'avenir?' (p. 93). Marie-Gabriel has no roots. This passage continues: 'Être orpheline, c'était être condamnée à vie à être vue par tous les autres comme un oiseau posé sur une branche nue en lieu et place d'une fleur enracinée' (p. 93). But we have already been told, right at the beginning of the novel, that the collective subject that is the island does not *need* roots – and this in the context of promoting a collective agency based, not on filiation and roots, but on *lateral* relationships between a number of rootless 'orphans':

> Qui marche seul n'avance pas. Qui meurt tout seul ne sème pas. Qui espère seul n'attend rien. La Guadeloupe est plus qu'un arbre. Même sans racines elle peut fleurir. Notre île est une vraie case, édifiée par notre grande famille d'orphelins fiancés. (p. 12)

The text invokes solidarity in the face of a common predicament, stressing commonality – as in 'Notre maison bien commune' (p. 28) – rather than difference. Lack of origin generates a form of agency that constructs its own 'floating' (Guadeloupe is the quintessential 'île flottante', p. 47) but mutually supporting lateral network of relationships with other equally disoriginated subjects; it is, by implication, because they are 'orphelins' that they are 'fiancés'.[17] The network is echoed in the shifting pronominal structures of the novel; while these, as I have argued, fissure and empty out the subject, by the same token they also present it as nothing over and above its relations with other subjects.

But this does not mean that the notion of rootedness is presented as simply negative. A major characteristic of the novel, as we have seen, is its habit of recasting oppositions as paradoxical coexistences; fragility is *equated* with strength, and the central metaphor of the house renders untenable the opposition between closure, solidity and protection on the one hand and openness, emptiness and freedom of movement on the other. Even the hurricane itself combines the negative idea of destruction with the positive value of clearing a space for renewal, and so is not simply an enemy: 'le cyclone de ce soir [...] qui *fait du mal avec du bien*, qui lave la terre et l'eau, bouscule et arrache *sans distinction nos cancers et nos santés*' (p. 62, my italics). In similar fashion, rooting oneself in the ground is sometimes a necessary act of resistance: 'Me rappeler que, même seule, il faut [...] enraciner les pieds s'il s'agit de tenir' (p. 63). But this positive version of rootedness reminds us that, like plants, we have to grow our own roots: they do not, as the usual but actually inaccurate metaphor of *finding* one's roots implies, pre-exist us.[18] More paradoxically, it does not exclude mobility and change: Paul Gilroy's distinction between 'roots' and 'routes' gives way to a single concept that includes both.[19] Thus the text refers to 'élans enracinés' (p. 84) and 'tes racines [...] réinventées' (p. 163), offering this explicitly as a new model of subjectivity: 'Mais ici, entre fuite et ancrage, vous trouvez un nouveau centre de gravité: l'errance enracinée' (p. 40).[20]

These strangely mobile roots are perhaps the most extreme example of the text's pervasive impulse to deconstruct oppositions. The form of agency that it advocates does not operate with clear-cut notions of good and bad, or success and failure. But, as well as stressing the flexibility and the paradoxical, insubstantial nature of resistance, it is as though deconstructing oppositions of itself releases an energy that makes action possible. In presenting this rootless, content-less, evanescent, deconstructing and deconstructed subject as an agent of resistance, *L'Île et une nuit* situates itself in a closer relation to Lacanian and Derridean versions of poststructuralism than to the more dominant paradigms of the postcolonial novel.

# PART II

# On Édouard Glissant

# *Discours* and *Histoire*, Magical and Political Discourse in *Le Quatrième Siècle*

Glissant's *Le Quatrième Siècle* is concerned with Martinican society and the island's history, and above all with the connections or lack of connections between the historical past and social experience in the present. The novel's narrative structure is determined by this thematic concern; so too is what one might term its *discursive structure*: that is, the way in which different types of fictional discourse interact in the text to produce a particular kind of representation of the past. I shall argue that while Benveniste's concepts of 'discours' and 'histoire'[1] are relevant and illuminating in relation to *Le Quatrième Siècle*, the novel also questions the distinction between these two categories; and that it does so by implicating them in a socio-political problematic that is not present in their original formulation.

The narrative is divided into four sections, which on one level form a straightforward chronological progression from 1788 – the date of the arrival in Martinique, on a slave ship, of two Africans who are later given the names Longoué and Béluse – up to 1946, the year in which Martinique acquired the status of a Département d'Outre-Mer. But the first three of these sections each juxtapose *two* periods of time: the historical past, and a narrative present which is situated in the 1940s and consists mainly of a series of conversations between Papa Longoué, an old man, descendant of the first Longoué, and an adolescent, Mathieu Béluse, descendant of the other transported slave Béluse. It is these conversations that lead into the historical narrative, on the basis of Mathieu's curiosity about the past, and Papa Longoué's role as a source of knowledge about it. These dialogues frame and at times interrupt the narration of the Longoué and Béluse family histories, and of the longstanding enmity between them. The 'present time' which the dialogues constitute itself extends over five years from 1940, when Mathieu is fourteen, to 1945, when Papa Longoué dies.

For the first two sections, the past consists of events occurring before Papa Longoué was born; in the third, they are contemporaneous with the first part of his life: his childhood and youth, marriage, the birth of his son, the death of his wife and the death of his son in the First World War; while as part of the fourth section, the 'present' of the first – Mathieu's visits to the old man in his cabin in the forest up in the hills – is retold as the 'past'. In the first three sections, therefore, there is a clear division between, on the one hand, a *present* which exists in the text mainly as spoken dialogue between two clearly identified individual speakers (the boy and the old man) and a *past* which is presented as a third-person account by an omniscient and anonymous narrator, in a fairly formal literary style. It includes direct speech between 'historical' characters, authoritative descriptions of their thoughts and feelings, free indirect speech, detailed and vivid descriptions of the settings and so on; it is, in other words, a typical realist fictional narrative.

The switch from one of these discourses to the other is usually (with some exceptions) very noticeable. In, for example, the narration of Longoué's arrival in the slave compound of the plantation to which he has been sold:

> Il avait compris qu'on les séparait là pour toujours, et arrivé plus tard devant la maison plate, tassée derrière les deux immenses troncs d'acajou, il avait su qu'enfin on le conduisait à l'enclos final préparé pour lui et ses compagnons. Avant d'y être poussé il put communiquer, d'un seul geste, avec les trois ou quatre autres spectateurs de la scène [...] Quoique ses deux mains fussent liées, il les leva vers l'enclos pour signifier qu'il n'entendait pas rester là: et peut-être que la femme avait vu le geste et qu'elle s'était préparée dès ce moment-là à venir le délivrer.
>
> -- Mais tu ne sais pas ce qui s'est passé là-bas dans le pays au-delà des eaux! Depuis si longtemps, depuis si longtemps, mon fils [...]
>
> 'Nous ne savons pas', pensa Mathieu. 'Nous. Nous! Et pas même toi le plus vieux ici [...]' (pp. 56–57).

Here the sudden intervention of the 'present' dialogue into the evocation of the past is unambiguous and clearly marked.

At first sight, therefore, it appears that there is a simple, regular correlation between, on the one hand, present time and 'discours' (i.e., language overtly produced by a known speaking subject and addressed to another subject) and, on the other hand, past time and 'histoire' (in Benveniste's sense of an impersonal, authoritative, neutral account of past events). Glissant has a longstanding interest in the relation between oral and written language, and the possibilities opened up by the use of 'oral' language in literature; in *Le Discours antillais* he writes:

> La seule manière selon moi de garder fonction à l'écriture (s'il y a lieu de le faire), c'est-à-dire de la dégager d'une pratique ésotérique ou d'une banalisation informatique, serait de l'*irriguer* aux sources de l'oral. Si l'écriture ne se préserve désormais des tentations transcendantales, par exemple en s'inspirant des pratiques orales en les théorisant s'il le faut, je pense qu'elle disparaîtra comme nécessité culturelle des sociétés à venir [...] l'écriture se renfermera dans l'univers clos et sacré du signe littéraire. (p. 193)

The kind of alternating pattern we find in *Le Quatrième Siècle* could be seen simply as a form of such 'irrigation'. In fact, however, it is not as simple as that: on closer examination, both of the oppositions so far brought into play – past/present, *discours/histoire* – turn out to be much less clear cut. As one reads the novel, for instance, it soon becomes obvious that the relation of past and present is something rather different from a straightforward contrast, or even a clear separation. One of the main themes, formulated repeatedly by Papa Longoué, is that the past continues to exist in the present: the past is *still here*. Very near the beginning, for instance, he says to Mathieu: 'Ils sont sots, par là-bas en bas. Ils disent: "Ce qui est passé est bien passé." Mais tout ce qui passe dans les bois est gardé au fond du bois!' (pp. 15–16).

As this also implies, however, this 'presence' of the past goes unrecognized by most people. That, in turn, is why it is also important (but also so difficult) to rediscover it; towards the end of the novel we read: 'Le pays: réalité arrachée du passé, mais aussi, passé *déterré* du réel' (p. 279, my italics).[2] This conception of the past is elaborated in various different ways. It means, for instance, that the past is not *linear*, not 'comme un palmiste droit et lisse avec la touffe au bout, non, il commence depuis la première racine et il va en bourgeonnant sans arrêt jusqu'aux nuages' (p. 147); it is, according to Papa Longoué, *multiple* and elusive: 'car le passé n'est pas simple, ah! il y a combien de passés qui descendent jusqu'à toi, tu dois faire la gymnastique si tu veux les attraper' (p. 204).

A number of images, also, describe the past as *mass* rather than line, and as something that accumulates: it is 'ce monotone entassement'

(p. 160). This is reinforced by the narrative structure of the novel. The overall, large-scale forward progression of the chapters through time coexists and contrasts with a pervasive habit of treating the events of the narrative as though they exist not in sequence but as a tangled mass which is experienced simultaneously. Thus in many of the most dramatic, potentially most suspenseful incidents, we are told the end of the story first, and what leads up to it is recounted only later: we know *that* Longoué escaped a long time before we learn *how*, and we know that Papa Longoué's wife was killed in a hurricane before we read the detailed and horrific account of this episode. Above all, we know that the enmity between Longoué and Béluse has its roots in something that happened in Africa and the account of this emerges bit by bit: in such a way, moreover, that we repeatedly think that we now have the full story, only to discover later that there is something more behind it. The systematic use of this narrative technique in itself creates an impression of the past as 'mass' – as both potentially accessible and inexhaustible.

The implicit thematic statement that the past is 'still here' seems to be open to two possible interpretations. It can, firstly, be taken as a fairly uncontentious assertion that past events actively determine the present. Thus in this passage the 'entassement' is a kind of web of necessary connections in the past which produce a particular outcome in the present:

> Ainsi, pour qu'un Longoué égaré parmi les Béluse montât, femme intrépide, de son plein gré sur les mornes [...] il avait fallu ce monotone entassement. Que Senglis entêté dans sa décrépitude s'obstine à garder sa plantation (que sa plantation ne soit pas ravagée par les marrons), que Béluse monte dans la case de Roche Carrée, qu'il se rapproche à mi-chemin des bois; que La Roche acharné à défricher laisse Longoué à ses hauteurs (que Longoué protège l'*Acajou*, du moins qu'il se garde d'attaquer l'*Acajou*), et que la 'voisine sur le bateau' enfante la mère de Stéfanise. (p. 160)

This interpretation includes the idea, central to all Glissant's writing, that the present is equally determined by the *repression* of the past. For a number of historical and psychological reasons, much of the Caribbean past has been forgotten or rejected. There is therefore a need to reclaim and reveal it, in order to achieve a fuller understanding of the present – an understanding which itself is important above all because it is a necessary condition for effective action in the future. As Mathieu says towards the end of the novel: 'Le passé. Qu'est le passé sinon la connaissance qui te roidit dans la terre et te pousse en foule dans demain?' (p. 280). Glissant in fact sees it as specifically the duty of Caribbean *writers*:

> Le passé, notre passé subi, qui n'est pas encore histoire pour nous, est pourtant là (ici) qui nous lancine. La tâche de l'écrivain est d'explorer ce lancinement, de le 'révéler' de manière continue dans le présent et l'actuel. Cette exploration ne revient donc ni à une mise en schémas ni à un pleur nostalgique. C'est à démêler un sens douloureux du temps et à le projeter à tout coup dans notre futur [...] C'est ce que j'appelle *une vision prophétique du passé*. (DA, p. 132, italics original)

The past is a need ('C'est le passé ce besoin', *Le Quatrième Siècle*, p. 59), and a value, because it gives identity and solidity to existence in the present, which is otherwise experienced as absence or emptiness: 'le clair lancinement du présent, ou plutôt de la vacance présente' (p. 261). At the same time it appears as though the present does not exist at all except as the lack of connection between past and future – the 'precipice' which the people of Martinique (here, 'l'homme') must cross:

> Il crie sur lui-même, il lui reste un précipice à franchir. Tant qu'il ne l'a pas franchi, c'est le passé qui continue; et au moment où il l'aura franchi, l'avenir commence. Il n'y a pas de présent. Le présent est une feuille jaunie sur la tige du passé, embranchée du côté où la main, ni même le regard ne peuvent atteindre. Le présent tombe de l'autre côté, il agonise sans fin. Il agonise. (p. 224)

This suggests the further idea that the opposition is perhaps not so much one of past and present in the simple sense, as that between *historical* and *ahistorical* time; the narrative present corresponds to the period in which Martinique, with its Vichy regime, was blockaded by the American navy and thus completely isolated from the rest of the world – a period of material deprivation and political impotence, described in the final section of the novel – whereas 1946 is seen by Mathieu as marking the point of its re-entry into the world and hence into history: 'Et dans sa certitude il y avait le monde enfin ouvert et clair, et peut-être si proche' (p. 286). In this perspective the notion of 'the past in the present' evokes the possibility of an alternative way of experiencing the *present* as *historical* time, and hence as dynamic and significant rather than static and empty.

The first of the two interpretations is thus a *political* one: a community rediscovering its history in order to free itself for political action in the present and future. But the novel also confronts its reader with another, simpler but more startling interpretation of the idea that 'the past is still here'. This presupposes a far more radically different conception of time, because it is entirely *literal*. In other words, Mathieu and Papa Longoué enter into a state of mind in which the past is directly and immediately experienced; the past, we are told several times, 'falls' on them (e.g., 'le passé soudain tombé sur eux', p. 76),[3] and this happens as a result of *magic*. That is, Papa Longoué is a *quimboiseur*[4] and so claims to have the power to see the past; we are told how he was initiated by his grandfather, Melchior, who 'entrait avec l'enfant dans la nuit vacillante où nul ne pouvait les suivre' (p. 209) and showed him his dead ancestors; later, Papa Longoué 'sees' the field hospital where his son died in Flanders (p. 243), and so on.

The status accorded to magic is somewhat ambiguous. It is not presented as matter-of-factly as in some of the canonical texts of magical realism (or in Depestre's *Hadriana dans tous mes rêves*), but nor is it discredited. On the one hand, the novel sets up an opposition between magic and *logic*, presented through arguments between Papa Longoué and Mathieu in which the latter is often very scornful of the *quimboiseur*'s powers, and the old man does not always defend himself very convincingly.[5] But Mathieu himself also enters into the magic vision of the past, and at the end of the novel, admittedly while delirious with fever, even creates his own: he 'sees' Papa Longoué's death. A characteristic feature of *Le Quatrième Siècle* is that the binary oppositions running through it – past/present, *discours/histoire*, and now magic/logic, and perhaps magic/politics – are all inextricably bound up with each other; and the best way to approach the problem of magic is perhaps to look at its most important *effect* in the text, which is on the latter's discursive structure, that is, the apparent opposition between *discours* and *histoire*.

On closer analysis, the status and provenance of the passages which I have provisionally defined as *histoire* – the subjectless omniscient narrative of the past – become questionable. Although most of the time this historical narrative seems to have nothing to do with Papa Longoué, there are also clear indications that it is actually to be read as emanating *from him*. After eight pages of impersonal narration, for instance, we suddenly read:

> Elle s'en alla; mais sitôt tournée, sitôt disparue. Marchant encore, visible encore sur le sentier qui menait à la maison haute, et déjà absente; comme si sa présence tenait surtout à son regard, à son visage, au poids possible de sa parole. L'homme (*dit Papa Longoué*) apprit ainsi dès le premier jour

que le maître n'existait réellement qu'au moment où il vous regardait. (p. 68, my italics)

Or the narrative will be interrupted by Mathieu in a way which makes it clear that he has been *listening* to what we have been reading: 'Plus vite, papa, plus vite, ça c'est connu, j'ai lu les livres' (p. 21); or he will intervene to *quote*, sarcastically, phrases which we have already read in the narrative (p. 121).

If, then, Papa Longoué is 'really' telling this story to Mathieu, one needs to ask why it is not presented in the text as an overtly oral 'storytelling' discourse. The reason *Le Quatrième Siècle* does not adopt this procedure is, I think, that it would entail presenting the narrative as a story whose authority was based solely on the trustworthiness of the storyteller. That is, whether or not it was 'true' would simply depend upon the perceived psychological characteristics of its individual narrator, and his objective situation in relation to the events described. The general and far more important issue of the very possibility of reconstructing the past would thus be elided. And of course a straightforward omniscient *histoire*, which is by definition valid in its own terms, would equally preclude this question – which is central to the whole novel – being posed.[6]

In other words, the use of either *discours* or *histoire* in their original pure Benvenistean state would make it impossible for the text to explore what is in fact its central problematic: whether and how a society can construct a valid representation of its historical past. To create a space in which this can be addressed, conversely, it has to set up a kind of intermediate or indeterminate discourse whose provenance and authority are uncertain. Thus Papa Longoué's 'authorship' of the narration is simultaneously posited and put into doubt when a passage of his speech is followed by:

Le vieillard médita sur ce flot de paroles, supputant s'il les avait réellement débitées, lui, ou plutôt un autre, un étranger inconvenant qui aurait pris sa place auprès du feu [...] Il s'étonnait d'un si long discours, et d'avoir pu l'écouter, à mesure qu'il le prononçait, sans impatience. (p. 33)

– implying that he is the medium rather than the conscious source of what he has said.

The situation is especially complicated in the third section of the novel, which covers events in his own life. Here passages in italic alternate with passages in roman type; they often deal with the same subject matter, but the italic passages are oral *discours* – Papa Longoué's reflections on his life – whereas those in roman type continue the third-person narrative as before, presenting Papa Longoué himself as a character described by an omniscient anonymous narrator. But at the same time the text suggests that the roman passages are also 'spoken' by him; the opening of this third section is:

> *Je te dis,*
> Quand il revint à La Touffaille où ils l'attendaient tous, la mère concentrée, les fils à crier sans raison, les filles évaporées dans leur attente [...].
> (p. 195, italics original)

– and another roman passage switches in mid-sentence to a new paragraph in italics with Papa Longoué complaining that Mathieu is not listening to what he *has been saying* (p. 217), as though it is meant to be read as one continuous discourse.

To sum up, then *Le Quatrième Siècle* presents us with a narrative which looks, stylistically, like *histoire*, but turns out to be a discourse whose status is different both from subjectless omniscience and from an overtly subjective account based on individual memory. It is at once 'spoken' and not spoken by Papa Longoué, and this affects its fictional truth status, since *histoire* is by definition diegetically true, while *discours* may or may not be. We therefore have to wonder what sense we can make of this quasi-*histoire*, which both does and does not 'belong' to an individual speaker, and which seems at times to transcend both his knowledge of the facts and his awareness of what he is saying. And if he is indeed saying it, how can he believe that he knows exactly what happened? How, also, can we as readers reconcile this vivid, third-person evocation of the past with the idea of a story being *told*, over five years, by an old man to a boy?

The only way of understanding this very ambiguous evocation of the past is through the agency of *magic*. In other words, magic turns *discours* into *histoire*, making it possible for Papa Longoué to produce a full and convincing *vision* of events of which he has no personal experience, and to communicate it to Mathieu.[7] It is significant that right at the beginning of the novel Mathieu says to Papa Longoué: 'Dis-moi le passé' (p. 15). It is a slightly odd request; we might perhaps have expected him to say: 'Raconte-moi le passé'. But this 'dis-moi' does not mean 'tell me *about* the past'; rather, it implies a kind of performative: a speech act which, magically, brings the past into real existence. Thus later Mathieu 'sees' the eighteenth-century ship's captain negotiating the price at which he will sell his cargo of slaves, in the same kind of realist detail as the impersonal narrative has supplied throughout:

soudain il vit la cabine étroite, à l'odeur forte [...] les fusils et les pistolets cadenassés au mur, le coffre avec les livres de compte qui sur ce bateau tenaient lieu de livre de bord, les flacons de ce rhum qui avait aidé à supporter le voyage, tous vides maintenant, et la caissette aux boules rouges pour marquer le nombre de morts dans la cargaison. Il vit le rhum nouveau sur le coffre, les six hommes entassés là autour des pots d'étain douteux, et il entendit les paroles, ne sachant même pas si Papa Longoué les redisait à son intention ou si c'était le vent, dans tout ce cri des ouvrages d'antan, qui enfin marchandait le prix de la chair. Car dans la lutte autour des noms et des secrets du passé, Mathieu pour la première fois se trouva directement cerné par le pouvoir du quimboiseur, sans loisir d'étudier le vrai. (p. 41)

In other words, there is here a direct equation between *histoire* and 'le pouvoir du quimboiseur', and we as readers find ourselves in the same position as Mathieu.

It is thus the power of the *quimboiseur* that not only explains the elision of the boundaries between past and present, but also transcends the distinction between *discours* and *histoire*. This in turn implies that the coherence of the novel's whole discursive structure depends upon the validity of the *quimboiseur*'s magic – which, therefore, the reader has to take seriously. It also shows that the discursive categories defined by Benveniste are not universal, but dependent on a Western cultural definition of knowledge as objective and rational.

*Le Quatrième Siècle*, then, offers two ways of interpreting the idea that 'the past is still here'. There is a socio-political one, based on rational knowledge, in which it indicates the possibility of liberation through a *prise de conscience* of history and its impact on the present; and, secondly, there is a magic one, involving fidelity to the past and the African heritage, as a route to another kind of knowledge. But, however incompatible these might appear in the abstract, the novel presents them as complementary rather than contradictory. In part, it achieves this by neutralizing the (slightly different) opposition between magic and *logic*. Papa Longoué, for instance, compares magic and logic to the sun and the moon when they are both visible in the sky at the same time, and adds: 'tu ne sais pas lequel éclaire l'autre. Si c'est la magie qui te fait comprendre le passé ou si c'est la mémoire la suite logique par-dessus le nuage qui devant toi brillent?' (p. 74). The argument is certainly never resolved for Mathieu; when he is ill, at the end of the novel, he plans to visit the old man again as soon as he is better, in order to 'donner avec Papa Longoué un semblant de conclusion à la chronique obscure, et

décider au moins si la "suite logique" avait à la fin dominé "la magie"'
(p. 274) – but Papa Longoué dies before he can do so.

Papa Longoué says to Mathieu: 'Et je sais que pour toi, un quimboiseur
c'est la folie et la bêtise. Mais ce n'est pas vrai. *On ne connaît pas tout
mais on connaît quelque chose*' (p. 137, my italics) – and this claim is
supported by the novel as a whole. Magic is seen as a relative, historically situated form of knowledge, which co-exists with political logic
and political action. It is embodied in Melchior, one of the strongest and
most respected figures in the novel, who through being a *quimboiseur*
also realizes the political ideal of autonomous and lucid action that is
inaccessible to everyone else. He is described as: 'Le seul, oui le seul qui
ait pu choisir sa destinée, le mener par la main sans dévier [...] Lourd et
clairvoyant, sans un accroc pendant tout le temps qu'il s'était tenu debout'
(p. 149); and we are told that 'il résume dans sa vie toutes les raisons,
présentes et passées, pour quoi il vivait' (p. 161). Melchior succeeds
in acquiring a sense of himself in history and hence in establishing
a continuity and purpose in his own life. The *quimboiseur*, in other
words, is not solely turned towards the past. Rather, his evocation of
the past has the same crucial relevance to the future that Glissant, in the
discussion of Caribbean writers already quoted, describes as a 'vision
prophétique du passé'. Thus, also, Mathieu's remark to Papa Longoué:
'tu prétends qu'il ne faut pas suivre les faits avec logique mais deviner,
*prévoir* ce qui s'est *passé*' (p. 58, my italics).

The magic hypothesis, therefore, is not antagonistic to the political
interpretation. It contributes an alternative mode of understanding, but
one which, just like the political one, is orientated towards the future and
the possibility of collective agency. If the aim of the recovery of history
is indeed to enable people to act and to determine their future, then we
can perhaps see that the diegetic truth of the *quimboiseur*'s representation – its authority as *histoire* – is less important than its ability – as
*discours* rather than *histoire*, therefore – to liberate people into action.
As in the original Benvenistean conception, in which *discours* was
primarily *inter*subjective – 'le langage mis en action, et nécessairement
entre partenaires' (*Problèmes*, p. 259) – so Mathieu's naïve 'Dis-moi le
passé', implying a performative utterance to which logical truth values
are irrelevant, takes on an additional level of meaning. It is not only an
*act*, but one which will open the way to other, not necessarily verbal,
acts. Magic may not give access to an objectively true vision of the past,
but it has real effects.

This argument can be taken one stage further. That is, the performative conception of the reconstruction of history in language is not only relevant to the magic narrative of the *quimboiseur*, but is ultimately to do with language in general. At this point we rejoin another major theme of the novel, which is the interdependence of language and action. That is, Glissant claims that one of the features of the particular form of oppression constituted by slavery in a plantation economy is the 'mutisme' imposed on the slaves; in 'l'implacable univers muet du servage' (*DA*, p. 277) the slaves had no language in which to articulate their situation. This is one of the major ways in which the past can be seen to weigh on the present: Mathieu in the 1940s comes to understand how the people

> pouvaient s'en aller, tarir sans descendance réelle, sans fertilité future, enfermés dans leur mort qui était vraiment leur extrémité, pour la simple raison que leur parole était morte elle aussi, dérobée. Oui. Parce que le monde, dont ils étaient une écoute acharnée ou passive, n'avait pas d'oreille pour leur absence de voix. Mathieu voulait crier, lever la voix, appeler du fond de la terre minuscule vers le monde, vers les pays interdits et les espaces lointains. Mais la voix elle-même était dénaturée. (p. 264)

The recovery of history is thus not the only necessary condition for political action; in addition, there is the necessity of acquiring or constructing an unalienated language. Moreover, if *this* is the significance of language, then it follows that it is important primarily as *discours*; and, conversely, that *discours* has acquired a political significance as *prise de parole*.[8] Thus in *Le Quatrième Siècle* the people are described as slowly and painfully struggling to find a language:

> Tressant, d'une sentence à l'autre, [...] la voix grossie de mystère d'où naîtrait leur clarté [...] Sans qu'ils osent croire que l'acte futur [...] ils le sentaient peut-être courir d'une de leurs phrases à l'autre. L'acte: pulsion qui raccordait déjà les mots entre eux, ou plutôt, articulation (syntaxe insoupçonnée) de leurs discours sans suite. (p. 153)

And although the conception of language as a political discursive *act* applies most obviously to the articulation of present needs and future actions, it is in fact equally relevant to the production of a representation of history, because what is at stake in representing history is not scholarly factual accuracy – which is in any case often impossible: as Glissant remarks, 'l'essentiel de l'histoire de la Martinique, histoire raturée, se lit par hypothèse créatrice' (*DA*, p. 161) – but an urgent political need to recover the capacity for action.[9]

There is thus no difference between the magic and the political interpretations of the past in so far as their status as *discours* or *histoire* is concerned, since from the political perspective, too, the significance of the 'historical text' lies in its force as *discours* rather than its authoritativeness as *histoire*. In other words, what makes the ultimate goal of meaningful historical agency possible is a collective *subjective* relationship to the past, materialized as a discourse, which can be either magical or political. History is not, after all, *histoire*, but a quasi-performative *discours*. Whether it is accomplished through the rhetoric of magic or of rational political liberation, the representation of history is revealed, not as something objective and given, but as a collective discursive enterprise.

# 8

# Collective Narrative Voice in *Malemort, La Case du commandeur* and *Mahagony*

In the introduction to *Le Discours antillais*, Glissant describes the Antillean Départements d'Outre-Mer as being trapped in a contradictory fantasy of assimilation that cuts them off from any real knowledge of themselves as a community. On the one hand, the numerous uprisings which occurred from the seventeenth century onwards not only failed in their immediate aims but incurred such brutal repression that 'il n'en est résulté chaque fois qu'une démission de plus en plus tracée de *l'élan* collectif, de la volonté commune qui seuls permettent à un peuple de survivre en tant que peuple' (p. 15). On the other hand, the abolition of slavery and then departmentalization offered at least some of the people the 'solution' of an illusory participation in metropolitan French society and culture, so that 'les Antillais sont ainsi conduits à se nier en tant que collectivité, afin de conquérir une illusoire égalité individuelle' (p. 17).

In *Le Discours antillais* Glissant sees this absence of a collective identity as one of the fundamental social problems of the islands, and as both a cause and an effect of their political passivity and stagnation. In this situation, he argues, 'cultural action' assumes a particular importance; writers have a significant role to play in trying to develop a collective consciousness in the people (pp. 208–19). He insists that Antillean literature – unlike that of Europe – is a collective practice: 'la parole de l'artiste antillais ne provient donc pas de l'obsession de chanter son être intime; cet intime est inséparable du devenir de la communauté' (p. 439). It is the writer's responsibility to help the Martinican people achieve a sense of itself as a political and historical subject – a community that can act in its own name. For this to be effective, the collective subject must be constituted in the actual structures of the literary text; as well as being represented thematically, it must occupy the position of narrating subject: a collective narrative voice. However – and this is the whole point – this voice does not (yet) exist in social reality; the fiction has to create it. There is for Glissant an exact parallel between the political and literary projects, not only because they are working towards the same goal but also because they are both in the situation of trying to bring into existence something as yet unformed:

> Une politique et une poétique de la libération ne peuvent qu'être sécrétées, non pas suggérées. Le premier mot collectif de cette poétique est encore à prononcer. Et malgré tant de combats héroïques et obscurs menés par le peuple martiniquais, l'acte initial et initiateur de cette politique est encore à accomplir. (p. 93)

The construction of such a collective narrative voice involves a number of problems. It will, for instance, be incompatible with a conventional realist framework, since it cannot be represented as an existing reality:[1] it can have no fictional referent in the usual sense. Equally important, however, is the political and also ethical question of the writer's legitimacy – what gives him or her the right to speak in the community's name? In saying 'nous', Glissant may appear to be laying claim to a unity that does not exist. It is therefore essential that the collective narrative voice does not impose a false, coercive uniformity; rather, it must be sufficiently fluid and flexible to include all the different voices within the community. And, if it is to do this without merely collapsing into vagueness, it must be able to situate these differences in relation to each other. Here, in other words, the literary problem of narrative voice connects with Glissant's concept of Relation, articulated in *Le Discours antillais* as a form of combined solidarity and openness, a promotion of 'le Divers' and 'la nécessité opaque de consentir à la différence de l'autre' (p. 256), and developed further in *Poétique de la Relation*[2] to transform the notion of community from a monolithic entity to a diverse, non-hierarchical collectivity, a constantly changing matrix within which identities, languages and narratives circulate:

> La Relation ne relaie ni ne relie des afférents, assimilables ou apparentables dans leur seul principe, pour la raison qu'elle les différencie à tout coup et les détourne du totalitaire – car son ouvrage change à chaque fois chacun des éléments qui la font, et par conséquent le rapport qui en naît et qui les change à nouveau. (*PR*, p. 186)

There is thus a shift in emphasis between *Le Discours*, in which the aspiration towards collective identity presupposes a certain at least strategic unity to facilitate political liberation, and *Poétique de la Relation*, which explicitly rejects such a communal unity in favour of a conception of community so diverse and dynamic that a single author could never speak in its name.[3]

As far as literature is concerned, this means that Glissant's 'projet', as Michael Dash puts it, 'peut être conçu comme un effort soutenu de dénouer la poétique de l'un et de rétablir les circuits qui rendent le nous possible'.[4] And establishing these 'circuits' implies that literature's task is to elucidate the relations between individual subjects, their community and what lies outside it. This is already evident in *Le Discours*, in what Glissant calls 'le roman de l'implication du Je au Nous, du Je à l'autre, du nous au nous'; and he goes on to say:

> La Relation dessine en connaissance le cadre de ce nouvel épisode. On me dit que le roman du Nous est impossible à faire, qu'il y faudra toujours l'incarnation des devenirs particuliers. C'est un beau risque à courir. (p. 153)

It is this 'risk' that I now want to trace through *Malemort*, *La Case du commandeur* and *Mahagony*, for it is in these texts, rather than in Glissant's first two novels or the subsequent ones, that the problematic of 'nous' can be seen to be working itself out most clearly, in a process whereby the theoretical position developed in *Le Discours antillais* and then *Poétique de la Relation* is gradually realized in the fiction.

*Malemort* is usually seen as the most uncompromisingly bitter of Glissant's novels in its representation of Martinican society as disunited, alienated and impotent. Glissant himself has described it as recording 'ce qui là (ici) se défait sans répit [...] Nous n'en finissons pas de disparaître, victimes d'un frottement de mondes' (*DA*, p. 15). Its structure is remarkably disjointed: the thirteen chapters recount, in no chronological order, separate episodes taking place between 1788 and 1974 and tenuously linked only by the recurrence of certain characters. They are also extremely heterogeneous as discourses: one chapter is a poem, one is a satirical monologue, one appears to be quasi-autobiographical, one creates a kind of mythical discourse, one reproduces the 'delirium' of the character Médellus, and so on. Running through them all, however, there is a persistent if rather desperate collective narrative voice: a 'nous' that seems to be trying to link everything together. Bernadette Cailler analyses the inauguration of this voice at the end of the first chapter and shows how from then on 'le "*nous*" envahira le tissu du texte, non pas tant côte à côte avec un narrateur omniscient de type hétérodiégétique, ou avec une voix à la première personne que plus ou moins clandestinement infiltré, installé, au cœur des divers discours'.[5] This is not an impersonal narration: it has many features of colloquial speech, so that it sounds like a distinct 'voice'; it addresses both other characters and the reader; and it speaks in the first person plural. But it is never clear who 'we' are. At the beginning of the second chapter, the reader is given a list of individual characters included in 'nous': 'Il nous semblait (Épiphane […] Colentroc […] monsieur Lesprit […], etc.' (*Malemort*, p. 22). But not only does this list include an indefinite number of 'ceux innommés qui en ce matin d'août de guerre lointaine attendaient devant la mer close un rien de sel et de manioc'– and a pig – but it is also clear that the list is merely a sample, not an exhaustive count; a different incomplete list is given at the beginning of the second paragraph (p. 22). The actions and thoughts attributed to 'us' are also, here, expressed in metaphorical terms, which do not help in specifying who 'we' are:

> et nous voir tourner autour de nous comme une troupe en marge du combat: ne bataillant qu'à nos lisières sans armes ni balles, mais ramassant parfois nos morts sous les trop réelles balles de l'autre – et nous voir contents rire nos larmes, nos crânes rasés suant la mort blanche. (p. 23)

In fact, the question of the identity of 'nous' is posed in the text precisely as an unanswerable question: 'nous, énorme question qui ne donne pas réponse' (p. 34). In other words, 'nous' has no determinate referent; the voice that speaks in the text is plural and inclusive, but also completely undefined and undifferentiated.

All the named characters are referred to both in the third person and in the first person plural, as part of 'nous'. Indeed, the three main characters – Dlan, Médellus and Silacier – seem to have been chosen at random to represent everyone: 'après tout donc, pourquoi pas ces trois-là, eux-mêmes nous, eux-mêmes fous' (p. 23). 'Themselves us', they are both 'them' and 'us', both narrators and narrated. The language they use is equally ambiguous, both separate and communal; Dlan, for instance, is described as: 'nous parlant déjà dans sa langue (notre langue) particulière, et ainsi commençant déjà d'être incompris des deux autres qui pourtant (Silacier, Médellus) étaient, sont partie de nous (nous, partie d'eux) et qui nous parlent chacun dans sa langue (notre langue) particulière' (p. 34). Thus although the 'nous' is beginning to counteract the splintered, dispersed existence of the community, it is still a very inchoate entity in which the relations between those who make it up have not yet been clarified. The same section of *Malemort* in fact alludes to the historical development of a collective consciousness from the first moment of revolt – the slave escaping into the forest: 'Quand "nous" (non différencié, intact, humilié, chose et âme) s'échappait dans les bois sans peut-être savoir ce qui l'y poussait, et pourtant plus vif, plus chaudement mort et vainqueur qu'il ne le serait jamais' (p. 23) – in a way which suggests that at this stage there is no individual consciousness and no explicit awareness of why the individual is acting in this way – although the ambivalence of the attributes ('intact'/'humilié', 'chose'/'âme', 'vif/mort/vainqueur') prevents us from undervaluing this state. But the text continues: 'et quand "nous" [...] apprenait à dire je, à penser je, à commencer (continuer?) son infinie agrégation, sa si infime totalité [...]' – and so seems to equate the beginnings of an individual subjectivity with the capacity for forming together into a collectivity: 'à commencer [...] son infinie agrégation' (p. 23). The narrative voice, however, never reaches this stage of differentiation in *Malemort*. The ideal of collective unity in difference is present only as the utopian dream of the mad Médellus, who imagines 'un seul chanter plein de voix diverses' (p. 200).

But the very fact that *Malemort* does not present an achieved collective consciousness of communal identity (Nancy's 'common being', see note 3) – so that the novel is usually seen, including by Glissant himself, as lamenting this failure – also means that the indeterminacy of its 'nous' actually preserves the radical diversity of its community, and counteracts in a positive sense the fully constituted, bounded conception of collective identity that it might seem to be presenting as an (unrealizable) ideal. Thus Jean-Yves Debreuille sees the narrative voice, in its unstructured plurality, as a positive resistance to unity and hierarchy: 'un "nous" qui loin d'assigner, d'ordonner, de hiérarchiser, entre en fusion avec cette indifférenciation [...] D'ailleurs, le propre discours de ce "nous" n'est nullement unifié, il s'étend à mesure qu'il décrit, et s'approprie les langages'.[6] *Malemort*'s ambivalent 'nous', in its very confusion and dispersal, can perhaps also be seen as a viable alternative to the structured relationality of 'un seul chanter plein de voix diverses' (p. 200).

*La Case du commandeur* represents Glissant's second attempt at 'le roman du Nous', except that the short central section, 'Mitan du temps', has an entirely impersonal narration. In the other two sections, however, the 'nous' is even more prominent than in *Malemort*. *La Case du commandeur* opens and closes with direct references to the problem of creating a collective identity. Firstly, we read: '*Nous* qui ne devions peut-être jamais former, final de compte, ce corps unique par quoi nous commencerions d'entrer dans notre empan de terre' (p. 15, italics original). And the final sentence of the narrative is:

> Nous, qui avec tant d'impatience rassemblons ces moi disjoints; dans les retournements turbulents où cahoter à grands bras, piochant aussi le temps qui tombe et monte sans répit; acharnés à contenir la part inquiète de chaque corps dans cette obscurité difficile de nous. (p. 239)

*La Case du commandeur* differs from *Malemort* in that it conveys a stronger sense of historical continuity; instead of the abruptly discontinuous episodes of the latter, we move steadily backwards in time, retracing a family history back through four generations, each one occupying one chapter of the first section. The third section then follows the life of the main character, Marie-Celat, straightforwardly from 1945, where it left off in Glissant's first novel *La Lézarde*, to the present year of 1979.[7] Perhaps because of this, the novel conveys a greater sense of hope and possible progress; although collective consciousness is still seen as far from achieved and still the major problem, the struggle towards it is more vigorous: for instance, in the phrase which is repeated until it becomes a kind of refrain running through the text: 'moi disjoints qui nous acharnions chacun vers ce nous' (p. 42).

To this extent, collective unity is by implication more forcefully promoted here than in *Malemort* (and, certainly, than it will be in *Mahagony*). But the 'nous' of *La Case du commandeur* nevertheless remains inchoate and indeterminate. In one of the final scenes Marie Celat, who has been more or less forcibly taken to a mental hospital, escapes, together with Chérubin, another inmate. The journey he takes her on through the forest is also a psychological journey, achieved through language ('Ils traversèrent la route et plongèrent dans les touffes: tout autant de la parole soudain sans faille de Chérubin que du lacis de feuilles et de souches qu'ils labouraient de leurs corps', p. 230). The new form of narrative which this produces is also first person plural; rather than 'nous', however, Chérubin says 'non-nous-encore': 'Non-nous-encore n'avons pas fini' (p. 230); 'regarder non-nous-encore déambuler' (pp. 230–31). After six occurrences, however, this suddenly changes to:

> mais voilà *non-nous-encore-mais-déjà* tss tss c'est non-nous-encore-mais-déjà qui levons de la terre immondice à l'entrée des bureaux est-ce que tu comprends la parole de Chérubin [...] c'est non-nous-encore-mais-déjà

qui levons du bureau pour embrasser la terre et connaître le tout-nouveau.
(pp. 231–32, my italics)

The 'mad' narrative of Chérubin, in other words, illuminates the status of the collective subject, revealing it dialectically to be both as yet unconstituted and already existing on the margins of 'normal' consciousness.[8]

As in *Malemort*, the 'nous' provides a narrative point of view that is different both from impersonal omniscience – because it is often overtly personal and subjective – and from the usual type of focalized narrative, which is limited to a single circumscribed point of view. But its similar lack of definition is also made to serve a new purpose: unlike in *Malemort*, its extreme elasticity, allowing it to move between different characters and different periods of time, in effect gives it a very unconventional, non-hierarchical kind of omniscience, on the basis of which it constructs a new kind of representation of intersubjective relations between the individual characters.[9] It implies that people's most intimate feelings are known to the community. The narrative, in other words, has some kind of communal knowledge of individuals, even if how it is acquired remains obscure: 'Mais Augustus avait déjà fait sa déclaration [...] (nous en savions les détails on dirait par les feuillages des tamarins d'autour)' (p. 90) – and this effect is created simply by the use of 'nous' as a narrative voice.[10] Knowledge also involves participation and a sense of responsibility; 'we' know, for instance, how Marie Celat is experiencing her nervous breakdown, and link her feelings to 'ourselves':

> Par un obscur besoin nous établissions, ceux d'entre nous qui hésitaient au bord de ce malheur, mesure et correspondance de cette passion de Marie Celat aux incertitudes qui nous épuisaient jour après jour: prononçant chacun à part soi qu'avec la fin de son tourment cesserait aussi pour nous cet insupportable contentement qui, nous le savions déjà sans rien savoir encore, était le seul butin de notre consentement à nous laisser mener. Nous n'avons donc jamais désespéré de la voir se remettre, remonter de la nuit. (p. 225)

In this sense the strength and flexibility of the collective voice are more clearly evident than in *Malemort*. But *La Case du commandeur*, ending with a restatement of 'cette obscurité difficile de nous' (p. 239), has still not really begun to work on 'l'implication du Je au Nous', which, as we have seen, is the basis for Relation.

This, however, is the principal structural concern of *Mahagony*, which in this respect represents a distinct break with the two previous novels. It is formally more complex, and it abandons the anonymous 'nous' in favour of a narrative divided into separate sections, which each have a named individual narrator. The most dominant of these – the narrator of five of the eighteen sections – is Mathieu, who has already featured as a character in all of Glissant's previous novels. But, in now assuming the status of narrator, Mathieu uses his new autonomy to criticize the author who had originally created and used him: in other words, Glissant himself, whom Mathieu calls 'l'auteur', 'le chroniqueur' or 'mon biographe'. He accuses him of 'me conférant une exemplarité dont j'étais loin d'approcher la mécanique simplicité' (p. 18), and also, more importantly, of underestimating the complexity and multiplicity of the other characters and events represented in *La Lézarde*, *Malemort* and *La Case du commandeur* – 'cette incommensurable dimension née de milliards et de milliards de rencontres, de hasards, de lois impitoyables et de pitoyables amours' (pp. 23–24).

This odd device of a character supposedly escaping from his author's control enables Glissant to present the reader with a critique of his own earlier work. One major aspect of this critique is the collective voice as used previously, the result of which was, according to Mathieu, to 'confondre les habitants, leur descendance, leurs visages, dans une même indistincte et trop puissante identité' (p. 33). The author, in other words, is guilty of obliterating the difference whose recognition is the necessary basis of Relation (as opposed to what in *Le Discours antillais* Glissant already calls 'les pseudo-collectivismes dans quoi le Nous a dilué le Je', p. 153). The undifferentiated collective voice is now seen as a kind of bad faith, 'la tentation [...] de me fondre dans un nous bienfaisant qui m'eût aussi permis de m'y effacer' (*Mahagony*, p. 85), whereas honesty requires that he retain his separateness and acknowledge that much of his narration is simply of no interest to the community on whose behalf he would be claiming to speak – in this case, an 'épisode qui avait apparemment laissé peu de trace dans ce nous que je désirais parfois d'exprimer ou de vivre' (p. 86). No one voice, in other words, can express the totality of the community's experience, and to attempt to do so is now seen as a kind of authorial arrogance. Instead, the solution is to have a number of narrators, each making a particular and different contribution to the narrative.

The narrative in question, moreover, is not wholly containable within the boundaries of *Mahagony* alone. Many of the events related here have already figured in Glissant's previous novels; but what *Mahagony* does is to show these earlier representations as incomplete and one-sided because of their unitary narrative point of view. *Mahagony* thus relates intertextually to the rest of Glissant's fiction, retelling the same stories but from a different perspective, enlarging and relativizing their original significance. Mathieu says: 'Je reprenais le texte du chroniqueur [...] La chronique avait enroulé le premier fil de l'histoire sans pour autant suffire à la trame: d'autres paroles devaient y concourir' (p. 16). The clearest example of this is the story of Beautemps, who disappeared into the forest and eluded capture for seven years after attacking the white master who had raped his woman, Adoline. This is a central incident in *Malemort*, but the new version of it in *Mahagony* introduces two previously unmentioned characters: Adélaïde, who tells the story, and Artémise. These are both women who were secretly in love with Beautemps, but Adélaïde's portrait of him is distinctly less heroic than that given in *Malemort*. Moreover, her narrative is supplemented in *Mahagony* by that of Papa Longoué (another character who appears in all the novels), who, we now discover, was secretly in love with Adoline and therefore has yet another perspective on the story.

If the character Mathieu has now become the 'author' of *Mahagony*, Glissant has conversely become a character/narrator in his own book, and as such has his own section of narrative (entitled 'Celui qui commente'). Marie Celat refers to him as the 'friend' who has previously (i.e., in *La Case du commandeur*) written her story (p. 173), just as she comments on Mathieu's role as author (p. 182). The various narrators, in other words, are all on the same textual level of reality and are aware of each other's existence. The text as a whole has become a perfect example of Bakhtin's dialogic novel: a matrix of interrelated voices, in which no single author or narrator has a privileged position.

This, however, is not immediately apparent in the case of Mathieu, who at first claims to have organized all the other narrators: it is he, he tells us, who has consulted the sources and put together the different partial accounts to arrive at the full picture; the other narratives are embedded in and dependent upon his. He stresses his ambition to be detached, objective and scientific; and this initial ambition, while it is humbler than the previous all-encompassing 'nous', is nevertheless still an assumption of control and an imposition of order. But it soon fails. The hierarchy of voices that he had hoped to set up falls apart and he finds himself 'compromised' by the others, rather than being able to reduce them to his own order: 'Je me retrouvais compromis à ces langages successifs que j'avais ambitionné de clarifier. J'étais un paroleur parmi d'autres, saturé d'un suc dont je n'étais pas capable de peser la teneur' (p. 31). Thus both Glissant as author and Mathieu as principal narrator are challenged and undermined by the plurality of the narration. Neither can keep their own voices 'pure' and supreme; both have to enter on equal terms into a dialogue of mixed voices; so, Mathieu concludes, 'la recherche de l'*ordonnance* cédait donc à la contamination' (p. 32, italics original).

A key verb that recurs in *Mahagony* – and which Glissant elsewhere links to Relation – is 'relayer'.[11] It describes the process of handing on information from one person to another, but also that of handing over control of the narrative, and, as 'se relayer', of working together to produce a collective but non-uniform narrative that will emerge out of the incomplete individual contributions. The narrators take it for granted that their story will be continued by others. Hégésippe, for instance, the slave who secretly learns to write but has to stop when he goes blind, buries his manuscript underground but still assumes that it will be found, read and completed:

> Ce qui s'ensuit n'est plus mon conte, incontinent je vais fouiller la terre déposer le résumé dans sa nuit avec mes yeux pour toujours jusqu'à la découverte. Mon ouvrage a terminé [...] que j'envoie au hasard ou à l'ouverture du temps, pour le bienheureux qui l'encontrera. Mes yeux finissent de fermer. (p. 70)

This pattern of handing on the story is repeated throughout, most explicitly in the third part of the novel, where, first of all, Marie Celat explains why she is unable to continue with the story and must hand over to her daughter Ida (p. 187); Ida then hands over to Mathieu (p. 211), who in turn hands over to the 'author': 'Ce qui suit ne saurait être que commentaire de mon auteur. Je lui laisse la place, je lui laisse' (p. 227). The cumulative effect of this process is that the events and characters of the stories become almost less relevant than the intersubjective structures of narrators that support and relay them. Nathaniel Wing comments: 'L'importance d'un contenu originel et du point d'origine d'un récit s'efface dans ces romans en faveur de la *relation*, dans la double signification d'acte de *relayer* de multiples versions d'un récit et de *rapport* établi entre ces diverses versions par un interprète, qu'il soit lecteur ou personnage romanesque'.[12]

The structure of *Mahagony* is superficially far more familiar and conventional than the 'nous' narrative, in so far as it fits unproblematically into the category of novels narrated from a number of different individual points of view, a category that includes such well-known texts as Sartre's *Chemins de la liberté*, for instance, or Gide's *Les Faux-Monnayeurs*. But there is an important difference between novels like these and *Mahagony*. For the European novel, the multiplicity of viewpoints is motivated by the divergences between them, and the overall effect is one of ironic disjunction arising from the way in which the different narrators undermine each other: the main point of Gide's *La Porte étroite*, for instance, is that Jérôme misunderstands Alissa's feelings for him, and the reader realizes this through having privileged access to their separate accounts. But in *Mahagony* the plurality of voices is not disjunctive: their differences supplement rather than contradict each other; nor, as we have seen, are the voices isolated from each other. The result is a kind of stereoscopic, multidimensional, open-ended representation of an interwoven fictional reality.[13] Moreover, towards the end of the novel there is the suggestion that, in fact, there is no end: the intertextual network or 'trame' will go on expanding indefinitely, extending beyond the existing corpus of Glissant's own novels to meet up with other stories and form new combinations. Mathieu refers to 'ce moment où toute histoire dilate dans l'air du monde, s'y dilue peut-être, y conforte parfois une autre trame, parue loin dans l'ailleurs' (p. 242).

Thus *Mahagony*, in basing itself on the notions of the relay and the 'trame', comes much closer than *Malemort* or *La Case du commandeur* to realizing the ideal of the dynamic, internally differentiated collective consciousness. The relays have to be clarified before we can effectively know ourselves and act together; Mathieu describes discussions with his friends as being like the different lights coming on and going out in the countryside as secret messages to Beautemps, the fugitive on the run: 'Ils s'éteignaient l'un après l'autre, en sorte que nous ne voyions pas le champ étoilé tout entier répandu sur la nuit. Nos lumignons se relaient, il leur reste à brûler ensemble' (p. 157). In other words, the collective voice is always a multiplicity of individual voices whose unity can only be based on the relations between them, relations here materialized as narratives. Glissant underlines the connections between 'relation', 'relative', 'relay' and also 'related' in the sense of 'told': the truth of Relation 'se donne dans un récit [...] Mais, son relaté ne procédant pas en réalité d'un absolu, elle se révèle comme la totalité des relatifs mis en rapport et dits' (*PR*, p. 40). In the same vein, *Mahagony* gives a final restatement of the relay, as Mathieu writes on the last page:

> Ainsi ai-je couru la courbe de ce récit aux voix mêlées [...] Si nous entendons consigner nos dérives ou nos futurs, il nous faudra bien à la ronde accepter de partager la tâche: car nos paroles valent d'autant

qu'elles se relaient. Écrire est étrange, quand un qui était considéré ou pris comme modèle, ou prétexte, entreprend à son tour de modeler. Ce va-et-vient correspond à nos humeurs. Il indique notre place parmi les étoiles futures, dans le relais infini des voix singulières. (pp. 251–52)

The evolution of the collective narrative voice from *Malemort* through *La Case du commandeur* to *Mahagony* reflects the parallel development of Glissant's theorizations of collective identity over the nine years separating *Le Discours antillais* (1981) from *Poétique de la Relation* (1990); the first two novels, published in 1975 and 1981 respectively, echo *Le Discours antillais*'s concern to build a militant collective consciousness that will rescue Martinique from its political alienation and stagnation, while *Mahagony*, in 1987, anticipates *Poétique de la Relation*'s more fully developed theorization of Relation as a refutation of unity, hierarchy and essentialist identity. But this does not mean that *Mahagony* therefore represents the successful conclusion of a process in which the two previous novels were no more than imperfect attempts. *Malemort*, as I have suggested above, turns failure into a strange kind of success: the distress of its chaotic, alienated characters is at once an acute social problem and an – equally chaotic – intimation of a new kind of unalienated but also unbounded community. *La Case du commandeur* combines the more forceful promotion of collective unity that Mathieu will reject in *Mahagony* with a 'nous' that escapes any restrictive definition and creates new forms of intersubjective participation in different individuals' experience. But it is in *Mahagony* that the question of collective *narration* is most fully and explicitly explored, as it puts in place its 'relais infini des voix singulières'. All three novels, however, demonstrate the interconnectedness of literary form and socio-political issues in Glissant's fiction: the formal problem of narrative voice is indissociable from the substantive political problem of the nature of collective identity.

# Fictions of Identity and the
# Identities of Fiction in *Tout-monde*

In *Tout-monde* we read: 'Nos identités se relaient, et par là seulement tombent en vaine prétention ces hiérarchies cachées [...] Ne consentez pas à ces manœuvres de l'identique [...] Ouvrez au monde le champ de votre identité' (p. 158). And in the course of an interview marking its publication in 1993, Glissant remarks, rather casually, 'Les éditeurs appellent ça un roman, donc je pense que le public peut le considérer comme tel'.[1] But he would clearly prefer not to have to assign it to any particular existing literary genre – and it is not hard to understand why. My starting point here is the juxtaposition of these two quotations. In other words, *Tout-monde* extends the critique of unitary identity that had become increasingly prominent in Glissant's work, exploring further the notion of plural, variable, relational *personal* identity; and at the same time it breaks down the boundaries that separate and distinguish the *generic* identities of novel, essay, autobiography, prose poem, travel writing, etc. This chapter will examine the possible connections between these two projects.

On a theoretical level they can be brought together via the notion of the *rhizome*, which Glissant takes from Deleuze and Guattari.[2] His enthusiasm for the multiply proliferating 'rhizome' as against the singular 'root' is evident not only in *Tout-monde* – which is dedicated to the memory of Félix Guattari – but also in *Poétique de la Relation*, where he writes:

Gilles Deleuze et Félix Guattari ont critiqué les notions de racine et peut-être d'enracinement. La racine est unique, c'est une souche qui prend tout sur elle et tue alentour; ils lui opposent le rhizome qui est une racine démultipliée, étendue en réseaux dans la terre ou dans l'air, sans qu'aucune souche y intervienne en prédateur irrémédiable. La notion de

> rhizome maintiendrait donc le fait de l'enracinement, mais récuse l'idée
> d'une racine totalitaire. La pensée du rhizome serait au principe de ce que
> j'appelle une poétique de la Relation, selon laquelle toute identité s'étend
> dans un rapport à l'Autre. (p. 23)

In the interview cited above, the opposition between root and rhizome
is exploited more specifically in the context of national identity; Glissant
says:

> Les identités à racine unique font peu à peu place aux identités-relations,
> c'est-à-dire aux identités-rhizomes. Il ne s'agit pas de se déraciner, il
> s'agit de concevoir la racine moins intolérante, moins sectaire: une
> identité racine qui ne tue pas autour d'elle mais qui au contraire étend ses
> branches vers les autres. Ce que d'après Deleuze et Guattari j'appelle une
> identité-rhizome. (*IPD*, p. 132)

This deconstructing of the classical notion of singular identity echoes
the opening sentences of Deleuze and Guattari's *Mille Plateaux*, which
affirm a provocative plurality – 'Nous avons écrit *L'Anti-Œdipe* à deux.
Comme chacun de nous était plusieurs, ça faisait déjà beaucoup de
monde' (p. 9) – and a subversive fluidity of personal identity: 'Non pas
en arriver au point où l'on ne dit plus je, mais au point où ça n'a plus
aucune importance de dire je ou de ne pas dire je. Nous ne sommes
plus nous-mêmes' (p. 9). But the conceptual implications of the rhizome
in fact go beyond questions of personal identity, whether individual
or collective. Its force is that of a very general principle, promoting
multiplicity and heterogeneity over unity and closure; and as such
it is also extremely relevant to the literary activity of constructing a
text. Thus the first few pages of *Mille Plateaux* are devoted to the
question of 'le livre', claiming that 'Un livre n'a pas d'objet ni de sujet,
il est fait de matières diversement formées, de dates et de vitesses très
différentes' (p. 9). The first 'principles' of the rhizome are 'de connexion
et d'hétérogénéité' (p. 13); anything can and should be connected to
anything else, and this includes the different types of discourse that
traditionally allow us to categorize different literary genres.

The rhizome thus provides a general conceptual matrix which can
bring together the two parameters of personal identity and literary
genre, and enable us to explore in more detail their interaction within
the text of *Tout-monde*. If *Tout-monde* is a novel, it is one which
transposes onto a literary level Jean-Luc Godard's famous remark: 'Il
faut *tout* mettre dans un film'. For instance, it includes extracts from
a 'Traité du Tout-monde' attributed to one of its characters – Mathieu

Béluse – but which has subsequently been published under Glissant's own name.[3] This latter includes the passages that figured in *Tout-monde* (for example, my opening quotation here from page 158 of *Tout-monde* reappears on page 68 of the *Traité du tout-monde*), but is itself equally heterogeneous: no more a pure theoretical essay than *Tout-monde* is a pure novel. As well as these 'quotations' from the 'Traité', the main body of the text of *Tout-monde* also at times reads like an essay: pages 435 to 436, for instance, discuss (complete with footnote) the problem of creating a relational, non-oppressive conception of identity.

A more prominent recurring borderline, however, is that between fiction and autobiography, which is almost constantly in question throughout the volume. Some sections are quite unambiguously fiction and not autobiography: 'L'Eau de volcan', for instance, if only because it is set in the eighteenth century. But even here the status of the fictional diegesis is subtly undermined by the quality of the characters' dialogue. This is often so exaggeratedly 'period' that one is irresistibly led to read it as a *parody* of the historical novel: 'Seigneur, à quoi tend donc votre élucubration?' (p. 66); 'C'est insupportable, cria Senglis. A quoi tend cet interrogatoire impertinent?' (p. 68). Equally parodic, surely, are the apparent attempts, typical of some historical novels (and films and television dramas) to establish a realistic historical context by means of fictional characters' heavy-handed references to real people of the period: 'Chacun prétend que ces marauds de Voltaire et de Rousseau sont des esprits forts qui nous préparent à fournaise, m'est avis que c'est plutôt son fait, à ce monsieur Diderot sans père ni mère ni descendants' (p. 65).

More often, the events of a particular section centre on a male protagonist, either referred to simply as 'il' or named as 'Mathieu' or 'Thaël', from whose point of view they are recounted. Some of these are characters we already know from Glissant's previous novels, such as Mathieu and Thaël themselves, or Papa Longoué in the section entitled 'Un pied de térébinthe', or Artémise and Marie-Annie in 'Bezaudin'. Some introduce new characters, who are also straightforwardly fictional: Rigobert Massoul, for instance, in 'Les tiques de Sénégal', has the same status as the fictional narrators of *Mahagony* discussed in the previous chapter. But others refer to real people: Glissant's friends, colleagues and family. 'Atala', for instance, tells the story of a summer spent in Corsica by two penniless students, one an unnamed Martinican from whose point of view the events are narrated, and the other the poet Roger Giroux; it also refers in passing to Michel Leiris and André Breton (p. 244).

Stylistically, too, it reads as the recollection of a real past rather than a constructed fictional narrative: a series of random events interspersed with abstract reflections and little direct speech. Conversations are reported with a casual vagueness, as in their unsuccessful attempt to hitch a lift to Paris; 'Le routier répondit qu'ils n'avaient pas de chance, ou que la chance n'était pas avec eux, ou que ce n'était pas leur jour de chance, un de ces lieux communs qui vous déracinent' (p. 259). The overall effect is of an autobiographical rather than a fictional discourse. This is reinforced, albeit somewhat ambiguously, by the section appended to the end of the main text, which purports to tell the reader to whom the names in the main text refer (p. 513). Here we learn, for instance, that 'Roger' is indeed Roger Giroux, that 'Maurice' is the writer Maurice Roche, that Patrick Chamoiseau appears as 'Gibier' and so on. But these names of real people are mixed quite indiscriminately with names that we recognize as those of fictional characters; and there are also some people whose real identities, we are told, have to remain hidden. In other words, the text refuses to make a clear separation between fiction and reality. One consequence of this pervasive ambiguity is that the autobiographical material is not restricted to sections with an anonymous *sujet d'énonciation*, but at times invades sections belonging to the character Mathieu Béluse as well: he meets Sylvie (i.e., Sylvie Glissant), for instance (p. 312). Occasionally a contradiction arises between fictional consistency and the pull of the author's biographical reality; thus we know from *Le Quatrième Siècle* that Mathieu was born in 1926, but in *Tout-monde* we read that he was born in 1928 (p. 309) – as was Glissant himself.

In one sense, of course, this can be considered a non-issue: much of what we read as fiction draws heavily on the author's own experiences, and there is perhaps a particular tradition of this kind of fictionalized autobiography in the French Caribbean.[4] But I want to argue that Glissant is doing something more radical than simply subsuming real-life experiences into a fictional framework. Rather, this is a deliberate interrogation of the relationship between fiction and the real,[5] and its effect is to open the text out onto the real in a way that is quite unusual. It enacts Deleuze and Guattari's pronouncement that 'le livre n'est pas image du monde [...] il fait rhizome avec le monde, il y a évolution aparallèle du livre et du monde' (*Mille Plateaux*, p. 18). Conventionally, if a book is to function effectively as a picture or representation of reality, it must be diegetically consistent and homogeneous *as* a (fictional) representation. Deleuze and Guattari are arguing against this traditional conception of the book as a 'model' (the rhizome is not a model, but a 'processus immanent qui renverse le modèle', p.31), and for a kind of book that celebrates its own discursive heterogeneity, and especially its deliberate mixing of fictional and real elements – in exactly the way that *Tout-monde* does. *Tout-monde*, from this point of view, 'fait rhizome avec le monde'.

Deleuze and Guattari even claim that the effect of mixing different signifying 'regimes' in this way is to move outside the domain of language and signification altogether. They imagine a situation in which the classic purity of the Saussurean sign is so fundamentally disrupted that the famous barrier between signifier and signified falls away:

> Dans un rhizome au contraire, chaque trait ne renvoie pas nécessairement à un trait linguistique: des chaînons sémiotiques de toute nature y sont connectés à des modes d'encodage très divers, chaînons biologiques, politiques, économiques, etc., mettant en jeu non seulement des régimes de signes différents, mais aussi des statuts d'états de choses [...] l'on ne peut pas établir de coupure radicale entre les régimes de signes et leurs objets. (p. 13)

The recurrent emphasis in *Tout-monde* on 'errance', and on the diverse trajectories of its characters moving around the world, acquires a further resonance here when juxtaposed with Deleuze and Guattari's definition of the kind of book they are promoting as 'écriture nomadique', which they explain as: 'le nomadisme de ceux qui ne bougent même plus et qui n'imitent plus rien. Ils agencent seulement. Comment le livre trouvera-t-il un dehors suffisant avec lequel il puisse agencer dans l'hétérogène, plutôt qu'un monde à reproduire?' (p. 35). The book which is thus 'agencé avec le dehors' abandons the homogeneity and closure necessary to representation in favour of a heterogeneous opening onto and connection with the world – or the 'Tout-monde'.

There are two features of Glissant's fiction that further facilitate these moments of crossing the boundary between fiction and autobiographical reality: his characteristic narrative structure, and his representation of place. Firstly, that is, the indeterminacy of the discourse as between fiction and real can be sustained only because Glissant's fiction has already jettisoned traditional notions of narrative structure and plot. In a conventional novel, the presence of a particular incident is motivated by the dynamic of the plot (or, as Barthes puts it, 'ce qui est noté est, par définition, notable'),[6] whereas an autobiography has greater freedom – it can recount an event for the simple reason that it 'really happened'. But the reader of *Malemort, La Case du commandeur* or *Mahagony* has already learnt to expect a non-linear, proliferating narrative that does not conform to the logic of plot.

Secondly, the extreme importance that Glissant attaches to *places* is also a central factor in the neutralizing of the distinction between the two genres. One major sub-category of autobiography is travel writing, and the 'carnets' that form the last part of the 'La Tragédie d'Askia' section of *Tout-monde* (pp. 443–59) seem to be preliminary notes for exactly this kind of text. Equally, however, realist novels are set in real places, and put invented characters into Paris, Rouen, Besançon, etc. A textual passage describing a place, then, if read out of context, will contain nothing that could tell the reader whether it comes from a fictional or a non-fictional text. But this indeterminacy is foregrounded in Glissant's case because for him place has always been more than simply setting: 'Le lieu est incontournable' (*Tout-monde*, p. 435). His long and intense descriptions of places – of Genoa and Vernazza, for instance, in 'Banians' (pp. 29–61) – thus in themselves serve to blur the boundary between fiction and the real.

The influence that places exert on people in his texts is also significant, both from the point of view of generic instability and from that of 'rhizomatic' identity. *Tout-monde* very explicitly links its rejection of the artifices of conventional fictional characterization with the notion that people are intimately bound up with particular places:

> Il y avait tant de personnages du monde qui étaient des paysages, et tout à fait inversement. Ce romancier, dont on pouvait dire qu'il partait aussi en poésie, essayait de tracer, de révéler les personnages par le paysage, (nous ne croyons plus avec lui au personnage du roman qui vous en impose, ni aux astuces de l'auteur: les descriptions rusées qui tâchent de présenter un quidam sans en brosser vraiment le portrait [...]) et ainsi d'arrimer le paysage sous l'apparent disparate, et de chanter le pays sous toute cette apparence. (p. 441)

Here the writer is both novelist and poet, and his characters are 'revealed' through their links with the landscape, rather than being constructed as they would be in conventional fiction.

In the same way, the plurality of relations with place that is inherent in 'errance' also serves to create a plurality within the individual's sense of identity: 'La pensée de l'errance débloque l'imaginaire, elle nous projette hors de cette grotte en prison où nous étions enfermés, qui est la cale ou la caye de la soi-disant unicité' (p. 124) – a plurality which is manifested in Caribbean migrants all over the world:

> C'était comme ça pour les Antillais. Ils partaient chacun de son côté mais forcément, ils menaient plusieurs vies à la fois. La vie en mouvement qu'ils poursuivaient au loin [...] la vie tout arrêtée qu'ils tenaient en réserve au plus secret [...] la vie hasardeuse enfin dont ils rêvaient [...] Il n'y avait aucun moyen de joindre ensemble ces vies-là. (pp. 280–81)

There are many other examples throughout *Tout-monde* of this phenomenon of multiple 'rhizomatic' identity. But it is particularly noticeable in those characters who occupy subject positions in the discourse of particular sections of the text; that is, while they are not necessarily first-person narrators, the text is written from their point of view and they therefore function as its *sujets d'énonciation*. The traditional authorial voice splits into a variety of different instances, some of which have proper names, while others are simply given a designation that expresses their status as *sujets d'énonciation*: 'le romancier', 'le chroniqueur', etc. Moreover, these latter do not remain stable. We do not know who they are, and – more importantly – we do not know whether they are in fact different people. The text lists them together several times, putting us on our guard against assuming that any one of them has authorial status:

> Le déparleur, le poète, le chroniqueur, le romancier, ne gagez pas que c'est l'auteur du livre, vous vous tromperiez à coup sûr. (p. 513)

– or assuming that they are the same person:

> Note du commentateur, qui n'est pas Mathieu Béluse ni Raphaël Targin ni Marie Celat ni ce chroniqueur, ce poète, ce romancier ni ce déparleur. (p. 516)

– or assuming that they are different people:

> Mathieu Béluse pourtant, qui ressemblait au déparleur, c'est-à-dire, dans ces riens qui importent tellement, et d'ailleurs vous n'avez pas oublié que Mathieu, déparleur, chroniqueur, romancier, c'était quatre-en-un, sinon davantage. (p. 345)

The cumulative effect of this is to construct a plurality of *sujets d'énonciation* for the text while simultaneously refusing to assign any definite identities to them; they remain as an ambiguously fissile and proliferating collective instance of narration:[7]

> Le poète quant à lui avait repris ce conte dans il ne savait plus quel ouvrage, et Mathieu Béluse avait fait de même, et aussi ce chroniqueur qui s'était tant mêlé des affaires de Mathieu, (remarquez ainsi la multiplication, à

partir de Mathieu Béluse: Mathieu, le chroniqueur, le poète, le romancier, sans compter celui ou cela-ci [*sic*] qui écrit là en ce moment et qui ne se confond ni avec Mathieu, ce chroniqueur, ce romancier ni ce poète, ils prolifèrent, peut-on dire qu'ils sont un-seul divisé en lui-même, ou plusieurs qui se rencontrent en un. (p. 271)

To complicate matters further, the ambiguities extend across diegetic levels, in a manner already evident in *Mahagony*, in/of which Mathieu is both character and author, as discussed in the previous chapter. This metadiegetic play is continued and extended in *Tout-monde*, where, in the 'Bezaudin' section, Mathieu's own narrative account of events in *Mahagony* is in turn challenged by Artémise and Marie-Annie (pp. 181–83). But this time Mathieu defends himself by saying that he was not in fact the author, because the story was actually told by someone else: 'Sauf qu'il y avait un autre raconteur, vous ne parlez jamais de lui. Sauf que ce raconteur a mis tout ça en méli-mélo et m'a enveloppé dedans' (p. 183).

This idea that there is another, rather shadowy, presence behind the apparent *sujet d'énonciation* is borne out by the way in which at several points the text of *Tout-monde*, having established a *sujet d'énonciation* for one particular section, then as it were pulls back from him and reveals another – always anonymous – presence in the background. This is true of the 'Bezaudin' section itself, which is consistently narrated from Mathieu's point of view until three pages from the end, when he is suddenly addressed by another voice, giving the reader a different point of view on him:

Ho Mathieu Béluse ho! Où piochez-vous dans cette errance? Où ça donc? N'est-elle pas moins dévirante que le tournoiement dans la tête qui vous prend, quand vous écoutez les deux puissances du jour et de la nuit? (p. 188)

A similar tactic is used in the section 'Stepan Stepanovitch ou la folie Marie Celat'. Here the narrator at first appears to be 'le déparleur', who tells the stories of Stepan and Marie Celat, piecing them together from what he has heard from others: 'Le déparleur raboutait ensemble ce qu'il avait entendu, directement ou par rapportage' (p. 342). The next page, however, abruptly introduces another *sujet d'énonciation*, who gives his point of view *on* 'le déparleur': 'Que cherche-t-il, le déparleur? Pourquoi mélange-t-il ainsi, ou du moins tente-t-il de le faire, des misères qu'il a devinées?' (p. 343). A similar effect is achieved by the use of the second-person pronoun intervening in Mathieu's vision of Genoa in

'Banians' – a series of occurrences of 'vous' which may at first seem to be addressing the reader, but soon become so biographically specific that they have to be read as addressing Mathieu: 'Tâchez de prendre pied sur ce cassis à Bezaudin où vous êtes né' (p. 58). In all these cases it is as though the source of the narration suddenly moves back, recedes from one diegetic level to another, resituating a narrator as a character and by the same token instituting a new narrator, but an unidentifiable and extremely elusive one.

And on one of these levels we get back to the voice of 'Glissant' himself, the autobiographical author, who never declares himself openly as such, but whose suspected interventions trouble the fictional reality effect with the intrusions of a different kind of reality. One striking example of this is in the section 'Air-plane'. This occurs near the end of the book (pp. 460–90), immediately following the two short texts that form the end of the preceding section and that consist of notes on places in Peru and Egypt. These two 'carnets' have no fictional content, but are simply the notations and reflections of an autobiographical 'je' visiting various temples and other sacred sites. 'Air-plane' starts as the same kind of discourse, with 'je' commenting on several real texts: Alejo Carpentier's *Le Partage des eaux*, and an extract, reprinted from *Antilla*, of an article by Félix-Hilaire Fortuné on the 'Géographie des rivières de la Martinique'. But it almost immediately introduces the fictional Mathieu Béluse as though he were a real person who knew the author – and knew him precisely as an author: 'Mathieu Béluse m'appelle "ce romancier-là"' (p. 461). A comparison of the novelist's work with that of the 'pacotilleuses'[8] is followed by an autobiographical narrative describing a plane flight threatened by an oncoming cyclone, as he and his family were travelling to Baton Rouge (where Glissant taught for several years), a visit to Alain Baudot in Toronto, Glissant's reactions to the Gulf War, a phone conversation with Maurice Roche, and so on. This is then once again suddenly interrupted by a reference to Mathieu Béluse (p. 467), which this time leads into a long dialogue between Mathieu and another fictional character, Jorge de Rocamarron, the descendant of the free mulatto whom we met in 'L'Eau de volcan', and Artémise and Annie-Marie (p. 468). Thus we have, apparently, moved from autobiography to fiction.

Soon, however, the confusion between novelist and autobiographer is compounded by a new confusion between novelist and character. Rather than simply mixing up real and fictional material (characters or events) this entails a collapsing of the diegetic boundary between author and character, similar to that which we have seen in *Mahagony*, except that, this time, it is from the point of view of the author: the 'je' here is Glissant, in other words, rather than Mathieu. In 'Air-plane' the author of the fiction in which the characters appear is present with them in the conversation – but in a rather elusive fashion. They seem to be aware of his presence – 'il savait donc que j'étais là' (p. 469) – but they ignore his increasingly petulant attempts to join in the conversation: 'J'aurais voulu mettre mon mot, mais rien à faire, apparemment je n'avais pas une place ni sur cette spirale ni sur ce cercle. Pourtant, j'aurais voulu mettre mon mot. Je suis romancier quand même, nous avons appris par ici ce que c'est qu'un roman quand même' (p. 470). By repeatedly telling the bewildered reader that 'c'était comme si je n'étais pas là' (pp. 471, 474) Glissant is of course asserting that he was there, that the autobiographical voice is also that of a 'romancier' and that the latter is also present as a character in his fictional creation.

The provocative playfulness of this manipulation of diegetic levels, first in *Mahagony* and now in *Tout-monde*, represents something new in Glissant's fiction. It echoes and is perhaps influenced by the general tone of *Mille Plateaux*. But it is also reminiscent of French avant-garde novels of the 1960s and 1970s, and the structuralist literary theory that accompanied them; the use of *mise en abyme*, in which different levels of representation are juxtaposed within the text, was a major feature of the work of *nouveaux romanciers* such as Alain Robbe-Grillet and Claude Simon.[9] The result, and the purpose, of the *mise en abyme* is to undermine the 'illusion référentielle', that is, the realist assumption underpinning conventional fiction, by producing texts which make it impossible for the reader to read them as representing a diegetic reality. On a theoretical level, Roland Barthes' work had an equally anti-realist focus in his promotion of the 'texte scriptible' over the conventionally realist 'texte lisible', and this involved the deconstruction of the figure of the *author* in a way that seems particularly apposite to *Mahagony* and *Tout-monde*: his recommendation in *S/Z* that 'l'entreprise critique [...] consistera alors à *retourner* la figure documentaire de l'auteur en figure romanesque, irrepérable, irresponsable, prise dans le pluriel de son propre texte' (p. 217, italics original) could serve as a description of the manoeuvres accomplished in these two novels.

Despite these similarities, however, Glissant's deliberate confusion of diegetic levels has a very different aim from the *nouveaux romanciers'* concern to undermine the realist basis of the novel. Glissant's agenda is not a *formalist* one. Rather, he follows Deleuze and Guattari in rejecting the notion of representation in order to construct a different relation between the text and the real: one in which the text 'fait rhizome avec le monde'.[10] Equally, he does not reject the notion of authorship *per se*, but relativizes it into an elusive plurality of instances. Thus in *Le Discours antillais* he argues that the contemporary Western theoretical 'demythification' of the author is relevant to Caribbean novels only in so far as they too need to 'demythify' the figure of the *individual* author, in favour of the communal authorship of the 'roman du Nous': 'Le texte doit être ici (dans notre vécu) mis en question, parce qu'il doit être mis en commun, et c'est peut-être par là qu'effectivement nous rejoignons ces propositions qui se sont fait jour ailleurs. L'auteur doit être démythifié, oui, parce qu'il doit être intégré à une décision commune' (*DA*, p. 258). This position, I would argue, is still valid in relation to his later novels: in other words, what is at work in *Mahagony* and *Tout-monde* is not the wholesale rejection of the novels' diegetic reality – although this is certainly problematized in a number of ways – but rather the insistence that no narrative or text can be under the control of a *single* author. The difference between these novels and those of the *nouveau roman* is that Glissant brings together his critique of generic boundaries and his critique of personal identity: neither the text nor the *sujet d'énonciation* has a unitary identity.[11] In other words, the connection that I posited at the beginning of this chapter, between rhizomatic personal identity and rhizomatic generic heterogeneity, turns out to be articulated through the indeterminate multiplicity of the *sujet d'énonciation*, because this latter includes a typically rhizomatic movement across different diegetic levels and ultimately across the boundary that normally separates the fictional from the real.

# Mixing up Languages
# in the 'Tout-monde'

It is widely accepted that Glissant's thought undergoes a dramatic change of perspective and of mood in the late 1980s and early 1990s; that is, between *Le Discours antillais* (1981) on the one hand, and *Poétique de la Relation* (1990), *Tout-monde* (1993), *Introduction à une poétique du divers* (1996) and *Traité du Tout-monde* (1997) on the other. *Le Discours antillais* was, as its title suggests, exclusively concerned with the French Antilles, and in fact mainly with Glissant's own home island, Martinique; and it gave an extremely pessimistic evaluation of Martinique as a 'morbid', politically stagnant, alienated and isolated society. The major texts of the 1990s, in striking contrast, expand their focus to encompass the whole world, and are dominated by a far more up-beat, exuberant celebration of hybridity and cross-cultural contact. The emphasis here is on dynamism and change; Glissant takes the Caribbean phenomenon of creolization and – in a move that is emblematic of his whole shift of perspective – reworks it on a global level, as a force capable of endlessly generating new forms of culture and experience. Creolization becomes a supercharged, *generative* version of *métissage*: 'le métissage sans limites, dont les éléments sont multipliés, les résultantes imprévisibles' (*PR*, p. 46). This new position is encapsulated in the concept of the 'Tout-monde': the world envisaged as a multiplicity of communities all interacting and all aware of each other's existence: 'Pour la première fois, les cultures humaines en leur semi-totalité sont entièrement et simultanément mises en contact et en effervescence de réaction les unes avec les autres' (*TTM*, p. 23).

The 'Tout-monde' thus comes to stand as a kind of shorthand for a 'good' version of globalization: contact which not only preserves diversity but creates new forms of it. Globalization in the negative sense of 'le règne des multinationales, la standardisation, l'ultra-libéralisme sauvage sur les marchés mondiaux'[1] cannot be resisted from a purely local standpoint; the first chapter of the *Traité du tout-monde*, entitled 'Le Cri du monde', argues eloquently that while it is necessary and important to fight to preserve one's own particular community, this must not preclude a more general awareness of and solidarity with other struggles across the world: 'nous acceptons maintenant d'écouter ensemble le cri du monde, sachant aussi que, l'écoutant, nous concevons que *tous l'entendent désormais*' (p. 17, italics original). An important aspect of the 'Tout-monde' is thus communication, and therefore *language*. Globalization has created the conditions both for much greater contact between different language communities, as a result of migration and hybridization, and at the same time for the increasing dominance of the major world languages at the expense of those spoken by smaller and economically weaker communities. How, then, does the 'Tout-monde' resituate languages in this context of generalized hybridity and creolization?

The texts of the 1990s are full of references to language, and languages; but so, equally, are Glissant's earlier works. In fact, it is arguably his position on language that changes most dramatically in the work of the 1990s. In the earlier texts there is a strong emphasis on the *lack* of any language adequate to the needs of the Antillean speaker, and indeed writer. In *L'Intention poétique*, for instance, he writes:

Et c'est à cette absence ce silence et ce rentrement que je noue
Dans la gorge mon langage, qui ainsi débute par un manque:
Et mon langage, raide et obscur ou vivant ou crispé, est ce manque
D'abord, ensuite volonté de muer le cri en parole devant la mer. (p. 44)

*Le Discours antillais* concentrates in particular on the tension between French and Creole, arguing that neither of these, for different reasons, can provide a ready-made idiom which will unproblematically fulfil the expressive needs of the subject, who is therefore marooned in the 'mutisme' which Glissant sees as the legacy of 'l'implacable univers muet du servage' (p. 277) in which 'S'exprimer est non seulement interdit, mais comme impossible à envisager' (p. 238). In *Tout-monde*, however, this scarcity of language is replaced by a 'chaotic' super-abundance of languages of all kinds, all apparently available to the speaker. Whereas in the earlier work language is sometimes imagined as the painfully thin trickle of water in a dried-up riverbed, in *Tout-monde* it is described as huge crashing waves; and the Antilleans, from hardly having one language at their disposal, are now seen as exuberantly 'surfing' a whole number of different languages: 'Alors encore vous entendez ces langages du monde qui se rencontrent sur les vagues le mont, toutes ces langues qui fracassent l'une dans l'autre comme des crêtes de vagues en furie, et vous entreprenez, tout un chacun applaudit, de bondir d'une langue dans l'autre' (p. 20).

The contrast between the two positions is immediately striking. However, there is also a less obvious level on which one finds a surprising degree of continuity in Glissant's view of language; in fact I am going to argue here that *Tout-monde*'s vision of multilingual surfing can be fully understood only if it is seen as developing *out of* the model of language and subjectivity which underlies earlier texts such *Le Discours antillais* – but also the even earlier *L'Intention poétique*, Glissant's collection of essays published in 1969, which in some ways has more in common with *Tout-monde*. Rereading *L'Intention poétique* today, one is struck by how presciently it already imagines a globalized and hybridized future of a kind that very few other writers were envisaging in the 1960s.

One of the key phrases of *Tout-monde*, much repeated throughout, is 'Mélanger les langues'. At times this acts as an exhortation, at times as a factual description of the existing situation. In its most obvious sense, it refers to individuals speaking more than one language and switching fluently from one to another – 'surfing' languages – and the book has various examples of fictional characters doing precisely this.[2] But 'mixing up languages' also has implications which extend beyond this, in two main ways which I want to explore in this chapter. The first is ethical and the second structural; both are somewhat problematic, but both also offer the possibility of an original and far-reaching theorization of how globalization in the positive sense of the 'Tout-monde' impacts on questions of language and language use.

'J'écris en présence de toutes les langues du monde' is a formula which recurs insistently in *Tout-monde*, *Introduction à une poétique du divers* and *Traité du tout-monde*. It relates in the first place to Glissant's concern to save minority languages from being obliterated by the domination of American English and, to a lesser extent, standard French. He insists that this has to be done on the basis of the equal importance of all languages – 'On ne sauvera pas une langue en laissant périr les autres' (*TTM*, p. 85) – because the battle cannot be fought purely on a local level without lapsing into the kind of linguistic sectarianism that he criticizes in some of the promoters of French Caribbean Creole.[3] Thus Anestor in *Tout-monde* argues:

> comment ferez-vous accepter à tous ces gens de se lever pour défendre ou sauver une langue créole ou une langue quéchoua ou une langue

islandaise, si vous ne commencez pas par changer leurs idées sur toutes les langues? S'ils ne consentent pas enfin que toutes les langues sont également importantes pour notre vie secrète ou public? (p. 397)

So far, this is a familiar argument, based on an analogy with the notion of *biodiversity*: all languages must be preserved because different languages incarnate different visions of the world, and so offer unique and valuable insights that are not accessible other than through the language itself: 'Car avec toute langue qui disparaît s'efface à jamais une part de l'imaginaire humain' (*TTM*, p. 85). But the biodiversity analogy, as usually formulated, has quite serious limitations. It relies upon the vision of reality incarnated in a particular language being *untranslateable*, because otherwise there is no argument for the need to preserve the language itself. Therefore, whereas the medicinal value, for instance, of a particular plant in the Amazon rain forest can in principle be made available to people all over the world, the philosophical value of a particular language's articulation of reality is only available to the speakers of that language and those who are prepared to learn it. And, since all languages are equally valuable, the only gain lies in speaking more than one, and preferably as many as possible. Simply preserving a language does not enable anyone other than its speakers to share in and benefit from its vision of reality.

Glissant avoids this problem by realizing that the insistence on inclusivity means that the claim for the value of every language cannot be based on its being intelligible to us, and shifting his argument away from the problem of *understanding* foreign languages, at least in the ordinary sense of the word.[4] In *Traité du tout-monde* he admits that 'il est vain d'essayer d'en connaître le plus grand nombre possible; le multilinguisme n'est pas quantitatif' (p. 26). Instead, he outlines a different, less concrete and more global, kind of awareness of them. 'Writing in the presence of all the world's languages' means that my text is 'inflected' by other languages, not because it incorporates lexical borrowings, for instance, but in the more negative sense that it is haunted by the knowledge that other languages, offering a vision of reality that lies beyond the scope of my own, are endangered. The act of writing *a* text in *a* particular language is experienced almost as an act of homage to all the other languages that are necessarily excluded from it, and that are perhaps destined to disappear, but whose spectral presence nevertheless makes an ethical demand on the writer. As he rephrases it in *Traité du tout-monde*, 'J'écris désormais en présence de toutes les langues du monde, dans la nostalgie poignante de leur devenir menacé' (p. 26).

This situation in turn alters my perception of my own language. Even if it is the only one I know, I can no longer inhabit it with the unreflexive confidence that normally characterizes the monolingual speaker; it no longer appears to me as complete and self-sufficient, but as existing only in its conflictual and fluctuating relations – and the connection with Glissant's central concept of Relation is very evident here – to all other languages:

> je ne peux plus écrire de manière monolingue. C'est-à-dire que ma langue, je la déporte et la bouscule non pas dans des synthèses, mais dans des ouvertures linguistiques qui me permettent de concevoir les rapports des langues entre elles aujourd'hui sur la surface de la terre – rapports de domination, de connivence, d'absorption, d'oppression, d'érosion, de tangence, etc. – comme le fait d'un immense *drama*, d'une immense tragédie dont ma propre langue ne peut pas être exempte et sauve. Et par conséquent, je ne peux pas écrire ma langue de manière monolingue; je l'écris en présence de cette tragédie, en présence de ce drame. (*IPD*, p. 40)

This multilingual awareness has, however, a further dimension. It can be seen as one form of Glissant's long-standing fascination with the phenomenon of *not understanding a language*. This has its roots in his childhood, when he used to witness the effect that unintelligible fragments of African languages surviving in the oral culture of Martinique had on those listening (*IPD*, p. 115). He suggests that it informs his concept of opacity; as he goes on to say, 'J'ai subi l'influence de cette présence non élucidée de langues ou de formules dont on n'a pas le sens et qui agissent quand même sur vous, et il est peut-être possible que toute une part de mes théories sur les nécessaires opacités de langage proviennent de là' (*IPD*, p. 116). Thus one of the principal ideas of his theoretical work is intimately connected with a very naïve, life-long affective engagement with foreign languages. Glissant's interest in exploring the kinds of relationship and communication we can have with individuals or texts whose language we do not understand is evident throughout his writing. In *L'Intention poétique*, for instance, he refers to 'la nostalgie consciente et fécondante des langues qu'il ne *comprendra pas*' (p. 46, italics original), and illustrates this with his experience of trying to read Hölderlin without speaking German, and the 'consciousness of a lack' which results from this.[5] Similarly, the much more recent *Traité du tout-monde* laments the fact that his inability to speak Arabic prevents him from appeciating the ways in which the Palestinian poet Mahmoud Darwich expands and reworks the language (pp. 224–25).

In other words, 'writing in the presence of the world's languages' is an ethical commitment to the equal importance of all languages and the need to defend their existence; and it is also a particular sensitivity to a mode of intersubjective and/or intertextual contact that does not depend on ordinary linguistic comprehension. What is less clear, however, is whether writing in this way is intended to make a difference which will be perceptible to the *reader*; and, if so, how exactly such a difference might be defined. Is there something about the way in which Glissant writes French that makes us realize he is not writing it 'monolingually'?

In a rather indirect way, we can perhaps find a clue to what this might be in the description of one of the characters in *Tout-monde*: an Italian woman called Amina who tells the narrator, Mathieu, that she can predict what will happen to him in the future. He therefore guesses that she is a gypsy; from the fact that she speaks French with no trace of an Italian accent he further guesses (without any actual evidence) that she also speaks a number of different languages that are unknown to him: 'Si elle était gitane, elle était capable de toutes les langues du monde' (p. 40). Amina is therefore an example of the fascination with 'secret' unknown languages; and she is also an example of an individual subject whose identity is not bound up with any one language: 'Elle était bien gitane, puisqu'elle ne se fixait dans aucun idiome privilégié' (p. 41). But what is given most emphasis in the text is her 'multilingual' way of speaking Italian; and this is not, as we might have expected, that her Italian is mixed up with fragments of other languages, but that she speaks it with a particular kind of 'hésitation légère au bord des mots' (p. 41). Rather than being solidly installed in a language that she takes for granted, it is as though her Italian is shadowed by the ghostly presence of all the other languages that she might have chosen to speak instead, and as though she is surprised to find herself in this language rather than another one:

> Amina par exemple, qui était bien italienne [...] avait une manière étonnée de commencer ses phrases, comme si l'usage de cette langue italienne lui était difficile, en sorte qu'on pouvait se demander si elle n'avait pas grandi dans les échos d'une autre langue qui pour l'instant dormait ailleurs, dans un lieu imaginaire d'où elle ne pourrait jamais la faire rejaillir. (p. 40)

But it is solely from the way in which she speaks Italian that Mathieu guesses she is multilingual; and this suggests that there is a way of using a language which makes it clear to one's listener that one does not identify exclusively with it, but is tentatively and provisionally choosing it among a number of possible other languages. Extrapolating from this example, one could perhaps conclude that this is also the impression that the *monolingual* writer who nevertheless writes 'en présence de toutes les langues du monde' creates in his or her readers; that is, Mathieu's relationship to Amina acts as a parallel to and an example of what Glissant hopes will be the *reader*'s relationship to the text written 'in the presence of the world's languages'.


'Mixing up languages', however, also has a second major implication: that the greatly increased contact between languages changes not just the behaviour of the speakers who 'surf' from one to another, but also the structures of the languages themselves, and perhaps even the way in which we define 'a language' in general. Glissant makes it clear that the mixing he envisages goes beyond the ordinary and unproblematic phenomenon of lexical borrowing. So, for instance, when he describes the way in which French Caribbean writers write a kind of French which is inflected by their knowledge of Creole, he emphasizes that he is not talking about the simple incorporation of isolated words and phrases of Creole – which he considers merely 'le côté exotique de la question' (*IPD*, p. 121) – but about the importation into French of the large-scale discursive 'structures' that are typical of the Caribbean folk-tale, for instance (*IPD*, p.121). It is only these, he argues, that will produce in the French reader the recognition of opacity – the experience of not understanding – which alone challenges the monolingual self-sufficiency that obliterates the 'presence of all the world's languages'. Faced with a new picturesque word, the French reader will merely be amused and intrigued by its exoticism; in contrast, 'la poétique, la structure du langage, la refonte de la structure des langages, lui paraîtront purement et simplement obscures' (*IPD*, p. 121).

The linguistic structures in question here are those of a 'poetics': the examples he gives are those of repetition, circularity and lists. In other words, they are stylistic and discursive rather than grammatical. Glissant does not here talk explicitly about *syntactic* structures; but the logic of his overall commitment to 'mixing up languages' would imply that ultimately it has to engage with these as well. His vision of languages morphing into one another is simply incompatible with the orthodox conception of a language as a discrete structure defined by a finite set of grammatical rules. This conception originates historically with Saussure's notion of the *language-system*; the whole thrust of Saussure's innovation in linguistics was to construct, out of a heterogeneous amalgam of 'faits de langage', a distinct, clearly defined structure, amenable to scientific analysis, that he calls 'langue' as opposed to 'langage', and that has the characteristic of being a coherent whole which cannot be modified by its individual speakers, and all of whose elements are held together by their relations to other elements in the system, so that it is clearly separated from all other language systems.[6] Saussure's 'langue', in other words, is constituted in such a way as to exclude the possibility of its being 'mixed up' with other languages; Glissant, in contrast, is asking us to consider what it would mean to conceive of a language which lacks definite, impermeable boundaries; and this would seem in the first place to mean a language which is not a 'language-system'.

There is in Glissant's recent work a prominent antipathy towards any kind of thought that relies upon the notion of a system; in *Tout-monde*, systems in general are characterized as oppressive and destructive: 'la pensée du système [...] est morte et mortelle, la pensée du système qui nous a tant régis, il faut en finir avec la pensée du système' (p. 237). The Saussurean language-system could thus be taken as just one example of this; and in the same text we find him also celebrating uses of language that transgress grammar or even bypass it completely. The character Mahmoud, for instance, an eleven-year-old tourist guide in Egypt, is introduced as someone who 'parle à peu près bien quatre langues touristiques. Il a appris auprès des gens de passage, qu'il pilote depuis bien longtemps. *Il parle par halètements et cris, n'ayant pas besoin d'une syntaxe suivie*' (*TM*, p. 451, italics original). But the idea of a language that does not have or need a grammatical system can also be traced back much further in Glissant's work, albeit in a somewhat different sense. The texts that he wrote in the 1960s and 1970s are dominated by an explicit anti-colonial emphasis that is largely superseded by the concept of the 'Tout-monde'. Language plays an important role in these; and *L'Intention poétique* includes a critique of linguistics which, like his more recent attacks on the idea of systems *per se*, may well have Saussure in mind:

> La linguistique, en tant qu'elle formule des constantes et des règles, se trouve déjà en retard sur ce vagabondage de langues et de parlers qui en chaque être (collectif) manifestera la présence de l'être au monde. Elle devra passer de l'analyse statique aux profils dynamiques, si elle veut englober cette condition; faute de quoi elle n'ira qu'à confirmer un anachronisme et se rendre solidaire des plus aveugles accommodements académiques. (p. 46)

But this remarkably modern perspective, in which linguistics is said to have been overtaken by the realities of a newly creolized world, is less typical of the early texts than a narrower focus on the situation of the colonized subject in relation to the colonial language; and here, Glissant's critique is not in fact aimed at the 'scientific' descriptive conception of Saussure, but at a more old-fashioned prescriptive, normative grammar which he links with nationalism and colonial domination. Teaching and learning French grammar, in other words, are one major aspect of the oppressive imposition of metropolitan norms of correctness on colonized subjects. In this context, grammatical structure has political implications; the language-system is a hostile force which Glissant calls on the colonized subject to attack or subvert. Thus in *L'Intention poétique* we also find linguistic correctness defined as a kind of purity with racial overtones: 'L'ère des langues orgueilleuses dans leur pureté doit finir pour l'homme' (p. 47), and the concern to promote it is equated with an aggressive nineteenth-century nationalism: 'toute nation hier encore se parfaisait dans la projection unique et souvent exclusive, aggressive, de son parler [...]', which he explicitly rejects: '[...] Mais je n'hérite pas de cette unicité, n'ayant même pas à réagir contre elle. Les épurations académiques de la langue ne me concernent pas (ne me satisfont, ne m'indignent ni ne me font sourire); me passionne par contre [...] mon affrontement à sa loi' (p. 45).

However, both the prescriptive notion of correctness and the Saussurean concept of systematicity have in common the basic criteria of purity and uniqueness, whether these are seen as obstacles to the free mixing up of languages or as manifestations of cultural domination, and Glissant's hostility to both presents some problems for other aspects of his ethical commitment to the notion of linguistic 'biodiversity'. Every language, as we have seen, is precious and worth saving because it contributes something different (*TTM*, p. 85), and he is careful to stress that mixing languages does not erase their distinctive characteristics; he evokes for instance 'un pays de terre où les paroles se mélangent sans se confondre ni se perdre, toutes les langues du monde' (*TM*, p. 236). But these unique features must surely include the syntactic peculiarities of a given language as well as its dominant stylistic features and the lexical items that he has characterized as more superficial and 'exotic'. The particular vision of the world that is represented in a language is expressed, one may think, more powerfully by the organization of time embodied in its system of tenses, or by how many gender distinctions it makes between nouns, for instance, than by the presence or absence of certain items of vocabulary. But it is difficult to see how the general syntactic structures that operate on the level of the language as a whole could survive a process in which the language is broken up and mixed with others. Is it possible, in other words, to conceive of syntax not as a single global system which, in Saussurean fashion, holds together by virtue of the necessary interrelatedness of all its parts, but as a more flexible and decentred phenomenon whose component elements could be *interchangeable* with structures taken from other languages?

The languages which, at least in some analyses, come much closer to this pattern than standard French or English are of course the different varieties of Creole, on which Glissant has written a great deal in *Le Discours antillais* and subsequent texts. In the former work, it was at the forefront of his concerns in the narrower context of anti-colonial resistance, and the difficult relation between French and Creole that, I have argued elsewhere, is at the root of his transgressive attitude towards French.[7] Later, just as the wider cultural phenomenon of creolization becomes a pattern for developments across the 'Tout-monde', so the Creole language itself also provides Glissant with a model for the way in which all languages are, or ought to be, developing ('je crois que toute langue à son origine est une langue créole', *IPD*, p. 28), in so far as it can be seen as providing an example of precisely the kind of fluid, non-totalizing syntax that Glissant's position requires. He subscribes, in other words, to what used to be a widespread view (although it has been contested by some linguists) that Creole is a language whose structure is *mixed* in its very foundations: 'une langue créole joue à partir de "zones" linguistiques différentes, pour en tirer sa matière inédite' (*TTM*, p. 25). Specifically, it is said to combine French vocabulary with 'African' syntax: 'c'est un vocabulaire des marins bretons et normands du XVIIe siècle "accordé" à une syntaxe qui n'a plus rien à voir avec; probablement une synthèse des sytaxes de la côte ouest de l'Afrique noire' (*IPD*, p. 52). At the same time it is a language which has never been subjected to the efforts of prescriptive grammarians to establish norms of correctness, and so allows a considerable amount of free variation in its syntactic use.[8] Glissant's promotion of 'mixing up languages' thus leads him to a new conception of the very principles of language structure – a conception in which Creole, no longer a marginalized exception to the rule, acquires exemplary status as a language which retains a concept of syntactic structures as distinctive, but no longer as necessarily bound to one particular total system.

But even if we accept that this creolization of languages is a general ongoing process, the question still remains of what kind of *agency* it involves. How, concretely, do different separate languages become mixed up with each other, recombined in new hybrid configurations? Glissant's descriptions of the process tend to be lyrical rather than analytical; but it is possible to construct a more substantial account of this new phenomenon by relating it to an idea that has been an important emphasis in his thought for much longer, from *L'Intention poétique* onwards, but that has undergone some significant modifications. This is his concept of 'langage', and its relationship to 'langue'.[9] Glissant's use of these terms is entirely different from that of Saussure. In his formulation, *langage* denotes the speaking subject's relation or attitude to the *langue* – French, English, Creole, etc. – that he or she uses, as that attitude is materialized in a particular practice of the *langue*. In *Le Discours antillais* he defines it as 'une pratique commune, pour une collectivité donnée, de confiance ou de méfiance vis-à-vis de la langue ou des langues qu'elle utilise' (p. 236). In the case of the Martinican community during the period that Glissant is writing about in *Le Discours antillais*, this attitude is determined by the tension inhabiting the colonized subjects' use of the colonial language: they speak French, but in a particular way that expresses their conflictual relationship with it.[10] It is a conscious, willed struggle for expression – the Caribbean speaker has to 'frayer à travers la langue vers un langage, qui n'est peut-être pas dans la logique interne de cette langue' (*DA*, p. 237) – and, as such, reflects the problems and the scarcity of language that characterize Glissant's representation of Martinique in this period.

But the distinction between *langue* and *langage* exists in all language communities; according to Glissant, one does not just 'speak French', or any other *langue*: one speaks one's *langage*, which is a personalized variant of the *langue*: 'Dans toute langue autorisée, tu bâtiras ton langage' (*IP*, p. 44). And, as the verb 'bâtir' suggests, this activity is both intentional and creative. Glissant's *langage* has interesting similarities with the phenomenological notion of the 'parole parlante' developed by Maurice Merleau-Ponty, and, although Glissant does not refer to him and has not been directly influenced by him, a comparison of the two concepts will help to illuminate the relation between *langue* and *langage*.[11] For Merleau-Ponty, linguistic meaning is possible only on the basis of the pre-reflexive intentionality of my embodied presence in the world; and speech, as distinct from language, emerges directly from this primary expressivity: '[la parole] prend son élan, elle est roulée dans la vague de la communication muette' (*Signes*, p. 32). The act of speaking precedes the existence of a constituted *langue*; and, like *langage*, it is 'creative' in a way that established language – which Merleau-Ponty also calls 'langage empirique' because it is the object of the empiricist philosophies of language that he is critiquing – is not: 'Distinguons l'usage empirique du langage déjà fait, et l'usage créateur, dont le premier, d'ailleurs, ne peut être qu'un résultat. Ce qui est parole au sens du langage empirique – c'est-à-dire le rappel opportun d'un signe préétabli – ne l'est pas au regard du langage authentique' (*Signes*, p. 72). The ability of the 'parole parlante' to create new languages corresponds to Glissant's view of the creativity of mixing up languages to form new ones.

One particular passage in *L'Intention poétique* is strikingly close to Merleau-Ponty's insistence on the primacy of speech – or in Glissant's terms, *langage* – over *langue*. *Langage* is defined here not only as the way in which the subject inhabits a *langue* but also as a very basic mode of expressivity, comparable to Merleau-Ponty's 'parole parlante': a disposition towards language in general that precedes the use of any particular *langue*; therefore, in the multilingual situation that Glissant is already predicting will become general in the future, *langage* also provides a means of relating one *langue* to another:

> On devra tenir compte de ce que l'être de demain parlera *naturellement* plusieurs langues; que chaque langage (chaque choix du dire) courra d'une de ces langues aux autres [...] que par conséquent l'analyse de chaque langage devra intégrer l'étude non seulement des langues intéressées mais encore de *leur réaction conjuguée dans l'être*. Définir un langage, ce sera définir l'attitude générale de l'être face aux mots dont il use, oui; mais aussi approcher le principe (en l'être) d'une symbiose élocutoire qui signifiera une des modalités de sa liaison à la totalité du monde. (*IP*, pp. 45–46, italics original)

It is this aspect of *langage* that is developed much further in the writings of the 1990s in the context of the 'Tout-monde'. Here, in other words, its most significant role becomes that of acting as a bridge between *langues* and thus making possible the process of 'mixing them up'. In the section of *Introduction à une poétique du divers* entitled 'Langues et langages' (pp. 33–57), for instance, Glissant argues that 'la construction d'un langage dans la langue dont on use permet la visée vers le chaos-monde: parce que cela établit des relations entre des langues possibles du monde' (p. 42); and goes on to claim that the writers of the Caribbean have a common *langage* that 'weaves' or mediates between the *langues* – English, French, Spanish and Creole – that they use (pp. 42–43). *Tout-monde*, similarly, returns again and again to 'la question des langues qu'on utilise, de la manière dont on les pratique, de la licence qu'on exerce à les mettre en relation avec d'autres langues, c'est-à-dire à en faire un langage' (p. 267). Here the mobile, dynamic quality of *langage* is stressed by presenting it as a 'journey' which traverses and hence weaves together different *langues*: 'Le langage est un voyage et voyez qu'il n'a pas de fin. Les langues sont des étapes' (p. 267). Finally, this in turn impacts on the *langues* themselves: it is *langage* which remixes them and relativizes the boundaries between them: 'le langage importe ici, qui dévie les limites des langues utilisées' (*TTM*, p. 76).

One major type of activity that involves putting languages in relation with each other is of course translation, and Glissant brings *langage* into play here too, to produce a theory of translation which makes of it a prime example of anti-systemic thought. In *Traité du tout-monde* he describes it as an elusive, creative activity based on 'l'esquive' and 'la trace', as opposed to the system: 'L'art de traduire nous apprend la pensée de l'esquive, la pratique de la trace qui, contre les pensées de système, nous indique l'incertain, le menacé, lesquels convergent et nous renforcent. Oui, la traduction, art de l'approche et de l'effleurement, est une fréquentation de la trace' (p. 28). Translation, in other words, is not simply a mechanical process of replacing one *langue* with another. It can work only through the invention of a new *langage* that bridges the two *langues*, but also produces something new and different from either of them: translation is thus by definition unpredictable – 'Le langage du traducteur opère comme la créolisation et comme la Relation dans le monde, c'est-à-dire que ce langage produit de l'imprévisible' (*IPD*, p. 45)– and will always contain an element of opacity (*TTM*, p. 29). When Anestor, in *Tout-monde*, asks his friend from the Ivory Coast to translate into his own language a fragment of French, he tells him: 'n'essaie pas de comprendre, seulement la machine à traduire, mais à traduire vraiment, hein, tout en poésie, tu brodes tant que tu veux' (p. 397). The work of the translator is as creative as that of the poet; and both work by exploiting the capacity of *langage* to transform and regenerate the *langue*: 'Une langue se rehausse de permettre que nous y traçions notre langage: la poétique de notre rapport aux mots' (*TTM*, p. 86).[12]

The concept of *langage* thus underpins both the early and the more recent stages of Glissant's theorization of language. Despite the apparently radical break between the difficulty and scarcity of language in *Le Discours antillais* and its ease and proliferation in *Tout-monde*, both positions, and the transition between them, are made possible by the distinction between a fully constituted *langue* and the primary subjective force of *langage*. Originally developed in response to the pressures placed on the colonized subject by the dominance of the French language and the resulting constraints placed upon any possibility of self-expression, *langage* recurs with equal relevance in the freer and much expanded environment of the 'Tout-monde', where one of its main functions becomes that of relating one *langue* to another, breaking down their boundaries and so enabling them to be 'mixed up'. In this context it acts on the *structural* features of language: by its position so to speak *between* the speaking subject and the *langue* (in the sense that I do not speak French, I speak my *langage* which draws on the resources of French), it redefines *langue* as a resource or reservoir of materials, rather than a structure; this in turn enables the subject to move between different *langues* and mix them up; and both of these factors have the effect of changing the *langue* itself, pushing at its boundaries.

But the concern with language that is so central to *Tout-monde* and Glissant's recent theoretical texts also has the ethical dimension discussed in the first part of this chapter, under the slogan 'J'écris en présence de toutes les langues du monde'. I want now to return to this aspect, to argue that *langage* has an equally important role to play in the question of our ethical relationship to other languages that we do not know. It is *langage*, in other words, that can enable us to 'understand' people speaking or writing in a language that we do not 'understand'; and that therefore acts as a bridge in this sense too, between what I have distinguished as the ethical and the structural aspects of Glissant's thought on language.

   In the first place, *langage* allows Glissant to resituate the relation between language and identity. He has almost from the start rejected the idea that personal identity involves the kind of straightforward identification with a *langue* that is in any case not accessible to colonized subjects. This is forcefully restated in the later work: in *Traité du tout-monde*, for instance, 'La langue n'est plus le miroir d'aucun être' (p. 85). But now it is because, rather than defining ourselves within one *langue*, we 'surf' them all ('vous entreprenez [...] de bondir d'une langue dans l'autre', *TM*, p. 20); and we are able to do this, as we have seen, through the agency of *langage*. It is *langage* that embodies the speaker's subjective relationship to the *langue* that s/he is using; so *langage* is in a sense an aspect of the speaker's identity, defined, however, not as a fixed separate entity but as an open-ended, multiple and mobile relation to others: 'La langue, c'est le creuset toujours bouleversé de mon unité. Le langage, ce serait le champ ouvert de ma Relation' (*TTM*, p. 112).[13]

Relation to other people includes, most crucially, other people whose languages we do not know; *Poétique de la Relation* insists that 'understanding', at least in the conventional sense, is unnecessary and even harmful to the proper exercise of Relation, which is ethically bound to respect the other's opacity.[14] But Glissant is able to develop this idea further by linking it specifically to *langage*: *langage*, that is, also opens up the possibility of a different mode of understanding the other's speech which does not depend either upon the reductive transparency he is opposing or upon ordinary linguistic knowledge. Here again the phenomenological characterizations of *langage* are very evident. Merleau-Ponty's definition of speech, as we have seen, places it in direct continuity with the primary 'communication intercorporelle' (*Signes*, p. 35) that is a basic given of my situatedness in the world. One major implication of this is that the meanings of words are not mechanically encoded as discrete units of language; rather, 'ils font tous ensemble allusion à une signification toujours en sursis, quand on les considère un à un, et vers laquelle je les dépasse sans qu'ils la contiennent jamais' (p. 143). And, just as in Glissant's view understanding should not be an introspective process but a relational openness to the other's speech which does not exclude opacity, so Merleau-Ponty argues that

> Nous n'avons pas, pour la comprendre [la parole], à consulter quelque lexique intérieur qui nous donnât, en regard des mots ou des formes, de pures pensées qu'ils recouvriraient: il suffit que nous nous prêtions à sa vie, à son mouvement de différentiation et d'articulation, à sa gesticulation eloquente. Il y a donc une opacité du langage. (p. 68)

Moreoever, understanding someone else is not a passive process of reception, but a matter of making their 'intention significative' (p. 143) converge with my own – as the translator of *Signes* puts it in his introduction:

> Every spoken word appears to me as a visible trace of the invisible significative intention which is constituting it, and I comprehend and respond to it by means of my own significative intentions. In my dialogue with other speaking men, expression and communication are polarized about significative intentions which converge through reciprocal encroachments in spoken words. (p. xxi)

Therefore, too, 'Men whose languages are different are able to communicate because they find within themselves a speaking power which lets them pass into the style of another language which encroaches on their own' (p. xxii). Thus, when Glissant claims that in his attempts to read Faulker's novels in English, 'j'accède immédiatement à la structure de l'œuvre de Faulkner avant d'accéder à la lettre de cet œuvre' (*IPD*, p. 116), or that when faced with a Haitian speaking an unfamiliar variety of Creole, you spontaneously translate it into your own variety – 'vous entendez son créole avec votre oreille' (*TM*, p. 386) – he is, I suggest, invoking something very close to the phenomenological concept of 'significative intentions'. But he himself locates this ability (to understand a language you do not understand) precisely in *langage*, which thus assumes the role of the phenomenological primary expressivity of my situatedness in the world, which precedes any *langue* and transcends the barriers between *langues*. Or, as Glissant puts it:

> La barrière de la langue tombe; dans une telle fonction c'est le langage qui opère [...] Chaque langage: sillon, faisceau de rapports par-dessus (et dans) les langues et leurs obstacles [...] Autrement dit: je te parle dans ta langue, et c'est dans mon langage que je te comprends. (*IP*, p. 52)

I have tried to show how Glissant's engagement with the topic of globalized multilingualism revolves around two main issues, neither of which are definitively resolved but both of which are explored in fruitful and illuminating ways. Firstly, how should we respond to the presence all around us of languages which we do not 'understand', in the normal sense of the word? Secondly, how does the existence of 'mixed', structurally heterogeneous languages, without fixed structural boundaries separating them, alter our conception of what 'a language' is? I have argued that both these questions need to be interpreted in the light of Glissant's distinction between *langue* and *langage* – a distinction which in fact goes back a long way before the recent work that is more explicitly focused on multilingualism. *Langage* is a central and richly multifaceted concept; it implies an extremely active, creative relationship to established languages – both those that we speak and those that we do not – and it is thus ultimately a major dimension of our Relation to the 'Tout-monde'.

# 'La parole du paysage'

## Art and the Real in
## *Une Nouvelle Région du monde*

Glissant is probably best known for his elaboration of concepts such as Relation, diversity, opacity, creolization and 'rhizomatic' identity, which all revolve around a respect for cultural difference. The more recent versions of these, from *Poétique de la Relation* onwards, have been influenced by the work of Deleuze, and in particular Deleuze and Guattari's *Mille Plateaux*.[1] But, alongside his writing on the politics of identity, Glissant has throughout his work shown a profound interest in *places* or (since most of them are rural) landscapes. This is an intense personal engagement which goes back to his infancy; in the section of *La Cohée du Lamentin* entitled 'Contestation du Morne, des Fonds et du Delta: Première vue des paysages'[2] he recounts how at the age of four weeks he was carried by his mother from the hills of Bezaudin down to Le Lamentin on the coast of Martinique, and describes his improbable conviction that he can actually remember the journey (p. 89) and his sense that ever since 'ces paysages se sont présentés à moi [...] comme des symboles vivants ou, plus audacieusement, comme des catégories de l'étant' (p. 91). This intimate relationship with landscape informs all his novels; indeed, in 'Le Roman des Amériques', he claims that a key difference between European literature and that of the Americas and the Caribbean is that 'Pour nous, l'élément *formellement déterminant* dans la production littéraire, c'est ce que j'appellerais la parole du paysage' (*DA*, p. 255, italics original).[3] Landscapes speak, in other words, and form a structural element of our being.

Places have always played a role in Glissant's overall network of Relation. But *Une Nouvelle Région du monde* is the first text to elaborate a specific connection between place or landscape on the one hand and, on the other, *difference*, which had previously been seen largely as a sociocultural phenomenon. That is, Glissant now articulates a new 'aesthetic' which, unlike his earlier 'poetics', covers both literary texts and the visual arts, and which both emerges out of the relationship between artist/writer and landscape and is based on difference. This entails producing a more explicitly theorized conception of difference that is influenced by, albeit not entirely congruent with, Deleuze; it also entails combining this with a conception of art as 'fusion' with the natural world, which goes back much further in Glissant's work and has little in common with Deleuzean theories of either difference or writing. In this chapter I shall look at how this new conjunction of landscape, fusion and difference is constructed; how it determines the relationship between the work of art and the real; and how it both takes up and departs from the ideas of Deleuze and Guattari.

Throughout *Une Nouvelle Région du monde* landscapes are seen as inherently expressive, meaningful and even 'textual'; it opens with an evocation of the Rocher du Diamant in Martinique and the beach opposite it, in which the waves breaking on the sand 'se relaient comme de la trame d'un texte' (p. 11) and the shape of the rock recalls enigmatic 'signes d'exclamation ou d'interrogation' (p. 12). More generally, 'chaque paysage s'obstine [...] il faudra exprimer aussi pourquoi leurs couleurs font un langage, qui révèle quoi? Et comment leurs formes, ainsi relevées, *correspondent*?' (p. 33, italics original). As this final verb suggests, Glissant's concept of fusion resonates with Baudelaire's famous 'correspondances', to which at one point (p. 99) he alludes:

La Nature est un temple où de vivants piliers
Laissent parfois sortir de confuses paroles
L'homme y passe à travers des forêts de symboles
Qui l'observent avec des regards familiers.

The language of landscapes is not clear – they are, precisely, 'confuses paroles' – and the task of the writer is not to clarify them, but echo their obscurity. The first section of *Une Nouvelle Région* is titled 'Langages obscurs', and throughout Glissant stresses the importance of an aesthetic that remains rooted in the 'inextricable' complexities and obscurities of the real, an aesthetic that is 'concret et dense et inentamable' (p. 67). In this way the writer remains as close as possible to the landscape – which is not an object of representation, with the distance and separation that that implies, but rather a kind of intertextual partner. The distance between a lucid representation and its mute, inert object gives way to the closeness of an expressive landscape and a dense, obscure text: 'l'affaire est d'exprimer l'inexprimable' (p. 38).

In an early article on Pierre Reverdy reprinted in a section of *L'Intention poétique* entitled 'Purs paysages', Glissant already emphasizes the poet's fundamental impulse to:

> établir [...]un contact plus étroit avec les forces de l'univers. Non pas les forces cosmiques, le déchaînement du Tout, mais l'humble et tenace courant de sève qui en chaque chose s'accomplit. Et l'homme peut vouloir susciter ce contact (malgré la densité que lui oppose le réel), parce que la nature *correspond* à l'esprit – par sa simple vérité, selon Reverdy. (p. 74, my italics)

and quotes Reverdy's remark: 'C'est la réaction de la nature sur la complexion de certains êtres qui produit la poésie' (p. 74). But to achieve this contact, the language of the poem must have an equivalent density and concreteness which renounces clarity and 'échappe tout à fait à la logique syntaxique ou du "sens", pour aller avant tout vers une correspondance quasi vitale' (pp. 75–76).[4] In *Une Nouvelle Région* Glissant develops this idea that writer and landscape need to be linked by a relation of what he now calls 'fusion' (and its synonyms: complicity, magnetic attraction).[5] The expressivity of the landscape is revealed through the poet's fusion with it, and, conversely, it is only because landscapes themselves 'speak' that the work of art can achieve fusion with them: a relation between two phenomena that are essentially continuous with one another. There is thus a necessary connection between the complicity of fusion and the expressivity of the world.[6]

But fusion is also presented as a phenomenon that the modern world has, to a large extent, lost. It underlies the very earliest forms of art: cave paintings, which Glissant interprets as 'une tentative [...] non pas pour dominer vraiment l'animal [...] mais pour se fondre en lui si possible' (p. 47). However, this ability to fuse with the animal – to some extent similar to Deleuze and Guattari's idea of 'devenir-animal' in *Mille Plateaux* (p. 285) – depends upon the animal not being a possession; Glissant constructs a schematic history in which the cavemen abandon their aesthetic of fusion at the point at which they come into conflict with other human groups and have to compete with them for resources: animals therefore become possessions (*NRM*, pp. 48–49). Thus fusion is opposed to possession, and these two basic attitudes to the world determine two different types of art: that which connects with the 'obscure' language of the natural world, versus a *realist* art that represents nature in an attempt to dominate and possess it: 'l'avènement de l'art qu'on a dit réaliste commencera là, et par une véritable prise de possession' (p. 50). In 'Le Roman des Amériques', Glissant already rejected realist art, arguing that for the writers of the Americas 'le réalisme, c'est-à-dire le rapport logique et consécutif au visible, plus que partout ailleurs trahirait la chose signifiée' (*DA*, p. 255). In realism the world is logical and static, because external – whereas for Glissant, as he goes on to say, 'il me semble, en ce qui me concerne, que mes paysages changent en moi; c'est probablement qu'ils changent avec moi' (*DA*, p. 255) – and if the object of representation is external and separate, it follows that it is of a qualitatively different order from the representation: it is only the text which speaks, not the landscape which it describes.[7]

Although realism has, according to him, been dominant for most of human history, Glissant claims that artists through the centuries have 'secretly' tried to revive the old aesthetic of fusion (*NRM*, p. 53). And in the 'new region of the world' a version of this will be reinstated as the basis of a new aesthetic, the 'intuition' of its original proponents which are *'après tout* constitutives de réalité' (p. 26, italics original) – in a manner which one might link to the Deleuzean concept of the virtual[8] – and it is now a question of trying to reverse the 'écarts' that have 'grandi entre les couleurs du monde et nos réflexes d'idées et de paroles' (p. 68).

Glissant here associates these 'écarts' primarily with the peoples who have come to dominate the world, whose desire for possession and mastery has led them away from fusion, as opposed to the oppressed communities who instinctively preserve it (p. 95). This represents a striking change from his earlier work, which stressed the particular alienation of the oppressed colonized people of Martinique from their surroundings and the difficulty they have in describing their reality. *Malemort*, for instance, presents the sensuous world as an overwhelming reality that language struggles to articulate:

La difficulté [...] d'avoir à articuler, autour des racines mauves, des fours à charbon sépulcraux dans leurs hardes de pluie, des fosses d'igname haut balancées, des plaques à cassaves sans yeux, des bâts de mulet en trapèze, des zébus lourds à la charrette, des chaudières rapiécées, des jambières de haillons sur la ligne de coupe de cannes, autour des cases sous les manguiers ou des bourgs de planchettes marquetés de terre grise, quelque cri que ce fût qui pût réellement se nouer en forme de langage. (pp. 69–70)

Here, the concrete elements of the landscape not only lack expressivity of their own, but actively resist expression in language. In *Le Discours antillais* Glissant explains the alienation between people and landscape as resulting from the people's dispossession: 'Aussi bien, si cet espace n'est pas l'espace ancestral, ce n'est pas non plus un espace possédé [...] La légitimité de cette possession collective n'est même pas esquissée. Il n'y a ni possession de la terre, ni complicité avec la terre, ni espoir en la terre' (p. 88). Thus possession and complicity in *Le Discours antillais* are aligned as part of the same problem: ultimately, it is not the fact that Martinique is not Africa, or even that the slaves were forcibly brought there, that prevents them from feeling connected to the landscape; it is the condition of slavery, in which one is oneself a possession and therefore cannot possess anything. So it is *Une Nouvelle Région*'s reformulation of 'complicity with the land' in a way which removes from it all connotation of possession, in fact sets it up as the opposite of possession, that allows Glissant to reinstate oppressed peoples as the primary exponents of fusion.[9] Nevertheless, as we shall see later, the emphasis is now more on indigenous than on transported peoples.

Rejecting representation in favour of fusion also, and most importantly, means that the work of art exists on the same *plane of reality* as the natural world:

> Un grand nombre de peuples ne considèrent pas cette autonomie éventuelle de l'œuvre comme constitutive d'une catégorie [...] Ils tiennent le cri de la mer et les accordailles des monts et des fleuves et le flot dévalant les nuages et l'errance du vent infidèle *à l'égal* des œuvres qu'ils créent de leurs mains. (p. 34, my italics)

This recalls the insistence in *Mille Plateaux*, to which I have already referred in chapter 9, that the work is not a representation *of* the world – 'le livre comme image du monde, de toute façon quelle idée fade' (p. 13) – but exists on the same 'plan de consistance' as the reality which surrounds it and with which it is 'agencé': 'Le livre, agencement avec le dehors, contre le livre-image du monde' (p. 34). The work 'fait rhizome avec le monde' (p. 18); and so is subject to the rhizome's 'principes de connexion et d'hétérogénéité' (p. 13); and indeed, of all Deleuze and Guattari's ideas, it is the rhizome that Glissant has most explicitly adopted in his later texts.

There is an important difference, however. Deleuze and Guattari stress the heterogeneity of the rhizomatic links between work and world; but in Glissant's formulation it is the inherent expressivity of the landscape that makes fusion, and hence poetry, possible; and if the landscape is already a kind of text, then the heterogeneity of the rhizomatic connection is replaced by a far more homogeneous kind of intertextuality. *Mille Plateaux* does, certainly, argue that semiosis extends beyond linguistic signification, but it remains restricted to human, social reality; and an important feature of the rhizome is that it connects signifying and 'asignifying' things (p. 13). One could even argue that while Deleuze reduces the properly signifying function of language in favour of a pragmatic emphasis on language as intervention in the world, Glissant makes the opposite move, in extending the power of signification beyond language to the natural world.[10]

As in Baudelaire's sonnet, however, the 'correspondances' are not just between man and nature, but also between different elements of the natural world. Thus, in the initial description of the beach at Le Diamant, Glissant asks 'comment la beauté de cet endroit-ci correspond-elle avec tant de hasard bleu à la beauté de cet endroit-là qui lui est si analogue [...]?' (*NRM*, p. 14). There is, in other words, a double relation: between the poet and the landscape (fusion, complicity, correspondance); and between one particular landscape and others, variously described as correspondance, repetition and difference. In fact, Glissant suggests here that landscapes' capacity to be meaningful actually depends on their 'repetition' creating patterns – in the shapes of rocks, for instance: 'une telle répétition du motif, les tempêtes frappent et sculptent partout de cette même manière, fait que vous voyez se dessiner là une ou plusieurs significations cachées' (p. 14). Repetition, however, is never exact; in fact, the landscapes that are said to correspond or repeat each other are often flagrantly different – Glissant goes on to list the 'analogous' landscapes in the quotation above as '[...] dans les végétations salines du Brésil ou dans les pires embruns bretons ou sous les caps tranchés net de la Terre de Feu ou à l'épais des enfouissures laquées de Norvège ou dans les lisérés à peines visibles des neiges et des glaces des côtes de Sibérie' (p. 14). Repetition always works together with difference, and here Glissant adopts a very similar formulation to that which Deleuze articulates in *Différence et répétition*: 'Et toujours, *c'est dans un même mouvement que la répétition comprend la différence* (non pas comme une variante accidentelle et extrinsèque, mais comme son cœur, comme la variante essentielle qui la compose)' (*Difference et répétition*, p. 370, italics original); in the Preface to the English edition, Deleuze envisages 'a single power of difference or of repetition, but one which operates only in the multiple and determines multiplicities' (*Difference and Repetition*, p. xiv).[11]

But if what is repeated is difference rather than sameness, it is equally true that difference is no longer sharply differentiated from resemblance. Difference now *precedes* the opposition between same and other: 'Ce n'est certes pas le même et l'autre, ni leur accord, qui tissent la Relation, c'est le différent, qui [...] permet que soient le même et l'autre' (*NRM*, p. 103) – an idea that is also central to *Différence et répétition*, where Deleuze insists that difference does not depend on a concept of identity.[12] This is not the position in *Le Discours antillais*; there, when Glissant talks about cultural differences between people(s), 'diversity' is systematically opposed to 'sameness', for example in the section entitled 'Le même et le divers' (pp. 190–98); opacity thus means respect for the *other* in his or her difference, in the conventional sense of the word (e.g., 'le Divers, la nécessité opaque de consentir à la différence de l'autre', *DA*, p. 256); the ethical responsibility to respect and relate to the other is important in so far as the other is *not like me*. But Glissant has always argued that it is only the inability or refusal to assume this responsibility that turns differences into conflicts or oppositions; and now, following Deleuze, he takes this idea to its logical conclusion in detaching difference explicitly from the notion of the other and distinguishing between 'les nuances de la différence' and 'des radicalités de l'altérité' (*NRM*, p. 104). Difference is thus a nuance and a correspondance; it produces continuity as well as diversities (p. 97), and so in fact becomes a quasi-synonym for Relation.

Difference as a general principle is not only more primary than the same-other opposition, it also *generates* all the particular differences and identities that are continuously evolving in Relation: 'Et les différences déroulent à leur tour d'autres différences [...] et ces différences engendrées produisent ensemble, par-delà les diversités, la continuité non prévisible du monde' (p. 97). Difference is 'la force opératoire du mouvement des variétés et des identités' (p. 108) and 'la matrice-motrice du chaos-monde' (p. 63). As such, it forms a basis for the new aesthetic that Glissant proposes, which makes use of the Deleuzean notion of quantity. Whereas beauty has conventionally been formulated as a particular, essential *quality*, the new beauty that characterizes the 'new region of the world' consists in the realization of a *quantity of differences* (p. 44). Beauty, in other words, is an aspect of Relation, the evolving matrix in which differences constantly generate other differences; '[la beauté [...] est et elle révèle dans une œuvre ou un donné *la force des différences qui dans le même temps s'accomplissent et déjà prédisent leur relation à d'autres différences'* (p. 45, italics original).

Glissant also uses his model of generative difference to explain how the work of art 'enters the real'. He has, in fact, already provided an account of this relation, albeit without the notion of 'entry', in terms of fusion: the work is situated on the same plane of reality as the natural expressiveness of landscape, as I have shown. Later on in *Une Nouvelle Région*, however, he gives an alternative explanation. He starts by asking 'Que serait-ce pourtant que d'"entrer dans le réel" [...]? Sera-ce un bâtiment où on s'introduit et d'où on sort à volonté?' (p. 117) – and goes on to explain that the 'entry' is, rather, made possible by the generative force of difference: since differences always produce other differences, those which structure the work itself irresistibly attract differences in the world outside the work:

> Si je dis [...] que l'art entre ainsi dans le réel, c'est que je conçois le moment où la quantité des différences réalisable qui palpite dans chaque œuvre d'art, et la tension de cette même œuvre vers tout ou partie des différences d'autour, commencent d'être perçues. (p. 117)

When this 'moment' occurs, the artist and/or spectator, 'reconnaissant cette tension et ces rencontres [...] les constitue d'instinct (avec cette œuvre) en éléments de relais dans ce qu'il devine être la quantité réalisée des différences du monde' (pp. 117–18); and 'Alors, l'œuvre de l'art entre réellement dans la quantité réalisée des différences du monde, elle est le repère de leurs rencontres, de leur Relation' (p. 118). It is the fact that both the work of art and the world are constituted by differences generating other differences, all attracting each other in a kind of magnetic force field, that allows them to, as it were, jump the boundary that in a more classical conception of art separates a representation from that which it represents. There is no difference in principle between the differences internal to the work and those in the world outside it.

We need to ask, therefore: how much difference is there between the two accounts of the work's relation to the real that coexist in *Une Nouvelle Région* – the 'fusion' model, which relies on the inherent expressivity of the natural world, and the model based on generative difference? In Glissant's presentation of the latter the equation of the real with the natural world is less prominent, and there would seem to be no particular reason why it should be limited to this; however, as I shall show at the end of this chapter, landscape retains a specific importance in modifying the kinds of change produced by generative difference; and, more generally, the focus throughout *Une Nouvelle Région* is very much on the writer's or artist's relation to *place*.

Glissant makes a point of bringing the two models together in the same paragraph or sentence (e.g., pp. 47, 64, 106); and, of course, both are inimical to the notion of representation. But, equally, each is quite adequate in its own terms; they do not actually need each other. The fusion model would be coherent on its own, without any recourse to difference and repetition: the expressivity of the landscape allows the writer to achieve a relation of fusion with it and thereby produce a text whose main quality is its being on the same level as the chaotic density of the real. Indeed, the early version of this model outlined in the article on Reverdy makes no mention of differences or correspondances between landscapes.

Conversely, the 'differences' model could quite well bypass fusion completely – not least because it does not appear to require a *subject* to operate the proliferation and attraction of differences; in fact, to the extent that it derives from Deleuze and Guattari's version of generative difference, it could be seen as a 'machine' explicitly designed to exclude any conception of a subject. In the fusion model, in contrast, the work itself is merely the means whereby fusion is achieved between the human subject (artist and/or community) and, for example, the animal depicted in the cave-painting: 'une tentative pour faire conjoindre les différences de l'animal par exemple et celles de la communauté qui le fréquente' (p. 47). But in fact Glissant's 'differences' model, while less necessarily committed to the agency of a human subject than the 'fusion' model – it is the work of art which 'enters the real', not the artist – is also not divorced from the subject like Deleuze and Guattari's conception. One of Glissant's principal areas of disagreement with Deleuze and Guattari concerns their promotion of the subjectless 'machine' and 'body without organs': on several occasions he pointedly prefers the organic to the mechanical.[13] Thus, while his conception of generative difference is in many ways very close to *Différence et répétition*, he criticizes Deleuze's version as being too 'passive' and 'neutral', and above all too mechanical: differences can generate other differences only if they are seen as an organic substance, 'des réalités vives et changeantes et préservées du tic-tac morne de la machine' (p. 100).

In Glissant's model, moreover, the work enters the real only when the differences are perceived by the artist and/or the spectator, who, as we have seen, 'les *constitue* d'instinct (avec cette œuvre) en éléments de relais dans ce qu'il devine être la quantité réalisée des différences du monde' (pp. 117–18, my italics). In other words, the process does in fact presuppose a subject. Representation, of course, also requires a subject, to represent the object, but Glissant's rejection of representation is not a rejection of the subject *per se*. Indeed, in the Hegelian and Marxist strand of his earlier work, the subject is a central concept (as, for example, in his distancing himself from Western poststructuralism's deconstruction of the subject in 'Le Roman des Amériques' (p. 258), to which I refer in chapter 9); and this can be seen to persist in the later writings, which, while they are vigorously anti-essentialist, never abandon a concept of the subject. There is still a certain tension between the differential conception of *meaning* constituted through multiple relations, implied by the differences model, and the pure expressivity released through the one-to-one fusion of writer and landscape; but the retention of the subject in the former allows us to conceive of a hybrid version in which landscapes 'speak' to the writer through the patterns of their differences, and the differences that constitute the text are continuous with those that constitute the world.

The two models also diverge in their implications with regard to movement and change. Fusion *per se* is not associated with movement.[14] In contrast, perceiving the 'repetitions' of numbers of different landscapes around the world (as in the list already quoted, *NRM*, p. 14) obviously presupposes the mobility to travel around to see them. Fusion and complicity, on the other hand, are more likely to be realized by people who *stay in one place*. Thus *Une Nouvelle Région* refers to the 'lieux imbougés où la connivence a pu se garder' (p. 39); it is from 'des lieux immobiles et enfouis' that we hear the voices preparing the 'new region of the world' (p. 40). In this they are contrasted with the 'discoverers' – in other words, they are the colonized and oppressed. So, while we are more used to Glissant contrasting colonizers with the transported colonized of the Caribbean, the opposition is now primarily between colonizers and *indigenous* peoples: alongside 'les explorateurs et les conquérants et les exploiteurs sans mesure' (p. 98) there are other, humbler and more obscure communities who 'ne bougèrent pas de leur lieu donné [...] c'était leur manière de continuer la connivence' (p. 98). Indigenous peoples who have survived into the present have been left on the sidelines of global progress, but for that very reason are in a position to initiate us into the old, but now new again, relationships with place that will inform the 'new region of the world' (p. 94). Thus the colonized are no longer characterized primarily by displacement and migration, as they have been from the early novels to *Tout-monde*; here, the opposition is between colonizers and 'stayers': 'Les humanités [...] exhortées à dominer le monde, celles qui se déplaçaient prenaient le pas sur celles qui *demeuraient*' (p. 49, italics original).

Staying in the same place of course also has a temporal dimension, underlined by Glissant's term for those who do: 'les demeurés' (p. 98) (with deliberate irony, he chooses a word which literally means 'those who have remained or stayed', but which is also a pejorative term equivalent to 'mentally retarded'). Fusion thus tends to go together with permanence in time as well as immobility in space. Here again this is foreshadowed in Glissant's praise for Reverdy, whom he quotes on the need to focus on 'ce qui est constant et permanent et la vraie substance des choses' (*IP*, p. 75). I noted earlier the similarity between Glissant's description of the cave-painter fusing with the animal he paints and *Mille Plateaux*'s notion of 'becoming-animal'; but the two conceptions also differ significantly in that for Deleuze and Guattari 'becoming' effects a change in both the man and the animal: the 'devenir-animal de l'homme' is indissociable from the 'devenir-autre de l'animal' (p. 291).[15] In Glissant's version, however, there is nothing to suggest that the fusion causes any changes in either man or animal. More generally, the way in which 'l'ancienne tentative originelle' (*NRM*, p. 53) at fusion has, in a secret and virtual form, been *preserved* over the millennia, in itself creates an impression of permanence.

The 'difference' model, in contrast, is a dynamic process which appears to be entirely based on change. But the combination of the two models moderates the force of change by a countervailing emphasis on permanence which is not at all Deleuzean, and gives *Une Nouvelle Région* a very different atmosphere from *Mille Plateaux* or *Différence et répétition*.[16] Crucially, moreover, this is facilitated by an aspect of the 'difference' model itself which, again moving decisively if unobtrusively away from Deleuze, allows Glissant to articulate a more explicit synthesis of change and permanence. He achieves this by integrating into it a *dialectical* conception of change – wholly antagonistic to Deleuze[17] – that, as Nick Nesbitt argues persuasively, featured more prominently in Glissant's earlier work (such as the novels I discuss in chapter 8) but persists throughout the later writings, in which Nesbitt analyses the contradictory coexistence of a Deleuzean 'discourse of immediacy, instantaneity, immanence' and a Hegelian 'dialectics of consciousness [and] historical experience'.[18] Relation can thus be seen as a dialectical totality (*Voicing Memory*, p. 174). Moreover, this dialectical conception does not undermine, but rather works together with, the concept of *identity* which is central to Glissant's thought and constitutes another profound difference between his position and Deleuze's implacable attack on identity.[19]

Identity for Glissant is relational and differential – not an essence, but defined by its differences from other identities. Equally, the *generative* force of difference also results in identities which are always changing over time; change is not a contingent attribute, it is what *makes* identity. In fact, rather than 'identity', Glissant sometimes prefers to use the term 'variety' – 'Toute identité est aussi une variété qui pour un temps a cessé de bouger' (*NRM*, p. 142) – to express the inseparability of identity and change. Therefore, an identity is defined by its difference from other identities, but also by the differences which cause it to go on changing: 'Nous découvrons qu'il y a au moins *deux qualités de différences* [...] celle dont se réclame chaque variété pour se constituer en variété, et celle dont chaque variété se charge pour varier justement et *ainsi se conformer à sa nature*' (pp. 106–07, my italics). In other words, it is only by changing that it remains true to itself: difference is *constitutive* of substance. Therefore, it is what allows substance to 'remain': 'Si la substance se connaît changeante, c'est bien la différence qui fait que la substance *demeure* en changeant' (p. 107, italics original).[20]

In the dialectical perspective, it is the internal contradictions of the object that necessarily cause it to change; the dialectic is based on the insight that, in Herbert Marcuse's paraphrase, 'reality is contradictory in character and a "negative totality" [...] every existence runs it course by turning into the opposite of itself and producing the identity of its being by working through the opposition'.[21] Glissant's preference for the notions of 'variation' and 'variety' conflicts significantly with the Hegelian concepts of contradiction and negation, and is closer to Deleuzean immanence. Nevertheless, his formulation of the 'two kinds of difference' has an unmistakable similarity with the thought of Hegel. In the first place, for Hegel the object exists only within a negative totality of relations with other things which are not it: 'the unity of the thing is not only determined but constituted by its relation to other things, and its thinghood consists in this very relation [...] The thing becomes itself through its opposition to other things' (*Reason and Revolution*, p. 108). But these contradictions are also internal to the object itself ('the negation that every thing contains determines its very being', p. 123) and drive the process of constant dialectical change: 'Contradiction [...] does not displace the actual identity of the thing, but produces this identity in the form of a process in which the potentialities of things unfold' (p. 124).

In particular, Glissant's statement that it is the object's capacity to change which ensures that it continues to exist as itself is strikingly close to Hegel's insistence that the object exists only through 'the negation of the negation', that is, through its return to itself after passing through otherness: 'Something is in itself in so far as it has returned to itself from Being-for-Other'.[22] Glissant's formulation 'un autre de l'autre' is, surely, to be read as a conscious echo of the 'negation of the negation': '*Le différent [...] constitue un autre de l'autre ou une variété du même, et qui n'est plus ni l'autre ni le même, sans cesser pourtant d'être l'autre, et par conséquent, et pour soi, le même*. La substance varie, sans cesser d'être elle-même' (*NRM*, p. 107, italics original). Indeed, he argues that it is the concept of the dialectic alone which allows modern Western subjects to grasp – in a way that was, he claims, natural to the 'demeurés' – this dynamic interplay of same and other:

> la dialectique nous fut enseignée précisément pour que nous puissions comprendre [...] l'autre et le même et l'en dehors et l'au-dedans et l'autre part et l'ici-même, toujours pour cette raison que pour nous ils ne ressortissaient pas à cette même et seule dimension. Bien des peuples du monde ne retiennent pas le même et l'autre pour donnés à part, et ces peuples n'ont pas besoin de l'art réparateur de la dialectique. (p. 131)

Change not only makes identity but, conversely, in its sense of changing-remaining, is itself *conditional* upon a concept of identity, which allows us to grasp the continuity of something through its evolving different states: we can perceive that something has changed only if we recognize it as the 'same' thing that it was previously. There are therefore good and bad forms of change. 'Bad' change is that which 'denatures' ('les identités varient sans se dénaturer', 'des différents qui les ont changé sans les dénaturer', p. 108), or which 'dilutes' identity (p. 105). The negative connotations attached to fluidity in *Une Nouvelle Région* – diluting, and 'dissolving' (p. 187) – contrast with Deleuze and Guattari's positive view of the real as a plurality of 'flows'.[23]

Glissant does not explicitly state what kind of change is denaturing or diluting, but he does suggest that 'good' change must be freely assumed rather than imposed (p. 105); and, more relevantly for my argument here, he attributes to *places*, specifically, the role of guarding against the danger of dilution or dissolution:

> Le lieu est ce qui dans la Relation, dans la quantité réalisée des différents du monde, est incontournable, c'est-à-dire que par le lieu nous voyons que la Relation n'est jamais une dilution des particuliers, un méli-mélo dans lequel tout se confond et se dissout. La Relation est la quantité réalisée de tous les lieux du monde. (pp. 186–87)

Place, as he has said many times before, is 'incontournable'. It seems to be the particular connection between landscape and fusion that leads Glissant to identify places as points of distinctiveness within the dynamic system of Relation.[24] (They construct a striated rather than a smooth space, in the terminology of Deleuze and Guattari.)[25] An informal version of the inseparability of change and permanence is already a theme in *Mahagony*, where it is closely associated with one of Glissant's most powerful and resonant places: the mahogany tree, presented both as a site of permanence and immobility – 'Qu'on parte ou qu'on reste, on revient au mahogani. Les lieux-communs sont là ensouchés. Ils ne voyagent pas, ils attendent' (p. 188) – and as a place which 'repeats': 'ce mahogani, multiplié en tant d'arbres dans tant de pays du monde' (p. 193). In fact, the phrase 'la substance *demeure* en changeant' (*NRM*, p. 107, italics original) is a clear echo of the novel's description of the landscape as seen over time by someone whose own identity is changing-remaining, in parallel with it:

> Le même disant, changé par ce qu'il dit, revient au même endroit de ce même pays, et voilà que l'endroit lui aussi a changé, comme a changé la perception qu'il en eut naguère [...] Les arbres qui vivent longtemps *changent toujours, en demeurant*. (*Mahagony*, pp. 15–16, my italics)

And later in *Mahagony* we find a very clear statement of the interrelation of change and permanence: 'Ces passages, de temps ou d'espace, légitiment le changement, le constitue en permanence. S'il n'y a pas eu passage, ce qui demeure ne mérite pas de durer' (pp. 169–70).

Despite the various tensions between the implications of fusion and of difference that run through *Une Nouvelle Région du monde*, it thus, I would argue, arrives finally at a synthesis rather than a contradiction. The new aesthetic that it constructs not only integrates Glissant's feeling of intimate connection to landscape with his more general theories of cultural diversity, but produces a more complex notion of difference that retains a concept of identity (as variation and relation), and, through the importance it attaches to place, achieves a balance between movement and stasis, between change and permanence. This synthesis in turn allows Glissant to articulate a radically new conception of the relationship between the text or the work of art and the real.

# APPENDIX

# 'Writing in the Present'

## Interview with Maryse Condé

CB   Does the idea of community have any meaning for you?[1]

MC   I think that there used to be a Guadeloupean community when the island was more turned in on itself, when people didn't travel, and didn't have the opportunity to look for work abroad. Then, there was a group of people who were more or less similar in the way they spoke, the way they dressed, ate and so on. I think perhaps my great grandmother or my grandmother lived in that community. But as soon as people started to leave Guadeloupe, to live abroad for six years, ten years, when they began to go abroad to look for work, and sometimes stayed away permanently, bringing up children who know nothing about Guadeloupe – the Antillean community has not ceased to exist, but it has radically changed. The idea of community has become a fantasy. People have started wanting to conform to the stories that their parents used to tell them.

CB   Even those who stayed in Guadeloupe?

MC   Yes, those who stayed are also faced with change. If you look at Guadeloupe now you will see that there is not a single family that does not have relatives abroad. Relatives who come back for the holidays. They have daughters who have married Frenchmen, 'whites' as we say at home, and that inevitably leads to a change in the community. Originally, there must have been a community, but it has changed – it has changed so much, been so transformed, that one can no longer define it. The day before yesterday I was with a group of young people, a reading club that had read *Desirada*,[2] and a girl asked me: 'But for you, where does the Caribbean begin and where does it end?' And it struck me as an excellent question.

CB    Actually, I've just read *Desirada*; I like it enormously, I think above all because it gives an absolutely contemporary feeling of what it is like to live in a big city …

MC    Yes, a city in which one was not born.

CB    Do you consider that to be a totally negative situation?

MC    No. For me, the fact of having to create one's own place, create one's group of friends, of constantly having to define oneself, make one's mark on one's surroundings, is an excellent thing. I have absolutely no nostalgia for those reference points of the past.

CB    Nevertheless, in *Desirada* Marie-Noëlle is not happy …

MC    Because of the conditions of her personal history. She was born in very confused circumstances. She doesn't know who her father is, her mother was very cold towards her. Her second mother, Ranelise, died. She left Guadeloupe when she was twelve years old. So, for her personally, a whole lot of things have meant that she is not happy. But it's not because she is recreating herself in America.

CB    In this new kind of open, migratory community, what are the changes that affect relationships between individuals? One has more choice …

MC    One has more choice, and in a way all those reference points, such as the family, such as biology, such as relationships based on kinship, are gradually disappearing. We find ourselves in the position of choosing a family or a community which may not be made up of people of the same origin as ourselves. We end up having American friends, friends from different countries. I consider this an enrichment.

CB    Does your idea of this have anything to do with Glissant's 'Tout-monde', or is it different?

MC    It's not very different. Except that Glissant is very intellectual; with him it is always, if I can put it like this, a more abstract question. Whereas I can only think in stories, I can only think if there are people and stories that I can make up. Sometimes I am not sure that I really understand what he is saying …

CB    Another thing I noticed in *Desirada* is that these relationships between people that are not based on family nevertheless involve a sense of responsibility …

MC   For example, Marie-Noëlle becomes the friend of an African-American woman, Anthea. For me, that is the perfect example of this new kind of relationship. People who do not think as you do. Not at all. People whose lives are different from yours – but with whom you can still have strong emotional ties. Marie-Noëlle and Anthea have nothing in common. Anthea goes to Africa and adopts a child, but these are personal choices.

CB   And that gives women a new position?

MC   I am not at all a feminist. I've already had a lot of trouble with my latest book,[3] which portrays a woman whom I conceived as a real shit-stirrer, but whom everyone else sees as a liberated independent woman, a symbol of liberation – and I am very uncomfortable with that kind of thing.

CB   But, compared with *Traversée de la mangrove*, for example, women like Marie-Noëlle, or like Thécla in *La Vie scélérate* do have far more autonomy.[4]

MC   Yes, but they have it rather in spite of themselves.

CB   To come back to *Traversée de la mangrove*, I'm sure you know Françoise Lionnet's article on it, in which she talks about a 'new humanism'.[5] I must admit that I found that rather puzzling, because the impression that I had of *Traversée de la mangrove* was of a very hostile world in which everyone felt imprisoned.

MC   Yes. They all want to leave, and at the end of the wake everyone feels as though they are going to start a new life elsewhere.

CB   At least, those who succeed, go away. So success means escape, simply.

MC   Success means having the strength to escape, yes. Having enough strength not to stay there. Repeating, repeating, repeating the same actions.

CB   Lionnet says that you emphasize universal experiences: rape, death, etc. – and so there is nothing specifically Guadeloupean or Caribbean in the characters' experiences.

MC   But is that entirely true? There is, in fact, a way of experiencing love that remains specific to the community, a way of approaching death also … I'm not sure that the idea of universality is altogether true. I think it is simply that the community changes, it introduces other elements, other kinds of connection. I don't believe that it dissolves completely into a universal model.

CB    So your criticism of Chamoiseau, for example, is not that he shows the Antilles to be different, but that he turns that difference into an essential value?

MC    It is a well-known fact that my literary views differ from those of the *créolité* writers. I don't want to come back to that again.

CB    Basically, *créolité* just becomes a new kind of exoticism, then?

MC    Yes, it might be if you take exoticism as a non-realistic vision of a society and its people.

CB    It seems almost inevitable that exoticism always recurs; it's a bit like the return of the repressed ...

MC    Well, it's because we are not read and published in our own islands; you must always remember that we write to be published elsewhere and for a public that is different from our own. That puts us into a position of exoticism. I believe that if we had local publishing houses, and if we had a population capable of reading us, we would have the possibility of writing differently.

CB    But you yourself have never given in to exoticism; you are almost the only one of the Antillean writers that I have read to have systematically rejected exoticism.

MC    I do my best ... I've never enjoyed the favours of the media, the press has never been infatuated with me. When they have these big articles in the *Nouvel Observateur*, for instance, on Antillean literature, I am never included; they always leave me out.

CB    But you have sold a lot of books ...

MC    Yes, but you have to make a choice. Either you remain true to yourself, to your first illusions: then people read you, but the press – who make a writer's reputation – regard you with slight suspicion. Or else you write what the press want to see, but you will perhaps be read less.

CB    But isn't rejecting exoticism more complicated than that? For example, it is perhaps possible to avoid it even when writing for a different readership. It is a kind of vigilance, don't you think? What does one have to do in order to represent an Antillean character for a readership whom one knows to be non-Antillean, to be European or North American?

MC   It's extremely difficult. However much we fight against exoticism, against the other's gaze, there are some elements that in spite of ourselves we want to include, that we can't reject. In all the novels I've done on the Antilles, there are these elements – the wake, for example – that I can't help describing because they seem to me to define the country's culture. There is no doubt whatsoever that if one looks at Guadeloupean society today the wake is extremely marginal, but, all the same, I can't help valorizing certain picturesque elements. That is a form of exoticism. But when it comes to the characters, there I think I do make an effort. People can no longer be described in the way that Joseph Zobel described Man Tine or José;[6] if one wants to be a writer and talk about the human heart, the human being, one must try to stick to the present. It's not easy, one is always tempted to add a little exotic touch, it's very difficult to eliminate it, but, honestly, as much as possible, 85 per cent of the time, I endeavour to free myself from it. For instance, in my next novel, which is coming out in May, you will see how I have really forced myself to talk about Guadeloupe in the present: with its rapes, with its robberies, with its strikes, with its people who longer believe in anything at all. And it was hard, you know, the narrative doesn't come easily, it doesn't flow, so one does have to make an effort in order to tell a story without using certain gimmicks. It's like a cook who doesn't add any salt, who doesn't add any spices or pepper, it's so much more difficult.

CB   And in order to avoid exoticism one has to show things that are genuinely unknown and new, because exoticism is in a sense a false unknown.

MC   Yes, you have to try to write in the present. As long as you remain in a sort of nostalgia, in the past, you lapse into exoticism. When you try to stick closely to the present, to the reality of today, the exoticism disappears. There is nothing exotic about Guadeloupe today: when you lock up your house at six in the evening because you are afraid that armed gangs are going to come and burgle you, that's not exotic at all. But, of course, one does not really want to put that in a novel.

CB   Why are there so many first-person narratives in your novels?

MC   Because when I write in the first person, I am truer to myself. I have a lot of trouble with the third person. I make an effort, but most of the time when I need to be really at ease with expressing nuances and subtleties, I find it better to use 'I'.

CB    In *Traversée de la mangrove*, you use the first person for the women and the third person for nearly all of the men – why is that?

MC    Because with the men there is a greater distance; when I write about a woman, it's a bit of myself, disguised as an Indian woman – Rosa Ramsaran – or disguised as Mira. It's always me. That comes easily.

CB    I've just read Fritz Gracchus's *Les Lieux de la mère*, and I'd like to ask you what you think of it?[7]

MC    It's a fantastic book.

CB    But very pessimistic!

MC    Yes, and sometimes very negative. But he writes very well about Fanon, for instance. No, it's a book that I like a great deal.

CB    Do you think he is right to say that the Caribbean mother has been idealized to such an extent?

MC    Well, obviously, I remember that when I read it I was a little shocked. He sees the mother as a kind of vehicle of alienation. I found that rather exaggerated. But when I thought about it, the more I read, the more I felt that it was true. I have more or less come round to his point of view.

CB    But this fantasy of the white father that he attributes to all the women – he has really got it in for Caribbean women, don't you think?

MC    He does try to be fair, though. He recognizes that it is not altogether their fault. It's the fault of the society, of slavery, of colonization. He considers the women more as sick than as guilty.

CB    In *Desirada*, the figure of Reynalda, Marie-Noëlle's mother, who was raped in her childhood …

MC    But it's not at all certain that she was raped, because, if you read the final pages carefully, you see that the man who made her pregnant was probably the priest; there must have been a love that was not reciprocated. The priest must have exploited her – perhaps! – but there was no rape.

CB    But she was so young.

MC   Yes, but ultimately there is nothing to prove that she was not in love with the priest. Perhaps. We don't know. It's a way of deconstructing the cliché that whenever there is sex between a white man and a black woman, it is always a rape. Whereas it can be a relationship, a love affair.

CB   That's just what Gracchus says ...

MC   Yes. I don't actually believe that all women were as he thinks they were, more or less attracted by power – no, I think there were the two kinds of women.

CB   Do you know Jacques André as well?

MC   Yes – he is French, but he lived in Guadeloupe for a long time and then left. He and I had a lot of discussions together; he knew Guadeloupe well, and I think his wife was Guadeloupean.

CB   The only thing that worries me in what he writes is the way he generalizes about a whole society.[8]

MC   Yes, but that, in my opinion, is the fault of everyone who writes essays. I think that we novelists have a sense of nuances, whereas the people who write essays and have theses that they want to prove are too definitive in what they say. They lack fiction – fiction introduces a sort of doubt, of questioning, which they don't have.

CB   And the fact that the novel presents individual characters ...

MC   Yes, I think that is the big difference with the novel. That's why I could never write an entire book of essays, and why they will never be able to write novels. For example, Glissant is an excellent writer of essays and sometimes less convincing in his novels, because in my view he has a more theoretical turn of mind: he is good at analysing, and he has theses that he wants to prove.

CB   And this novel that you are bringing out in May, what is it about?

MC   It's a novel called *La Belle Créole*.[9] It's the name of a boat. It's set in an island which is not named, but which is contemporary Guadeloupe – robberies, rapes, strikes, in particular a power strike and a strike of the refuse collectors. So everything happens in darkness. And it stinks everywhere. A young man who killed his mistress has just been released from prison, and he spends the night going round his friends looking for somewhere to stay. Everyone closes their doors to him. He ends up alone and in the end kills himself, aboard his boat 'La Belle Créole'. What had happened between him and this white woman? That is the issue. She had never loved him – she had been his mistress, but without ever loving him. The publishers are delighted, of course, they're calling it 'Lady Chatterley in the tropics' …

CB    Well, you've already done a *Wuthering Heights*[10] … Is it important for you to write about Guadeloupe in your novels, rather than the United States, for instance?

MC    The United States have not yet really inspired me … New York is a city that I like a lot, but which has not yet inspired me … Boston, where I have lived, is in *Desirada* – I hated Boston so much that I wanted to write about it. But as regards New York, I have not yet found anything … but I will do – it's simply a question of waiting for inspiration.

CB    And in *Les Derniers Rois mages*, is Spéro's wife, with all her cultural activities, a kind of American caricature?

MC    Yes, but it's a caricature based on a real person, because I cannot write in the abstract; I have a friend who is exactly like Debbie – it's when we were in Virginia, and I saw that kind of naivety in action.

CB    It's something that one doesn't find in the Caribbean.

MC    No. Because there the world is not judged so much in black and white terms … it's a different attitude, that's all. And also the Americans have an aggressive side that we don't have.

CB    In Confiant's novels there is a lot of sexuality – but in yours as well, in a different way: you are much less prudish than most other Antillean writers.

MC    Yes!

CB    And is that also part of being modern?

MC    At first it was a reaction against a literature that did not want to talk about sex. I remember, it was at least twenty years ago, Glissant was in Paris, and I asked him: 'Why is there no sex in your novels?' And he replied: 'Well, after all, people make love, but one doesn't write about it'. And I wondered why. It seems to me on the contrary to be a very good subject – and so, I wanted to react against this over-cerebral literature. So, for my part, I continue to write about sexuality, but I try to do so in a different way from male writers.

New York, 13 March 2001

# Notes

## Introduction

1 *Tropiques* has been re-edited in book form (Paris: Jean-Michel Place, 1978).

2 Gisèle Pineau, *L'Exil selon Julia* (Paris: Éditions Stock, 1996); André and Simone Schwarz-Bart, *Un Plat de porc aux bananes vertes* (Paris: Éditions du Seuil, 1967); Maryse Condé, *Traversée de la mangrove* (Paris: Mercure de France, 1989. Page references to the Folio reprint of 1996); Daniel Maximin, *L'Île et une nuit* (Paris: Éditions du Seuil, 1995).

3 Édouard Glissant, *Le Quatrième Siècle* (Paris: Éditions du Seuil, 1964); *Malemort* (Paris: Éditions du Seuil, 1975); *La Case du commandeur* (Paris: Éditions du Seuil, 1981); *Mahagony* (Paris: Éditions du Seuil, 1987); *Tout-monde* (Paris: Gallimard, 1993); *Une Nouvelle Région du monde* (Paris: Gallimard, 2006).

4 B. Ashcroft, G. Griffiths and H. Tiffin, *The Empire Writes Back* (London: Routledge, 1989).

5 Helen Tiffin, 'Post-colonial Literatures and Counter-discourse' in Bill Ashcroft, Gareth Griffiths and Helen Tiffin (eds), *The Post-colonial Studies Reader* (London and New York: Routledge, 1995), pp. 95–98, p. 95.

6 Although René Ménil claims, in a related sense, that 'notre conscience antillaise est nécessairement parodique parce qu'elle est prise dans un jeu de dédoublement, de redoublement, de miroitement, de séparation face à la conscience coloniale française [...] Pour une telle conscience divisée et soucieuse, la naïveté dans l'art est interdite' (*Antilles déjà jadis (précédée de Tracées)* (Paris: Jean-Michel Place, 1999), pp. 225–26).

7 Gayatri Spivak, *Death of a Discipline* (New York: Columbia University Press, 2003).

8 Nicholas Harrison, *Postcolonial Criticism* (Cambridge: Polity, 2003); Eli Park Sorensen, *Postcolonial Studies and the Literary* (Basingstoke: Palgrave Macmillan, 2010); Patrick Crowley and Jane Hiddlestone (eds), *Postcolonial Poetics: Genre and Form* (Liverpool: Liverpool University Press, 2011).

9  The best-known formulation of this is Fredric Jameson's 'Third-World Literature in the Era of Multinational Capitalism', *Social Text*, 15 (1986), pp. 65–88.

10  Peter Hallward, *Absolutely Postcolonial: Writing Between the Singular and the Specific* (Manchester: Manchester University Press, 2001); Chris Bongie, *Friends and Enemies: The Scribal Politics of Post/Colonial Literature* (Liverpool: Liverpool University Press, 2008).

11  In Jean-Paul Sartre's *Qu'est-ce que la littérature?* (Paris: Gallimard, 1948), for instance, or more generally in humanist Marxist literary theory.

12  Sorensen quotes Neil Lazarus: 'I am tempted to overstate the case [...] and declare that there is in a strict sense only one author in the postcolonial literary canon. That author is Salman Rushdie' (Lazarus, 'The Politics of Postcolonial Modernism' in Ania Loomba et al. (eds), *Postcolonial Studies and Beyond* (Durham, NC: Duke University Press, 2005), pp. 423–38, p. 424, quoted in Sorensen, *Postcolonial Studies*, p. 11.

13  Cf Harrison's rather different view: 'My argument is that what emerges from critical "readings" in the mode of literary indeterminacy is *not*, finally, a more accurate or nuanced view of a text's ideological "message" or orientation. Rather, criticism of that sort problematizes the identification of any such orientation' (*Postcolonial Criticism*, p. 149, italics original).

14  Jean Bernabé, Patrick Chamoiseau and Raphaël Confiant, *Éloge de la créolité* (Paris: Gallimard, 1989).

15  Graham Huggan, *The Post-colonial Exotic: Marketing the Margins* (London and New York: Routledge, 2001).

16  Gilles Deleuze and Félix Guattari, *Kafka. Pour une littérature mineure* (Paris: Éditions de Minuit, 1975) and *Mille Plateaux* (Paris: Éditions de Minuit, 1980). Gilles Deleuze, *Différence et répétition* (Paris: PUF, 1968).

17  I am not, of course, suggesting that I am unique in doing this. Nicholas Harrison's *Postcolonial Criticism*, for instance, makes substantial use of Derrida, Blanchot and Genette; although, like me, he does feel the need to comment on this fact (p. 6). Lise Gauvin's *Écrire, pour qui? L'écrivain francophone et ses publics* (Paris: Karthala, 2007) is a good example of a basically narratological approach which illuminates the social situation of francophone writers in their negotiations with a metropolitan readership.

18  For instance, Aijaz Ahmad's *In Theory: Classes, Nations, Literatures* (London: Verso, 2000) considers that any recourse to metropolitan theory risks undermining the specificity of postcolonial literature. Arif Dirlik makes a similar argument in his 'The Postcolonial Aura: Third World Criticism in the Age of Global Capitalism', *Critical Inquiry*, 20.2 (1994), pp. 328–56.

19  'L'effet de langage, c'est la cause introduite dans le sujet. Par cet effet il n'est pas cause de lui-même, il porte en lui le ver de la cause qui le refend. Car sa cause, c'est le signifiant sans lequel il n'y aurait aucun sujet dans le réel. Mais ce sujet, c'est ce que le signifiant représente, et il ne saurait rien représenter que

pour un autre signifiant: à quoi dès lors se réduit le sujet qui l'écoute' (Lacan, *Écrits II* (Paris: Éditions du Seuil, 1966), p. 200).

20  Spivak also makes the more general point that poststructuralism's use of the term 'text' is not reducible to a verbal text, but 'a network, a weave [...] politico-psycho-sexual-socio, you name it [...] that notion that we are effects within a much larger text/tissue/weave of which the ends are not accessible to us is very different from saying that everything is language' (*The Postcolonial Critic: Interviews, Strategies, Dialogues*, ed. Sarah Harasym (New York: Routledge, 1990), p. 25).

21  See, for example, Chinua Achebe, 'The African Writer and the English Language', in *Morning yet on Creation Day* (London: Heinemann, 1975), pp. 62–75; Edward Kamau Brathwaite, *History of the Voice: The Development of Nation Language in Anglophone Caribbean Poetry* (London and Port of Spain: New Beacon, 1984); Ngugi wa Thiong'o, *Decolonizing the Mind: The Politics of Language in African Literature* (London: James Currey, 1981].

22  Frantz Fanon, *Peau noire, masques blancs* (Paris: Éditions du Seuil, 1952).

23  Émile Benveniste, *Problèmes de linguistique générale* (Paris: Gallimard, 1966).

24  Mikhail Bakhtin, *Problems of Dostoevsky's Poetics* (Minneapolis, MN: University of Minnesota Press, 1984), p. 195. His related concept of the 'heteroglossia' of the novel was the basis for Julia Kristeva's theorization of intertextuality ('Le mot, le dialogue et le roman', in her *Recherches pour une sémanalyse* (Paris: Éditions du Seuil, 1969), pp. 82–112), to which I refer in chapter 4.

25  Bakhtin, *The Dialogic Imagination* (Austin, TX: University of Texas Press, 1981), p. 282. There are interesting similarities between Bakhtin's position and Derrida's much later poststructuralist formulation ('Je n'ai qu'une langue et elle n'est pas la mienne', p. 7) in *Le Monolinguisme de l'autre – ou la prothèse de l'origine* (Paris: Éditions Galilée, 1996). For a nuanced discussion of *Le Monolinguisme* in the context of Derrida's relation to postcolonialism, see Michael Syrotinski, *Deconstruction and the Postcolonial: At the Limits of Theory* (Liverpool: Liverpool University Press, 2007) pp. 12–25.

26  Roland Barthes, *S/Z* (Paris: Éditions du Seuil, 1970) p. 10. The 'texte scriptible' makes of the reader a 'producer' rather than a 'consumer' of the text, engaging the reader in its open-ended production of meaning, rather than providing a complete, finished representation of reality.

27  Pierre Macherey, *Pour une théorie de la production littéraire* (Paris: Maspero, 1966); Terry Eagleton, *Criticism and Ideology: A Study in Marxist Literary Theory* (London: Verso, 1976); Catherine Belsey, *Critical Practice* (London: Routledge, 1980).

28  'Le réalisme occidental n'est pas une technique "à plat", hors profondeur,

mais le devient quand il est adopté par nos écrivains. La misère de nos pays n'est pas seulement présente, patente. Elle comporte une dimension d'histoire (d'histoire non évidente) dont le seul réalisme ne rend pas compte' (*Le Discours antillais* (Paris: Éditions du Seuil, 1981), p. 198).

29 René Depestre, *Hadriana dans tous mes rêves* (Paris: Éditions Gallimard, 1988).

30 'Habiter ce pays, la Guadeloupe', *Chemins critiques*, 1.3 (1989), pp. 5–14, p. 13.

31 The representation of a collective consciousness that does not yet exist as a social reality, to which I refer in chapter 8, involves a further, rather different relationship to the real, which stems from the dialectical aspect of Glissant's thought. See also chapter 11 for a discussion of Glissant's use of dialectics.

32 Harrison invokes Derrida's notion of 'suspension' as a different kind of attempt to give nuance to the realist/anti-realist divide. He quotes Derrida: 'There is no literature without a *suspended* relation to meaning and reference. *Suspended* means *suspense*, but also *dependence*, condition, conditionality' (Derrida, *Passions* (Paris: Galilée, 1993), p. 94) and comments: 'This notion of suspension should be distinguished, then, from any concept of literary fiction that makes it appear wholly non-"referential", that *opposes* semiosis to mimesis, or that dwells exclusively on its "unreality"' (*Postcolonial Criticism*, p. 139).

## Chapter One

1 In the interview with Jacqueline Leiner that forms the preface to the re-edition of *Tropiques* in book form, Césaire describes the impact which Breton's presence had on the review (p. vi). Martin Munro emphasizes *Tropiques'* enthusiasm for the possibilities which surrealism offered them in establishing the autonomy of Martinican culture: 'The pages of the review are replete with almost fervent references to surrealist ideas, and are marked by a real sense that through this European movement [...] the Western mind-set might be subverted, and that the colonized Martinican self might finally be able to assert itself ' (*Shaping and Reshaping the Caribbean: The Work of Aimé Césaire and René Depestre* (London: MHRA Texts and Dissertations, vol. 52, 2000), p. 65).

2 Michel Leiris, *Contacts de civilisation en Martinique et en Guadeloupe* (Paris: Gallimard, 1955), p. 108.

3 James Arnold makes a similar argument: 'Surrealism was to serve the Martinican [Césaire] as an instrument for making contact with his own African heritage construed as biological and presumably waiting to be tapped in the reservoir of the collective unconscious' (*Modernism and Negritude: The Poetry and Poetics of Aimé Césaire* (Cambridge, MA: Harvard University Press, 1981), p. 95).

4 See Sartre, 'Orphée noir', preface to Léopold Sédar Senghor (ed.), *Anthologie de la nouvelle poésie nègre et malgache de langue française* (Paris: Presses Universitaires de France, 1948).

5 In 1932 Ménil was one of the editors of the journal *Légitime défense*, which combined the surrealism which its title, a quotation from André Breton, implies, with a Marxist critique of Antillean society.

6 'L'exotisme colonial', originally published in *La Nouvelle Critique* (1959); reprinted in René Ménil, *Antilles déjà jadis*, pp. 20–27, p. 22.

7 In this Ménil is repeating Sartre's characterization of Césaire's poetry in his preface to 'Orphée noir'. I have given more details of these connections in 'Freud, surrealism and ethnography', the first chapter of my *Race and the Unconscious: Freudianism in French Caribbean Thought* (Oxford: Legenda, 2002), pp. 6–27, to which this chapter is, in a sense, a companion piece.

8 Since the 1978 reprint of *Tropiques* is a facsimile edition and therefore not continuously paginated, my quotations from *Tropiques* are followed by the issue number and then the page number.

9 Hédi Bouraoui, for instance, argues that the editors of *Tropiques* are above all attracted to surrealism because it corresponds to their desire for revolt and liberation. ('*Tropiques* ou la découverte du temps de l'interprétation', *Éthiopiques*, 19 (July 1979), http://www.refer.sn/ethiopiques/imprimerarticle. php3?id_article=968).

10 I discuss this issue in greater detail in 'Freud, surrealism and ethnography'.

11 Jeremy Lane interprets Ménil's article differently, seeing it as exploiting the Vichy regime's promotion of (French) folklore in order to camouflage his radical political agenda; but I think this overlooks the connection made by *Tropiques* between Antillean folklore and Negritude. See Lane, *Jazz and Machine-Age Imperialism: Music, "Race" and Intellectuals in France, 1918–1945* (Ann Arbor, MI: University of Michigan Press, 2013), p. 171.

12 A collection of Lafcadio Hearn's writing, edited and introduced by Mary Gallagher, has been published under the title *Esquisses martiniquaises* (Paris: L'Harmattan, série 'Autrement mêmes', vols I and II, 2004).

13 Another example of this is Suzanne Césaire's evocation of 'survivances africaines aux Antilles' (4, pp. 55–62), which reproduces three extracts from a 'Recueil des contes populaires de la Sénégambie recueilli par L.J.B. Bérenger-Féraud', published in Paris in 1885. For the second of these, moreover, the corresponding Martinican form of folk culture is identified via a collection of Antillean riddles published by a certain Paul Labrousse under the telling title 'Deux vieilles terres françaises'.

14 One way in which they try to solve the problem is by invoking a notion of the unconscious – as René Hibran briefly does. The most sustained attempt, however, is an article by Suzanne Césaire, 'Malaise d'une civilisation' in *Tropiques* no. 5; I have discussed this in 'Freud, surrealism and ethnography'.

15 See Martin Munro's discussion of the influence of Frobenius on the

Negritude movement and on *Tropiques* in his *Shaping and Reshaping the Caribbean*, pp. 54–58.

16 Michael Richardson emphasizes the parallels between Lam and Césaire: 'Césaire's return to his homeland was not to be the only one in this period. Certainly, Wifredo Lam's return to Cuba in 1941 was equally significant, having similar ramifications in the plastic domain to those raised in the poetic domain by Césaire: Lam's *The Jungle*, painted in Cuba in 1942, may I think be seen as the visual companion piece to Césaire's *Notebook*. Pierre Mabille's essay "The Jungle", which was published in *Tropiques*, brings out this importance' (*Refusal of the Shadow: Surrealism and the Caribbean* (London: Verso, 1996), p. 8.)

17 'Wifredo Lam, peintre cubain', *Présence africaine*, 4 (1948), pp. 590–94, p. 591. Madeleine Rousseau was the editor of the art periodical *Le Musée vivant*, and in 1948, together with Cheik Anta Diop, devoted a special issue of it to *l'art nègre*. Her article in *Présence africaine* offers an interesting insight into the way in which the French perception of the relationship between surrealism and primitivism changes in the post-war years; she notes the negative reception which greeted the exhibition of Lam's paintings that Pierre Loeb had mounted in Paris in 1946, and attributes it to Parisian disillusionment with surrealism: 'pour nous, Occidentaux de Paris, elle n'apportait rien de plus qu'un néo-surréalisme littéraire dont nous commencions déjà à être saturés' – a 'néo-surréalisme' which had become 'le nouveau conformisme de l'après guerre' (p. 591). In this she compares Lam unfavourably with Césaire: 'Césaire est actuel et dépasse le surréalisme dont Lam ne sut pas franchir les limites devenues trop étroites' (p. 593). The solution for Lam, she continues, is to abandon surrealism *in order* to realize successfully his intention to express in his art the African side of his personality: he needed, she suggests, to go back to Cuba to 'renouer le contact avec la nature antillaise', because it is in the Caribbean 'que ce peuple s'éveille, que le grand souffle créateur des ancêtres africains renaît' (p. 594). Surrealism, in other words, is now hindering rather than helping Caribbeans to find their African roots.

## Chapter Two

1 Originally published in *La Nouvelle Critique*, the French Communist Party journal. Reprinted in René Ménil, *Antilles déjà jadis*, pp. 20–27. Page references are to this edition.

2 'L'exotisme est une constante de la conscience coloniale axée – économiquement, socialement et culturellement – en dehors d'elle-même, sur la Métropole [...] ce mal ne disparaîtra qu'en brisant le système colonial lui-même pour remplacer les structures coloniales par des structures humaines' (p. 22, italics original).

3 Régis Antoine, *La Littérature franco-antillaise: Haiti, Guadeloupe et Martinique* (Paris: Karthala, 1992), pp. 331–50.

4 Roger Toumson, 'L'Exotisme. Problématiques de la représentation de l'autre et de l'ailleurs', *Revue française d'histoire du livre*, 60–61 (1988), pp. 433–50, p. 433.

5 'Comment décrire un cocotier? Comment dire qu'une plage de sable blanc est belle? Cocotier et sable blanc, tout le paysage en final de compte, ont été réifié par le discours exotique européen' ('Questions pratiques d'écriture créole', in Ralph Ludwig (ed.), *Écrire la parole de nuit, la nouvelle littérature antillaise* (Paris: Gallimard, 1994), pp. 171–80, p. 173).

6 Cf Condé's comment: 'However much we fight against exoticism, against the other's gaze, there are some elements that in spite of ourselves we want to include, that we can't reject' (Interview, p. 173).

7 See, for example, Francis Affergan, *Exotisme et altérité* (Paris: PUF, 1987); Chris Bongie, *Exotic Memories: Literature, Colonialism and the Fin de Siècle* (Stanford, CA: Stanford University Press, 1991); Charles Forsdick, 'Travelling Concepts: Postcolonial Approaches to Exoticism', *Paragraph*, 24.3 (2001), pp. 12–29. Forsdick argues cogently for the 'rehabilitation' of exoticism, distinguishing between the actual encounter with radical otherness and 'the process whereby such radical otherness is [...] translated, transported, represented for consumption at home' (p. 14); and points out that a new kind of postcolonial exoticism has created an equal, two-way relationship in which – in narratives of Africans visiting Europe, for instance – the postcolonial gaze illuminates the otherness of the West (pp. 25–26). But neither of these positive versions is relevant to auto-exoticism, which by definition involves no genuine radical otherness nor any exotic perspective on the metropole. Martin Munro argues for a positive sense of exoticism in the work of exiled Haitians Jacques-Stephen Alexis and René Depestre, but here again their situation of enforced physical separation from the society they are writing about is very different from that of Antillean writers (Martin Munro, *Exile and Post-1946 Haitian Literature* (Liverpool: Liverpool University Press, 2007), pp. 41–49, 127–28).

8 Régis Antoine, in his *La Littérature franco-antillaise*, gives some revealing statistics on literary texts set in the Antilles: he has found 325 metropolitan French writers writing about the French Antilles between 1635 and 1940; of these, 50 had lived there for a number of years, 75 had visited as travellers, and 200 had never been there at all (p. 331).

9 Confiant, *Le Nègre et l'amiral* (Paris: Éditions Grasset, 1988), p. 326.

10 For an extended analysis of the familial discourse which pervades metropolitan formulations of the relationship between France and the Antilles, see Richard Burton, *La Famille coloniale: la Martinique et la Mère Patrie* (Paris: L'Harmattan, 1994).

11 Michel Leiris defines the particular charm of Martinique and Guadeloupe – as opposed to Haiti, for instance – precisely in terms of this combination of the familiar and the strange, in a lecture entitled 'Antilles et poésie des carrefours' (in *Zébrage* (Paris: Gallimard, 1992), pp. 67–87). I have discussed this text in

detail in Britton, 'Dual Identities: The Question of "Départementalisation" in Michel Leiris's *Contacts de civilisations en Martinique et en Guadeloupe*', *French Cultural Studies*, 22.1 (2011), pp. 61–72.

12 In the introduction to her book on Chamoiseau, Maeve McCusker comments: 'More than in most other postcolonial societies, after all, Antillean writers bear the cultural and theoretical imprint of the metropolitan centre, however vociferously they may assert their differences from its institutional networks' (*Patrick Chamoiseau: Recovering Memory* (Liverpool: Liverpool University Press, 2007), p. 4).

13 See, for example, Maryse Condé, 'Chercher nos vérités', in Maryse Condé and Madeleine Cottenet-Hage (eds), *Penser la créolité* (Paris: Karthala, 1995), pp. 305–10); Michel Giraud, 'La créolité: une rupture en trompe-l'œil', *Cahiers d'études africaines*, 148 (1997), pp. 795–812; Richard and Sally Price, 'Shadow-boxing in the mangrove', *Cultural Anthropology*, 12.1 (1997), pp. 3–36; Richard Burton, '"Ki Moun Nou Ye?" The Idea of Difference in Contemporary French West Indian Thought', *New West Indian Guide*, 67.1 & 2 (1993), pp. 5–32.

14 Ménil does not explicitly name Confiant or Chamoiseau here, but a previous reference to a recipe for 'touffé-requin' clearly alludes to an episode in the latter's novel *Solibo magnifique* (Paris: Gallimard, 1988). His allusions to hummingbirds and butterflies are actually rather unfair to Chamoiseau, whose novels contain very little description of nature.

15 See the interview with Condé in this volume: 'you must always remember that we write to be published elsewhere and for a public that is different from our own. That puts us into a position of exoticism' (p. 172).

16 In a more general sense, this is of course the situation of all francophone writers, who, as Lise Gauvin comments, have to 'trouver des stratégies aptes à rendre compte de leur communauté d'origine tout en leur permettant d'atteindre un plus vaste lectorat. Comment en arriver à pratiquer une véritable "esthétique du divers" (Segalen) sans tomber dans le marquage régionaliste ou exotique?' (*Écrire, pour qui?*, p. 6). Gauvin also quotes Confiant's very explicit declaration that he is writing both for Martinican and international readers: 'J'écris pour deux types de lecteurs: d'abord pour les Martiniquais; quand j'écris c'est eux que j'ai en tête. Mais j'écris aussi pour un lecteur virtuel mondial amoureux de la littérature' (Confiant, *Archipels littéraires*, quoted in *Écrire, pour qui?*, p. 107).

17 Dominique Chancé analyses in depth the motives and the effects of this valorization of orality over the written literary text, seeing it as a desire on the part of the *créolité* authors to identify with the traditional figure of the Creole storyteller. See *L'Auteur en souffrance: essai sur la position et la représentation de l'auteur dans le roman antillais contemporain* (Paris: PUF, 2000).

18 Later in the text, they give a more guarded account of the possible pitfalls of this 'interlect' or mixed French-Creole discourse, that is, its tendency

to lapse into cliché and stereotype, or simply to appear comic (pp. 49–50). These variations of emphasis may of course result from divergences between the three authors.

19 Graham Huggan's influential study *The Post-colonial Exotic: Marketing the Margins* analyses the commodification of postcoloniality and the dependence of Third World cultural products on globalized markets. In the light of this analysis, it would be naïve to assume that *any* such product that was as commercially successful as Chamoiseau and Confiant's novels, whatever its literary or political qualities, could avoid the necessity of pleasing the metropolitan reader.

20 Condé, 'Chercher nos vérités', p. 308.

21 As Huggan asks: 'To what extent does the value ascribed to [postcolonial writers] and attributed to their writing depend on their capacity to operate, not just as *representers* of culture but as bona fide cultural *representatives*? And is this representativeness a function of [ …] the mainstream demand for an "authentic", but readily translateable, marginal voice?' (*Post-colonial Exotic*, p. 26, italics original). See also his discussion of a number of critiques of the commodification of authenticity (pp. 157–62).

22 Huggan writes: 'as the process of commodification clearly illustrates, cultural difference also has an aesthetic value, a value often measured explicitly or implicitly in terms of the *exotic*' (*The Post-colonial Exotic*, p. 13).

23 Condé sees this as unduly prescriptive, commenting that: 'The tedious enumeration of the elements of popular culture which is made in the first pages of the manifesto leaves very little freedom for creativity' ('Order, Disorder, Freedom and the West Indian Writer', *Yale French Studies*, 83.2 (1993), pp. 121–35, p. 130).

24 In an interview with Chamoiseau, Chancé asks him: 'Il faut combattre l'aliénation par une nouvelle image de soi?' – and his reply, revealingly, is: 'En principe, mes livres devaient *positiver* quand même l'image qu'on a de soi-même, de ce que nous sommes' (*L'Auteur en souffrance*, p. 203, my italics).

25 Cf Bongie: 'As one of the privileged modes of recuperating this lost individuality, the exoticism project attempts to diffuse the supposed threat of homogenization that mass society poses' (*Exotic Memories*, p. 38). Condé also sees exoticism as essentially nostalgic, arguing that in order to combat it, 'one must try to stick to the present' (Interview, p. 173).

26 Cf Richard and Sally Price's comment that '[Chamoiseau and Confiant] foster an illusion of diversity by peopling the island with a reified set of categories drawn from crosscutting kinds of schemata (class, "race", national origin, etc.)' ('Shadow-boxing in the mangrove', p. 10).

27 'Creole orality is (rather too unproblematically) associated with plenitude, immediacy and memory' (McCusker, *Patrick Chamoiseau*, p. 86).

28 Gauvin's narratological approach in *Écrire, pour qui?* accords detailed attention to the paratextual status of footnotes translating Creole words for the

French reader, and emphasizes how they implicitly confer a superior status on the latter: 'Toute glose, voire tout procès de traduction inscrite dans le texte, donne à la culture du récepteur un statut supérieur à celle de l'émetteur' (p. 31). Chamoiseau's ludic reversal of this relation makes the same point.

29  See Ronnie Scharfman, '"Créolité" is/as Resistance: Raphaël Confiant's *Le Nègre et l'amiral*', in *Penser la créolité*, pp. 125–34; and Adlai Murdoch, 'The Language(s) of Martinican Identity: Resistance to Vichy in the novels of Raphaël Confiant', *Esprit créateur*, 47.1 (2007), pp. 68–83.

30  This self-reflexive stance is developed much further in some of Confiant's later novels; Gauvin's analysis of the *Trilogie tropicale* (i.e., *Bassin des ouragans* (Paris: Éditions Mille et une nuits, 1994), *La Savane des pétrifications* (Paris: Éditions Mille et une nuits, 1995) and *La Baignoire de Joséphine* (Paris: Éditions Mille et une nuits, 1997)) highlights the parodic staging of relations between author, reader and critic (Gauvin, *Écrire, pour qui?*, pp. 119–22), which results in what she calls 'une *méta-créolité*, dans la mesure où l'écrivain lui-même devient son propre critique en choisissant de mettre en scène, voire de parodier, le discours produit par les diverses instances littéraires' (p. 125). The knowing irony with which both Chamoiseau and Confiant signal their awareness of the trap of auto-exoticism is also somewhat comparable to the functioning of Barthes' 'ironic code' (*S/Z*, pp. 51–52) in that it allows them to assert control over their texts, and distance themselves from the 'code' of exotic stereotypes without actually eliminating them from their own discourse. I refer to the ironic code more fully in chapter 5.

31  '"C'est par ce systématisme que se renforcera la liberté de notre regard', *Éloge*, p. 40.

32  See A. James Arnold, 'The Erotics of Colonialism in Contemporary French West Indian Literary Culture', *New West Indian Guide*, 68.1 & 2 (1994), pp. 5–22. Arnold argues that these writers react against the 'feminization' of colonized cultures by asserting an aggressively masculine attitude, and comments that: 'Concerning relations between the sexes, the *créolistes* reproduce in their fiction and their memoirs an aggressive heterosexual eroticism, envisaged from the perspective of a more or less predatory philandering male, whose activities can be justified – if need be – through the claim of verisimilitude' (p. 17). Arnold's explanation, which in fact contains nothing specific to *Caribbean* colonization and slavery, is supplemented by the argument of Fritz Gracchus that Caribbean men have been emasculated by the history of slavery, which denied them the role of husband and father (Gracchus, *Les Lieux de la mère dans les sociétés afro-américaines* (Paris: Éditions Caribéennes, 1986).

33  As expressed in the closing words of *Éloge de la créolité*: 'l'harmonisation consciente des diversités préservées: la DIVERSALITÉ' (p. 55).

34  Patrick Chamoiseau and Raphaël Confiant, *Lettres créoles* (Paris: Hatier, 1991).

35 Martinican Michel Giraud argues vigorously that Chamoiseau and Confiant in fact remain committed to an essentialist conception of identity based on origin, that this identity is largely a fantasy, and that its main function is to secure the authors' position as leading intellectuals in the Antilles: 'C'est cet enjeu de contrôle du champ politique par la médiation du contrôle du champ intellectuel qui constitue, selon nous, la motivation profonde de ce qui nous apparaît comme une adhérence continue des principaux tenants de la créolité, en dépit de leurs dénégations, à la problématique fautive de l'origine en matière d'identité culturelle. Leurs discours et leurs actes tendent en effet à réduire – précisément sous les espèces de la créolité – les identités antillaises à un patrimoine, qui est certes vu comme le produit d'une histoire complexe, mais d'une histoire cristallisée en une tradition à laquelle ils veulent qu'on reste fidèle alors même qu'ils l'idéalisent largement et, donc, la reconstruisent en fonction de leurs exigences présentes et de l'avenir auquel ils aspirent' ('La créolité: une rupture en trompe-l'œil', p. 800).

36 See for example Bhabha, 'The Third Space', in Jonathan Rutherford (ed.), *Identity: Community, Culture, Difference* (London: Lawrence and Wishart, 1990), pp. 207–21.

37 Mary Gallagher comments that 'the essentialism that is sometimes much in evidence within the Caribbean *creolité* movement perfectly illustrates the point that the postcolonial promotion of cultural hybridity can be not just culturalist, but also paradoxically and dogmatically, if not coercively, fundamentalist in effect' ('Postcolonial Poetics: l'exception francophone?', *Modern and Contemporary France*, 18.2 (2010), pp. 251–68, p. 256).

## Chapter Three

1 Huggan makes a similar argument for 'Indian literature in English, as a literalised *consumer item*' (*Postcolonial Exotic*, p. 59, italics original), but in this case there is much less evidence of an actual connection with food.

2 Jack Corzani, La Littérature des Antilles-Guyane française (Fort-de-France: Désormeaux, 1978), p. xv.

3 Alain Rouch and Gérard Clavreuil, *Littératures nationales d'écriture française* (Paris: Bordas, 1987), p. 192.

4 Ernest Pépin's novel *L'Envers du décor* (Paris: Le Serpent à plumes, 2006) contains a bitterly humorous evocation of tourists' illusions that they are encountering the 'real' Guadeloupe, while in fact they never succeed in penetrating to 'the other side of the décor'. See Britton, 'Secret worlds: Incommunicability and initiation in three novels by Ernest Pépin', *Francophone Postcolonial Studies*, 6.1 (2008), pp. 7–23, pp. 11–13.

5 An early and somewhat atypical example is Simone and André Schwarz-Bart's *Un Plat de porc aux bananes vertes*, in which, as I argue in the next chapter, her memory of the dish in question becomes for the narrator exiled

in France a symbol of Martinique as a whole: but the grimly tragic tone of the novel is far removed from the pleasures of the edible text.

6  As Condé wearily complains: 'Are we condemned *ad vitam aeternam* to speak of vegetable markets [... ?]' ('Order, Disorder, Freedom, and the West Indian Writer', p. 130.)

7  Hoffmann, 'L'image de la femme dans la poésie haïtienne', *Présence africaine*, 34–36 (1960), pp. 183–206, p. 199.

8  While generally conforming to the Caribbean exotic, this novel also significantly departs from it in that its heroine Hadriana, object of the sexual fantasies of the Haitian first-person narrator, is in fact French. See Martin Munro, *Exile and Post-1946 Haitian Literature* for a discussion of this (pp. 126–29). Munro comments: 'The idealization, or mythologization, of Hadriana is more than a simple reversal of colonial eroticization of its tropical other. Hadriana *is* objectified, but the erotic is underplayed in Depestre's fantastic presentation of her as an embodiment of flawless (French) femininity' (p. 127).

9  As early as 1949, Michel Leiris described the multi-ethnic nature of Antillean society, and the fascination it held for him, in these terms: 'Véritable *chaudron* de sorcière où s'est élaborée l'une des mixtures les plus rares et les plus chatoyantes que puisse avoir à *goûter* un Européen comme moi qui, certes, est bien loin de n'avoir que mépris pour la forme de culture qui est *son pain quotidien*, mais qui est avide, intensément, d'une *nourriture plus savoureuse et plus stimulante* susceptible de porter à son potentiel le plus élevé son imagination ('Antilles et poésie des carrefours', p. 71, my italics. Originally a lecture given in Paris in 1949, the text is published in *Zébrage*.) Once again it is the mixed nature of Caribbean society that constitutes its attraction, which Leiris compares to an exotic food that stimulates his imagination, so that the fantasy of oral consumption leads to further fantasies.

10  Quoted in Mary Gallagher, 'Lafcadio Hearn's American Writings and the Creole Continuum', in Martin Munro and Celia Britton (eds), *American Creoles: The Francophone Caribbean and the American* South (Liverpool: Liverpool University Press, 2012), pp. 19–39, p. 32.

11  Confiant, 'La littérature créolophone des Antilles-Guyane', *Notre Librairie*, 104 (1991), pp. 56–62, p. 62.

12  As in Confiant's rather ostentatious explanations of non-standard French usages – for example, Amédée's prostitutes, which 'il s'efforçait de choisir bleues – ce qui veut dire plus que noire dans notre parlure' (p. 61)

13  Marie-José N'Zengou-Tayo, 'Littérature et diglossie: créer une langue métisse ou la "chamoisification" du français dans *Texaco* de Patrick Chamoiseau', *TTR: traduction, terminologie, rédaction*, 9.1 (1996), pp. 155–76, p. 165.

14  'De la négritude a la créolité: éléments pour une approche comparée', *Études françaises*, 28.2–3 (1993), pp. 23–38, p. 27. Quoted in Gauvin, *Écrire, pour qui?* p. 112.

15 'Questions pratiques d'écriture créole', p. 180.

16 Delphine Perret observes, along similar lines but in relation to Chamoiseau, that the French reader, like an armchair traveller, is afforded the luxury of at least partially fantasized access to Creole without having to leave the comfort of his or her own language: 'Serait-on donc dans une autre langue tout en restant étrangement en français? Si c'est vrai, un lecteur non créolophone doit reconnaître qu'il a une certaine chance ici. Il fait un voyage linguistique (non entièrement fantaisiste) tout en restant dans un fauteuil assez confortable (la structure générale et la plus grande partie du lexique de sa propre langue)' ('Lire Chamoiseau', in Maryse Condé and Madeleine Cottenet-Hage (eds), *Penser la créolité*, pp. 153–72, p. 164).

17 The distinctively oral style in which she opens her narrative is characteristic of the whole: 'A beau dire à beau faire, la vie ne se mesure jamais à l'aune de ses douleurs. Ainsi, moi-même Marie-Sophie Laborieux, malgré l'eau de mes larmes, j'ai toujours vu le monde dessous la bonne lumière. Mais combien de malheureux ont tué autour de moi l'existence de leurs corps?' (Chamoiseau, *Texaco* (Paris: Gallimard, 1992), p. 47).

18 The privileging of spoken over written language could also be analysed in Derridean terms as phonocentrism and 'the metaphysics of presence'. In the first chapter of *De la grammatologie* (Paris: Éditions de Minuit, 1967) he defines phonocentrism as 'proximité absolue de la voix et de l'être, de la voix et du sens de l'être', and goes on to say: 'On pressent donc déjà que le phonocentrisme se confond avec la détermination historiale de l'être en général comme présence' (p. 23). The notion of presence is entirely congruent with the ideology of consumerism, in which, as I have already argued, the object, in order to be consumed, must be immediately and unproblematically present.

19 Bakhtin's concepts of dialogism and heteroglossia have, however, been adapted to a cross-cultural context by James Clifford, *The Predicament of Culture* (Cambridge, MA: Harvard University Press, 1988). See pp. 41–50.

20 Glissant's *Mahagony* is an excellent Caribbean example of a dialogic novel, as I suggest in chapter 8. Also, a particular type of double-voiced discourse is *skaz* or oral vernacular first-person narration, typical of Russian folktales, which defines the narration of, for example, *Texaco*. See *Dostoevsky*, p. 185, pp. 190–91.

21 'The consciousnesses of other people cannot be perceived, analyzed, defined as things – one can only *relate to them dialogically*. To think about them means to *talk with them: otherwise they immediately turn to us their objectivized side*' (*Dostoevsky*, p. 68, italics original).

22 'La littérature créolophone des Antilles-Guyane', p. 62. Jacques André links the fear of being assimilated/devoured to the suffocating presence of the 'mother' country: 'Au désir d'assimiler a succédé la crainte d'être absorbé/détruit. L'abondance de l'aide, l'invite étouffante à consommer, l'absolu de la prise en charge et de l'assistance, le vampirisme de l'émigration, autant

d'atteintes au sentiment même d'exister, autant de menaces mises au compte d'une mère orale: dévorante et insatiable' (*L'Inceste focal dans la famille noire antillaise* (Paris: PUF, 1987) p. 257).

23  See Lacan, 'Le stade du miroir comme formateur de la fonction du Je', in *Écrits* vol. 1, pp. 89–97. For Althusser's use of the mirror stage, see for example his *Pour Marx* (Paris: Maspero, 1966), p. 240.

24  'L'idéologie, qu'elle soit religieuse, politique, morale, juridique ou artistique, transforme elle aussi son objet: la "conscience" des hommes' (*Pour Marx*, p. 168); 'Une idéologie existe toujours dans un appareil et sa pratique, ou ses pratiques. Cette existence est matérielle' ('Idéologie et appareils idéologiques d'État', in Althusser, *Positions (1964–1975)* (Paris: Éditions Sociales, 1976), p. 105.

25  'Toute idéologie interpelle les individus concrets en sujets concrets, par le fonctionnement de la catégorie du sujet' ('Idéologie et appareils idéologiques d'État', p. 113).

### Chapter Four

1  Roger Toumson, 'Deux figures du destin', *Portulan*, 2 (1998), pp. 9–18.

2  *Réflexions sur la question juive* (Paris: Gallimard, 1947). Daniel-Henri Pageaux comments: 'Juifs et Noirs traversent l'œuvre de Jean-Paul Sartre. Ils apparaissent, d'un point de vue littéraire, sous des formes diverses: types, motifs, thèmes. Mais la condition juive et la condition noire, la "situation" juive et la "situation" noire, pour reprendre un mot clé de la pensée sartrienne, sont problématisées dans deux textes qui ont fait date. Parus quasiment coup sur coup, dans les premières années de l'après-guerre, *Réflexions sur la question juive* et "Orphée noir" [...] constituent encore aujourd'hui une double leçon de lucidité et de courage' ('Sartre, les Juifs, les Noirs ... et les autres', *Portulan*, 2 (1998), pp. 229–46, p. 229).

3  'Quand il s'agit du Juif, le problème est net: on s'en méfie, car il veut posséder les richesses ou s'installer aux postes de commande. Le nègre, lui, est fixé au génital; ou du moins on l'y a fixé. Deux domaines: l'intellect et le sexuel' (*Peau noire, masques blancs*, p. 136).

4  Finkielkraut's notorious interview with the Israeli newspaper *Ha'aretz* (17 November 2005), although mainly directed at Muslim Africans, contains the claim that: 'If you want to put the Holocaust and slavery on the same plane, then you have to lie. Because [slavery] was not a Holocaust' ('Quelle sorte de Français sont-ils?' (http://questionscritiques.free.fr/edito/haaretz/finkielkraut_171105.htm). See also Jean-Yves Camus' account of the extent to which the campaign during the 1990s to get the French government to publicly recognize the role France played in the slave trade modelled itself on the Jewish community's campaign for recognition of French responsibility for the holocaust ('The Commemoration of Slavery in France and the Emergence of a Black Political Consciousness', *The European Legacy*, 11.6 (2006), pp. 647–55).

5 Kristeva, 'Le mot, le dialogue et le roman', p. 83, italics original. Therefore, as John Frow formulates it: 'The form of representation of intertextual structures ranges from the explicit to the implicit. In addition, these structures may be highly particular or highly general [...] Texts are made out of cultural and ideological norms; out of the conventions of genre; out of styles and idioms embedded in the language; out of connotations and collocative sets; out of clichés, formulae, or proverbs; and out of other texts [...] What is relevant to textual interpretation is not, in itself, the identification of a particular intertextual source but the more general discursive structure (genre, discursive formation, ideology) to which it belongs.' John Frow, 'Intertextuality and ontology', in Michael Worton and Judith Still (eds), *Intertextuality: theories and practices* (Manchester and New York: Manchester University Press, 1990), pp. 45–55, pp. 45–46.

6 Placoly, *La Vie et la mort de Marcel Gonstran* (Paris: Denoël, 1971).

7 Samuel Selvon, *The Lonely Londoners* (London: Longman, 1956). The name of Selvon's central character, Moses, is another obvious reference to the Old Testament.

8 Daniel Maragnes, 'L'identité et le désastre (origine et fondation)', *Portulan*, 2 (1998), pp. 273–80.

9 Sam Haigh analyses the 'racial melancholia' suffered by both Maréchal and Man Ya in 'Migration and Melancholia: From Kristeva's "dépression nationale" to Pineau's "maladie de l'exil"', *French Studies*, 60.2 (2006), pp. 232–50.

10 See Haigh's 'Migration and Melancholia' for a detailed analysis of Maréchal's ambivalent melancholic/euphoric attitude to migration to France.

11 Although Pineau also seems to echo Fanon quite closely here, in the distinction he makes between the Jew whose appearance does not necessarily declare his race, and the black person who is always immediately recognizable as such (*Peau noire, masques blancs*, p. 95).

12 André Schwarz-Bart, *Le Dernier des Justes* (Paris: Éditions du Seuil, 1959).

13 *Discours sur le colonialisme* (Paris: Présence Africaine, 1955), pp. 11–12.

14 Myriam Warner-Vieyra's *Le Quimboiseur l'avait dit* (Paris and Dakar: Présence Africaine, 1980), whose protagonist is a young Guadeloupean girl forcibly interned in a mental hospital in France, is another example of the theme of exile as psychiatric incarceration.

15 See Martin Munro, *Shaping and Reshaping the Caribbean*, for an analysis of the image of Africa in Césaire's poetry and plays.

16 Selvon's *The Lonely Londoners* expresses a rather similar ambivalence towards the prospect of returning to the Caribbean; in the novel's closing pages Moses reflects on his constant postponement of the decision to return home and starts to wonder whether he really wants to leave London: 'Every year he vowing to go back to Trinidad, but after the winter gone and birds sing [...] and

then the old sun shining, is as if life start all over again, as if it still have time, as if it still have another chance [...] but it reach a stage, and he know it reach that stage, where he get so accustom to the pattern that he can't do anything about it [...] Why you don't go back to Trinidad. What happening man, what happening' (pp. 140–41).

17  Indeed, in the notes at the end of the novel, Simone apologizes to her Martinican friends for using Guadeloupean rather than Martinican Creole phrases in the text (p. 213).

18  Kathleen Gyssels emphasizes the 'traumatic' nature of Mariotte's actual memories of Martinique (*Filles de solitude: essai sur l'identité antillaise dans les (auto)biographies de Simone et André Schwarz-Bart* (Paris: L'Harmattan, 1996), p. 190).

## Chapter Five

1  Condé, in Françoise Pfaff, *Entretiens avec Maryse Condé* (Paris: Karthala, 1993), p. 49.

2  Régis Antoine, 'Postface', in Pfaff, *Entretiens*, p. 179; Leah Hewitt, 'Condé's Critical Seesaw', *Callaloo*, 18.3 (1995), pp. 641–51, p. 641.

3  Pfaff, *Entretiens*, p. 49.

4  'Habiter ce pays, la Guadeloupe', p. 13. Her realism does, of course, involve a particular attitude towards that reality, one which emphasizes its disorder and unpredictability; as Leah Hewitt writes: '[Condé's] particular version of the literary real is defined by its heterogeneity, contradictions, myriad assimilations (resistances, displacements), and, most important, its critical self-consciousness' (*Autobiographical Tightropes: Simone de Beauvoir, Nathalie Sarraute, Marguerite Duras, Monique Wittig, and Maryse Condé* (Lincoln, NE: University of Nebraska Press, 1990), p. 167.

5  This is evident from many of the titles of critical studies on Condé, for instance: Alain Baudot, 'Maryse Condé ou la parole du refus', *Recherche, Pédagogie et Culture*, 57 (1982), pp. 30–35; N. Araujo (ed.), *L'Œuvre de Maryse Condé: questions et réponses à propos d'une écrivaine politiquement incorrecte* (Paris: L'Harmattan, 1996); Lisa Bernstein, 'Demythifying the Witch's Identity as Social Critique in Maryse Condé's *I, Tituba, Witch of Salem*', *Social Identities*, 3.1 (1997), pp. 77–89; Madeleine Cottenet-Hage and Lydie Moudileno (eds), *Maryse Condé. Une nomade inconvenante* (Guadeloupe: Ibis rouge Éditions, 2002).

6  *Traversée de la mangrove* (Paris: Mercure de France, 1989). See for instance Lydie Moudileno, 'Les Écrivains de Maryse Condé: face à la filiation et à l'affiliation', in her *L'Écrivain antillais au miroir de sa littérature* (Paris: Karthala, 1997); Jean-Xavier Ridon, 'Maryse Condé et le fantôme d'une communauté inopérante', in Christiane Albert (ed.), *Francophonie et identités culturelles* (Paris: Karthala, 1999), pp. 211–26; P. ffrench, 'Community in

Maryse Condé's *Traversée de la mangrove*', *French Forum*, 22.1 (1997), pp. 93–105.

7 *Mythologies* (Paris: Éditions du Seuil, 1957). Barthes has occasionally figured in studies of Condé's work. Ann Smock uses his concept of the 'punctum' in her article on *Les Derniers Rois mages* ('Maryse Condé's *Les Derniers Rois mages*', *Callaloo*, 18.3 (1995), pp. 668–88); Delphine Perret refers to Barthes' *Le Plaisir du texte* (Paris: Éditions du Seuil, 1973) in her 'L'écriture mosaïque de *Traversée de la Mangrove*', in Maryse Condé (ed.), *L'Héritage de Caliban* (Pointe-à-Pitre: Éditions Jasor, 1992), pp. 187–200, p. 189.

8 Interview with Marie-Clotilde Jacquey and Monique Hugon, 'L'Afrique, un continent difficile', *Notre Librairie*, 74 (1984), pp. 21–25, p. 24. In a slightly different context Mireille Rosello comments: 'Condé's discourse shows that she is keenly aware that the island is a discursive, symbolic and evolving construction rather than a natural reality' ('Caribbean insularization of identities in Maryse Condé's work from *En attendant le bonheur* to *Les Derniers Rois mages*', *Callaloo*, 18.3 (1995), pp. 565–78, p. 570.)

9 'L'écriture mosaïque de *Traversée de la Mangrove*', p. 197.

10 'Introduction à l'analyse structurale des récits', *Communications*, 8 (1966), pp. 1–27, p. 7. Henceforth 'Introduction'.

11 '[T]oute unité qui appartient à un certain niveau ne prend de sens que si elle peut s'intégrer dans un niveau supérieur [...] Pour mener une analyse structurale, il faut donc d'abord distinguer plusieurs instances de description et placer ces instances dans une perspective hiérarchique (intégratoire)' ('Introduction', p. 5). Thus the three levels of narrative structure that he identifies are 'liés entre eux selon un mode d'intégration progressive: une fonction n'a de sens que pour autant qu'elle prend place dans l'action générale d'un actant' (p. 6).

12 Pfaff, *Entretiens*, p. 106. Suzanne Crosta also refers to Condé's subversive 'manipulation of the conventions of detective plots' in her 'Narrative and discursive strategies in Maryse Condé's *Traversée de la mangrove*', *Callaloo*, 15.1 (1992), pp. 147–55, p. 154.

13 An example is Sancher's cryptic 'Est-ce que tu as entendu parler de Carlotta?' (p. 97). This breaks another rule of the hermeneutic code, that the referents of its clues should be likely to be known by the average reader: 'Carlotta' divides the text's readership into the (presumably) small minority of ageing left-wing intellectuals who recognize that the reference is to 'Operation Carlotta', the Cuban intervention in Angola in 1976, versus the majority who do not. A detailed account of the campaign can be found in Gabriel Garcia Marquez's article 'Operation Carlotta', *New Left Review*, 101–2 (1977), pp. 123–37.

14 Suzanne Crosta comments that 'It is impossible to reconstruct the identity of the deceased because the referential data is sometimes misleading, sometimes suppressed, sometimes exaggerated, sometimes altered altogether'

('Narrative and discursive strategies', p. 153). I would add that it is also often impossible to decide what counts as 'referential data' in the first place.

15 Rosello outlines a parallel between the presentation of geographical places in Condé's *Les Derniers Rois mages* (Paris: Mercure de France, 1992) – 'None is really more important, or more original, or more authentic than any other' – and 'the paratactic structure of the novel (the constant and sudden leaps from one character to another, one story to another, the retelling of episodes at various times and various junctures in the book)' ('Caribbean insularization of identities', p. 574).

16 'L'ironie joue le rôle d'une affiche et par là détruit la multivalence qu'on pouvait espérer d'un discours citationnel. Un texte multivalent n'accomplit pas jusqu'au bout sa duplicité constitutive que [...] s'il n'attribue pas ses énoncés (même dans l'intention de les discréditer) à des autorités explicites, s'il déjoue tout respect de l'origine, de la paternité, de la propriété' (*S/Z*, p. 51).

17 See *S/Z*, pp. 210–12. He stresses how difficult it is to 'critiquer le stéréotype (de le vomir) sans recourir à un nouveau stéréotype: celui de l'ironie' (p. 212). These cultural stereotypes and their ironic treatment are far more prominent in *Les Derniers Rois mages* – 'a scathing satire of the religion of racial heritage' (Smock, 'Maryse Condé's *Les Derniers Rois mages*', p. 671) – than in *Traversée de la mangrove*.

18 Jean-Bertrand Aristide was of course a key political figure in Haiti from the mid-1980s until his election as president in 1990. If Condé has named her weak and selfish character after him, this would constitute another example of Barthes' classical irony. In any case, the juxtaposition here of 'Aristide' with the topic of Haitian elections serves to blur further the hierarchy of meanings.

19 Mohammed Taleb-Khyar, 'An Interview with Maryse Condé and Rita Dove', *Callaloo*, 14.2 (1991), pp. 347–66, p. 351.

20 Michael Lucey, 'Voices accounting for the Past: Maryse Condé's *Traversée de la Mangrove*', in Maryse Condé (ed.), *L'Héritage de Caliban*, pp. 123–32, p. 132.

## Chapter Six

1 For instance: Françoise Lionnet, *Autobiographical Voices: Race, Gender, Self-Portraiture* (Ithaca, NY and London: Cornell University Press, 1989), and *Postcolonial Representations: Women, Literature, Identity* (Ithaca, NY and London: Cornell University Press, 1995); Sidonie Smith and Julia Watson (eds), *Women, Autobiography, Theory* (Madison, WI: Wisconsin University Press, 1998); Carole Boyce Davies and Elaine Savory Fido (eds), *Out of the Kumbla: Caribbean Women and Literature* (Trenton, NJ: Africa World Press, 1990); Joanne M. Braxton, *Black Women Writing Autobiography* (Philadelphia, PA: Temple University Press, 1989); Mary Jean Green, Karen Gould and Micheline Rice-Maximin (eds), *Postcolonial Subjects: Francophone*

*Women Writers* (Minneapolis, MN: Minnesota University Press, 1996); Carole Boyce Davies, *Black Women, Writing, and Identity: Migrations of the Subject* (London and New York: Routledge, 1997).

2 Betty Wilson, 'Introduction' to Miriam Warner-Vieyra, *Juletane*, translated by Betty Wilson (London: Heinemann, 1981), pp. v–xv, p. ix.

3 Christiane Chaulet-Achour describes this as a 'ronde de pronoms personnels', and shows in detail how in all three of Maximin's novels 'l'écriture [...] refuse le "sujet plein" et multiplie les énonciateurs et les points de vue pour interroger les représentations individuelles et collectives' (*La Trilogie caribéenne de Daniel Maximin* (Paris: Karthala, 2000), p. 15). On a different level, the 'voice' of the text is also problematized by its very high level of intertextuality. It contains fragments from a large number of French Caribbean and French writers, as well as from Maximin's own earlier novels. Most readers will probably recognize just enough of them to guess how many more there must be. The experience of reading Maximin is thus one of peculiar uncertainty, because one is never sure of the origin of what one is reading: is this the author's voice, or is it a quotation from another writer? As a result, the status of Marie-Gabriel's voice, already circumscribed as we have seen, is further undermined by the uncertainty surrounding the narrative voice that ostensibly frames it. Ronnie Scharfman describes the similar structure of Maximin's first novel *L'Isolé soleil* (Paris: Éditions du Seuil, 1981) as 'permeated by and with other voices, constituted by them, so that the authority of authorial voices is multiplied and therefore relational rather than hierarchical. The writing itself seems to enjoy that undifferentiated moment in human development which Freud characterized as polymorphously perverse' ('Rewriting the Césaires', in Maryse Condé (ed.), *L'Héritage de Caliban* (Pointe-à-Pitre, Guadeloupe: Éditions Jasor, 1992), pp. 233–45, p. 235).

4 For example, Glissant's *Malemort* and *La Case du commandeur*; Vincent Placoly's *La Vie et la mort de Marcel Gonstran* and *L'Eau de mort guildive* (Paris: Denoël, 1973); and Simone Schwarz-Bart's *Pluie et vent sur Télumée Miracle*.

5 Simon Gikandi, *Writing in Limbo: Modernism and Caribbean Literature* (Ithaca, NY and London: Cornell University Press, 1992).

6 'Feminist Studies/Critical Studies: Issues, Terms and Contexts' in Teresa de Lauretis (ed.), *Feminist Studies/Critical Studies* (Bloomington, IN: Indiana University Press, 1986), pp. 1–19, p. 10.

7 As Smith and Watson put it, 'Numerous critics have argued for the multivoicedness of women's autobiographical texts as a crucial way to reframe issues of agency and ideological interpellation' ('Introduction', *Women, Autobiography, Theory*, pp. 30–31).

8 'Experience', in S. Smith and J. Watson (eds), *Women, Autobiography, Theory*, pp. 57–71, p. 66.

9 Unlike de Lauretis, however, Lionnet sees this as more or less continuous

with the poststructuralist conception of the subject: 'The past [...] is represented and redefined according to criteria that correspond roughly to the decentering of the subject effected by contemporary philosophy' (p. 175).

10 'We have to articulate [...] new concepts that allow us to think *otherwise*, to bypass the ancient symmetries and dichotomies that have governed the ground and the very condition of possibility of thought, of "clarity", in all of Western philosophy. *Métissage* is such a concept and a practice: it is the site of undecidability and indeterminacy, where solidarity becomes the fundamental principle of political action against hegemonic languages' (*Autobiographical Voices*, p. 57).

11 E.g., Simon Gikandi, *Writing in Limbo*; Françoise Lionnet, *Postcolonial Representations*; Chris Bongie, *Islands and Exiles: The Creole Identities of Postcolonial Literature* (Stanford, CA: Stanford University Press, 1998). See also the debate between Linda Hutcheon ('Circling the Downspout of Empire') and Diana Brydon ('The White Inuit Speaks') in Ian Adam and Helen Tiffin (eds), *Past the Last Post: Theorizing Post-Colonialism and Post-Modernism* (Brighton: Harvester, 1991), pp. 9–16, 191–203. Glissant is a good example of a writer whose novels have followed this trajectory, from the 'modernist' *Le Quatrième Siècle, Malemort* and *La Case du commandeur* to the 'postmodern' *Mahagony, Tout-monde* and *Sartorius* (Paris: Gallimard, 1999).

12 Jeanne Perrault, 'Autography/Transformation/Asymmetry', in Smith and Watson (eds), *Women, Autobiography, Theory*, pp. 190–96, p. 191.

13 Dominique Chancé gives an explicitly Lacanian interpretation of Maximin's novels, arguing that their subject is brought into existence through the play of unconscious signifiers (*L'Auteur en souffrance*, pp. 150–55).

14 'Là est proprement la pulsation temporelle où s'institue ce qui est la caractéristique du départ de l'inconscient comme tel – la fermeture [...] l'*aphanisis* est à situer [...] au niveau où le sujet se manifeste dans ce mouvement de disparition que j'ai qualifié de létal. D'une autre façon encore, j'ai appelé ce mouvement le *fading* du sujet' (Lacan, *Les Quatre Concepts fondamentaux de la psychanalyse (Le Séminaire Livre XI)* (Paris: Éditions du Seuil, 1973), p. 232).

15 The impermanent, insecure quality of the Caribbean house and its significance in fiction have been less positively evaluated by Edward Kamau Brathwaite, who comments on the difficulty that the West Indian writer has in writing about houses that do not conform to the Western European norms of solidity and clearly defined boundaries ('Houses in the West Indian Novel', *The Literary Half Yearly*, 17.1 (1976), pp. 111–21).

16 Christiane Chaulet-Achour comments in similar vein, but without developing the idea further, that 'Le discours du roman s'empare du vide – comment accepter le cataclysme à l'échelle de l'humain? – pour se construire et aider à vivre' (*Trilogie caribéenne*, p. 194).

17 Once again Ronnie Scharfman's comments on *L'Isolé soleil* apply equally

to *L'Île et une nuit*: 'In this text of generational engenderings, lateral relations are always valorized just as positively as parental ones – perhaps even more' ('Rewriting the Césaires', p. 237).

18  This can involve a temporal reversal. The idea of growing roots from the present back into the past, hence reversing the direction of heredity and filiation, is exemplified in Marie-Gabriel's reconnecting herself to the mother she has never known in a backwards movement which her mother anticipates in her diary as: 'Mon enfant se recréera une mère en moi comme une nouvelle source remodèle la mer à son débouché' (p. 80). Lydie Moudileno discusses this curious imaginary relationship which allows the daughter to 's'inscrire dans l'Histoire en renversant les jeux d'ascendance et de descendance' (*L'Ecrivain antillais au miroir de sa littérature*, p. 187).

19  Paul Gilroy, *The Black Atlantic: Modernity and Double Consciousness* (Cambridge, MA: Harvard University Press, 1993).

20  Another intertextual allusion: a short section of Glissant's *Poétique de la relation* (pp. 49–54) is titled 'Une errance enracinée'.

## Chapter Seven

1  These are elaborated in chapters XIX, XX and XXI of Benveniste's *Problèmes de linguistique générale*.

2  Glissant sees this conceptualization of the past as one of the deepest differences between European and American literature (i.e., the literature of the American continent, including the Caribbean), with the latter as a whole participating in the chaotic 'presence' of the past. He writes: 'Le romancier américain, quelle que soit la zone culturelle à laquelle il appartient, n'est pas du tout à la recherche d'un temps perdu, mais se trouve, se débat, dans un temps éperdu. Et, de Faulkner à Carpentier, on est en présence de sortes de fragments de durée qui sont engloutis dans des amoncellements ou des vertiges' (*DA*, p. 254).

3  Or, as Papa Longoué says: 'Car le passé est en haut bien groupé sur lui-même, et si loin; mais tu le provoques, il démarre comme un troupeaux de taureaux, bientôt il tombe sur ta tête plus vite qu'un cayali touché à l'arbalète' (p. 213).

4  This is the name given in Martinique to the men who are descendants of the African sorcerers, with powers of healing and magic.

5  For instance, Mathieu protests: 'Ce qui veut dire que je ne crois pas! L'abbé qui porte une épée, c'est dans les gravures, pas dans le pays! […] Ensuite, parce que nous connaissons géreurs et commandeurs sans oublier les économes, pourquoi veux-tu qu'on les appelle géreurs et commandeurs, dans le temps […] – Foutez-moi la paix, dit majestueusement le vieillard (p. 122).

6  An alternative explanation for the ambiguity attaching to *histoire* might be that it is designed to subvert the notion of omniscient narrative *per se*; but

this is very unlikely, given the *importance* of the events recounted in *histoire*, which makes it difficult to read them as a mere pretext for the undermining of a particular form of narration – a project which is, in any case, largely alien to Glissant's fiction as a whole, as I have discussed in the Introduction.

7 Glissant in fact sees the development of magical realism in American literature as a direct consequence of the necessity, and the difficulty, of representing *history* – 'La misère de nos pays [...] comporte une dimension d'histoire (d'histoire non évidente) dont le seul réalisme ne rend pas compte [...] Jacques Stéphen Alexis a compris cette nécessité de ne pas utiliser sans détour les techniques du réalisme quand il a développé une théorie du *réalisme merveilleux* dans la littérature haïtienne (*DA*, p. 198).

8 In the critical literature on Glissant's work this theme has received considerable attention, particularly when the *prise de parole* takes the form of *naming*. In an article titled 'Se nommer soi-même', for example, Priska Degras refers to the 'douleur ancienne des noms imposés que transcende ou annule parfois la décision d'inventer son "nom propre"' (59), and argues that 'Le Nom, le Nom propre, le nom de famille est en effet déjà langage: c'est lui qui permet de donner forme et cohérence à une obscurité et un désordre anciens, c'est lui qui permet aussi l'articulation d'un indicible (innommable) passé et d'un futur à inventer' ('Se nommer soi-même', *Carbet*, 10 (1990), pp. 57–64, p. 61).

9 Nathaniel Wing makes a rather similar point on 'la vérité historique produite dans ces romans', concluding that: 'Les récits sont vrais non parce qu'ils reproduisent et interprètent les événements et les acteurs d'un passé compris dans un développement logique et consécutif, mais ils sont vrais parce qu'ils mettent en relation les épisodes, les inventions, les bribes de prophéties, les paroles des protagonistes, constituant ainsi l'appréhension d'un passé complexe, non dévolu mais vivant encore dans les actes et dans l'imaginaire des acteurs' ('Écriture et relation dans les romans d'Édouard Glissant' in Yves-Alain Favre (ed.), *Horizons d'Édouard Glissant* (Biarritz: J. & D. Éditeurs, 1992), pp. 296–303, pp. 298–99.).

## Chapter Eight

1 It belongs rather to the dialectical strand in Glissant's thought: reality is not a given state of affairs, but a constant process of change driven by its contradictions. I discuss this in more detail in the context of his later texts in chapter 11.

2 *Poétique de la Relation* (Paris: Gallimard, 1990).

3 I have discussed these different conceptions of community more generally in *The Sense of Community in French Caribbean Fiction* (Liverpool: Liverpool University Press, 2008), in relation to Jean-Luc Nancy's concepts of 'common being' and 'being-in-common'; chapter 2 of the book analyses the similarities and differences between Glissant's and Nancy's views of community.

4 Michael Dash, 'Le Roman de nous', *Carbet*, 10 (1990), pp. 21–31, p. 30.

5 Bernadette Cailler, *Les Conquérants de la nuit nue: Édouard Glissant et l'H(h)istoire antillaise* (Tübingen: Gunther Narr, 1988), p. 163.

6 Jean-Yves Debreuille, 'Le langage désancré de *Malemort*', in Yves-Alain Favre (ed.), *Horizons d'Édouard Glissant* (Biarritz: J. & D. Éditeurs, 1992), pp. 319–28, pp. 324–25.

7 Glissant, *La Lézarde* (Paris: Éditions du Seuil, 1958).

8 In answer to a question about the connection between *La Case du commandeur*'s narrative style and 'verbal delirium', Glissant stresses the latter's significance as a mode of understanding and enlightenment: 'Le délire verbal est une projection désespérée vers une syntaxe, un ordre de raisons, une relation au monde, dont on cherche sinon à maîtriser du moins à vivre continûment le déroulement. N'est-ce pas là, au désespoir près, le statut de l'écrivain dans nos pays?' ('Entretien du *CARÉ* avec Édouard Glissant', *CARÉ*, 10 (1983), pp. 17–25, p. 25).

9 As Cailler comments, 'Si le narrateur est "omniscient", et il l'est dans *La Case du commandeur*, cette omniscience est d'une nature vraiment communautaire, non attachée à des catégories individualistes du sujet' (*Les Conquérants de la nuit nue*, p. 166).

10 Barbara Webb makes the point that by this kind of presentation Glissant is working against the Western tradition that tends to isolate the individual from the community: 'The source of [Marie Celat's] alienation is not conflict with her community but the lack of community. The "we" narrator stands as a constant reminder of this absence' (Barbara Webb, *Myth and History in Caribbean Fiction* (Amherst, MA: University of Massachusetts Press, 1992), p. 123).

11 I have also discussed this question in 'La poétique du relais dans *Mahagony* et *Tout-Monde*', in Jacques Chevrier (ed.), *Poétiques d'Édouard Glissant* (Paris: Presses de l'Université de Paris-Sorbonne, 1993), pp. 169–78.

12 Nathaniel Wing, 'Écriture et relation dans les romans d'Édouard Glissant', p. 297, italics original.

13 Or, as Catherine Mayaux puts it: 'Loin d'enfermer le réel dans un prisme, ces multiples points de vue semblent au contraire étendre le champ de vision et pousser plus loin l'investigation des autres et du monde' ('La structure romanesque de *Mahagony* d'Édouard Glissant' in Favre (ed.), *Horizons d'Édouard Glissant*, pp. 349–63, p. 359).

## Chapter Nine

1 'L'écrivain et le souffle du lieu', interview with Lise Gauvin, given in Martinique in 1993, reprinted in Glissant, *Introduction à une poétique du divers* (Paris: Gallimard, 1996), pp. 129–35, p. 129.

2  In their *Mille Plateaux*, in particular the opening chapter: 'Introduction au rhizome' (pp. 9–38), which is a revised version of their earlier short text *Rhizome* (Paris: Minuit, 1976).

3  Glissant, *Traité du tout-monde* (Paris: Gallimard, 1997).

4  For instance, in novels which are often seen as having inaugurated the region's literature, such as René Maran's *Batouala* (Paris: A. Michel, 1921) or Joseph Zobel's *La Rue Cases-Nègres* (Paris: J. Froissart, 1950). See also Betty Wilson's characterization of French Caribbean women's writing, quoted in chapter 6.

5  Another piece of evidence for my argument that the boundary between fiction and the (autobiographical) real is not simply erased, but made the object of questioning and play is the occurrence of Glissant's name in the text as an author of 'real' works of fiction, but juxtaposed with the works of an unnamed 'fictional' author, in the speech of a 'real' author (Maurice Roche): '"Et de fait," faisait observer Maurice [...] "avez-vous noté les analogies de titre avec les romans de Glissant? L'un a écrit *La Lézarde*, l'autre *La Tarentule*, celui-là *Le Quatrième Siècle*, celui-ci *L'An II*, vous ne trouvez pas ça troublant?"' (p. 266). (The 'Sur les noms' appendix at the end of the book notes enigmatically that 'L'auteur de *La Tarentule* se fera connaître quand il publiera ses livres' (p. 515).

6  'Introduction à l'analyse structurale des récits', p. 7. See chapter 5.

7  While this is clearly similar to the 'relaying' of narrators in *Mahagony* analysed in chapter 8, the much greater elusiveness of these *sujets d'énonciation* would also suggest that they serve less to embody the ideal of 'relational' collective identity than a problematizing of narrative voice in the text.

8  These are the women who travel round the Caribbean buying up and re-selling objects for tourists: so-called local carvings, cheap jewellery, etc.

9  Simon's *Triptyques* (Paris: Minuit, 1973), for instance, juxtaposes three locations, each of which figures as a picture of some kind in the two others, so that none of them can be established as the 'real' setting. See Lucien Dällenbach, *Le Récit spéculaire* (Paris: Seuil, 1977), pp. 163–68.

10  I discuss this further in chapter 11.

11  Interestingly, however, Gérard Genette sees the deconstruction of the opposition between identity and difference as a central feature of Robbe-Grillet's fiction – but in a far more formalist way. Gérard Genette, 'Vertige fixé', in his *Figures I* (Paris: Éditions du Seuil, 1966), pp. 69–90.

## Chapter Ten

1  'Édouard Glissant avec *Les Périphériques vous parlent*', novembre 2002. http://www.lesperipheriques.org/article.php3?id_article=34.

2  The Caribbean migrants who are described as 'le sel de la Diversité', for instance: 'ils ont dépassé les limites et les frontières, ils mélangent les langages,

ils déménagent les langues, ils transbahutent, ils tombent dans la folie du monde' (*TM*, p. 407).

3 The criticism here is implicitly directed at the authors of *Éloge de la créolité*, with whom, as we have already seen (chapter 2), Glissant had a markedly ambivalent relationship. In *Introduction à une poétique du divers* he writes: 'Certains défenseurs du créole sont complètement fermés à cette problématique. Ils entendent défendre le créole de manière monolingue, à la manière de ceux qui les ont opprimés linguistiquement. Ils héritent de ce monolinguisme sectaire et ils défendent leur langue à mon avis d'une mauvaise manière' (p. 113).

4 This is not the case in *l'Intention poétique*, where he is still assuming that multilingualism in the ordinary sense will become the norm in the future (*IP*, p. 45).

5 *Le Quatrième Siècle*, similarly, contains an important scene in which the maroon Longoué meets, in the forest, the plantation owner from whom he escaped ten years previously; rather than speaking to each other in Creole, each chooses to use their mother tongue – respectively, the African language which Longoué has not used for years, and standard French – so that they cannot in fact understand what the other is saying but choose to remain 'respectueux [...] de cette incompréhension mutuelle dans laquelle ils se retrouvaient solidaires' (p. 111).

6 Ferdinand de Saussure, *Cours de linguistique générale* (Paris: Payot, 1968), p. 31.

7 Britton, *Édouard Glissant and Postcolonial Theory: Strategies of Language and Resistance* (Charlottesville, VA and London: University Press of Virginia, 1999), pp. 25–30, 140–48.

8 Derek Bickerton's schema of 'levels' of Creole has been influential in francophone conceptualizations of Creole, such as the work of Jean Bernabé and the GEREC group at the Université des Antilles-Guyane. Bickerton analyses Creole as a continuum going from a 'basilect' through a 'mesolect' to an 'acrolect' which shades off into the standard language; in other words, exactly the model of unfixed, permeable frontiers that Glissant is also putting forward. See Bickerton, *Dynamics of a Creole System* (Cambridge: Cambridge University Press, 1975); Jean Bernabé, *Fondal-Natal: grammaire basilectale approchée des créoles guadeloupéens et martiniquais* (Paris: L'Harmattan, 1983).

9 The English term 'language' covers both of these and does not allow one to make the distinction between them, so I am retaining the French terms in my discussion.

10 *Langage* thus acts as the basis for the concept of counter-poetics, which results from the struggle Antillean speakers have in constructing for themselves a means of expression that simultaneously *uses* and *contests* the existing languages that are in theory available to them – Creole, but more particularly

standard metropolitan French. 'Counter-poetics' both reflects and resolves the tension with which, as postcolonial subjects, they relate to the colonizer's language. I discuss this more fully in *Édouard Glissant and Postcolonial Theory*, pp. 30–34.

11 See Maurice Merleau-Ponty: *Signes* (Paris: Gallimard, 1960; translated into English by Richard G. McGleary, *Signs* (Evanston, IL: Northwestern University Press, 1964).

12 A little later in *Traité du tout-monde*, Glissant elaborates on the poet's relation to *langue* and *langage* to emphasize even more clearly the *creative* force of the latter: 'Le poète, par-delà cette langue dont il use, mais mystérieusement dans la langue même, â même la langue et dans sa marge, est un bâtisseur de langage' (p. 122).

13 It is significant in this context that in *L'Intention poétique* and *Le Discours antillais*, *langage* is seen as a collective phenomenon, while in the later work individuals create their own particular *langage*. This is especially true of individuals whose lives are marked by displacement and migration; a striking example in *Tout-monde* is Stepan Stepanovich, who responds to the devastation of war by creating his own 'secret' *langage* (p. 341).

14 In the section entitled 'Pour l'opacité', he contrasts opacity with the 'transparency' that reduces the other to its own norms and preconceptions: 'Si nous examinons le processus de la "compréhension" des êtres et des idées dans la perspective de la pensée occidentale, nous retrouvons à son principe l'exigence de cette transparence. Pour pouvoir te "comprendre" et donc t'accepter, il me faut ramener ton épaisseur à ce barème idéel qui me fournit motif à comparaisons et peut-être à jugements' (*PR*, p. 204).

## Chapter Eleven

1 Peter Hallward claims that '[Glissant] stands today as perhaps the most thoroughly Deleuzian writer in the francophone world' (*Absolutely Postcolonial*, p. 7).

2 *La Cohée du Lamentin* (Paris: Gallimard, 2005), pp. 88–98.

3 Dominique Chancé sees this emphasis on landscape, in Glissant and also in Césaire and Maximin, as fundamental to a conception of literature 'of the Americas' (or at least the Caribbean) as a whole: 'Ces auteurs se réfèrent a une île ou à un archipel, à ses volcans, montagnes Pelée ou Soufrière, à ses mornes, à la mer. Leur antillanité s'inscrit dans ce paysage, au-delà des clivages linguistiques, de telle sorte que leur esthétique rejoint sans difficulté celle des poètes et des écrivains de Cuba, de la Barbade ou de Sainte-Lucie' (*L'Auteur en souffrance*, p. 138–39).

4 Another rather different manifestation of this primacy of the concrete is Glissant's fascination with the opacity, the absolute particularity, of the word 'cohée', which occurs only as the name of a particular part of the beach at Le

Lamentin – a word, that is, that in linguistic terms has only one referent and no signified – which provided the challengingly opaque title for his preceding book, and to which he returns in *Une Nouvelle Région* (pp. 114–15).

5 In another indication of how far back in his life this idea goes, he at one point attributes it to his teacher at the Sorbonne, Gaston Bachelard: 'nous recevons enfin la leçon des recherches de Gaston Bachelard, et nous concevons que les couleurs des paysages […] ces couleurs que nous rapportons à l'étant du monde, sont solidaires de nos réactions les plus secrètes, ou élémentaires ou élaborées' (*NRM*, p. 73).

6 He also uses the term 'géomorphisme', which, as against an anthropomorphism which interprets the world as an extension of man, 'essaie, par un mouvement tout opposé, de ramener les constituantes des humanités prises dans leur généralité à une géographie et à une géologie poétiques qui les dépassent en les intégrant' (*NRM*, pp. 176–77).

7 Glissant also sees *perspective* as imposing a clarity and a distance which are incompatible with fusion; in assigning a distinct point of view to the artist and spectator, perspective embodies their separation from the real. He notes how, in contrast, the lack of perspective which characterizes much non-Western art draws us into the density and mobility of the real, 'dans le tourbillon et dans la spirale, où la ligne perspective n'a pas encore frayé son chemin, et nous renonçons pour le coup à la représentation, pour approcher toujours les inapprochables limailles magnétiques et les réalités tremblantes de la Trace' (*NRM*, p. 157). He gives a fuller statement of the same idea in *La Cohée du Lamentin*, p. 53.

8 See for example *Mille Plateaux*, p. 125.

9 In his *Faulkner, Mississippi* (Paris: Gallimard, 1996) Glissant already notes Faulkner's tendency to attribute to his black characters, slaves or descendants of slaves like those in Martinique, a closer relationship to the natural world than that of the white characters – a relationship which Glissant describes as a 'une science secrète' and a 'capacité de conjunction et de fusion' (p. 88). He also emphasizes Faulkner's conviction, expressed particularly in *Go Down, Moses*, that the white settlers' appropriation of the land from the Indians, by turning it into a possession, brings about 'la mort de l'ordre naturel' (pp. 165–68).

10 See chapter 4 of *Mille Plateaux*. Jean-Jacques Lecercle analyses Deleuze's pragmatics in 'Another Philosophy of Language: The New Pragmatics' in his *Deleuze and Language* (Basingstoke: Palgrave Macmillan, 2002), pp. 154–73.

11 In *La Cohée du Lamentin*, Glissant describes the interrelatedness of places through difference-repetition as 'ce qui informe le Tout-monde', and links the idea explicitly with *Mille Plateaux* (pp. 136–37).

12 E.g., 'Que l'identité n'est pas première […] qu'elle tourne autour du Différent, telle est la nature d'une révolution copernicienne qui ouvre à la différence la possibilité de son concept propre, au lieu de la maintenir sous la

domination d'un concept en général posé déjà comme identique' (*Différence et répétition*, p. 59).

13 For example, in contrasting his positive version of globalization – 'mondialité' – with the economic neo-liberalism of 'mondialisation': 'les mécanismes déshumanisés et les froids dénis des mondialisations sont à combattre d'abord par les organicités vives de la mondialité' (p. 82).

14 Indeed, the early version of fusion exemplified by the article on Reverdy values the poem's ability to *arrest* movement: 'La tâche est donc de fixer le mouvement' (*IP*, p. 77).

15 Cf also: 'Supposons qu'un peintre "représente" un oiseau; en fait, c'est un devenir-oiseau qui ne peut se faire que dans la mesure où l'oiseau est lui-même en train de devenir autre chose, pure ligne et pure couleur' (*Mille Plateaux*, p. 374).

16 As Tamsin Lorraine comments, 'The work of Gilles Deleuze develops a way of conceiving reality in terms of dynamic process that privileges difference rather than identity, movement rather than stasis, and change rather than what remains the same' ('Ahab and Becoming-Whale: The Nomadic Subject in Smooth Space', in Ian Buchanan and Gregg Lambert (eds), *Deleuze and Space* (Edinburgh: Edinburgh University Press, 2005), p. 159–75, p. 159.

17 'Deleuze's most radical anti-Hegelian argument concerns pure difference: Hegel is unable to think pure difference which is outside the horizon of identity/ contradiction; Hegel conceives a radicalized difference as contradiction which, then, through its dialectical resolution, is again subsumed under identity'. Slavoj Žižek, 'Deleuze's Platonism: Ideas as Real', http://www.lacan.com/ zizplato.htm.

18 Nick Nesbitt, *Voicing Memory: History and Subjectivity in French Caribbean Literature* (Charlottesville, VA and London: University of Virginia Press, 2003), p. 171. His argument seems to me equally applicable to *Une Nouvelle Région du monde*, which appeared after his book's publication. What he describes as 'a potent reworking of dialectical thought, inherited from Hegel and Marx, one that [...] freely adapts and reconstructs Hegelian insights' (p. 174), appears at various points in *Une Nouvelle Région*, as for example in the very Hegelian definition of being as 'la connaissance absolue et la reconnaissance de cette quantité (ou totalité réalisée) des différences' (*NRM*, p. 44); the casual alternation between the Hegelian 'totality' and the Deleuzean 'quantity' rather provocatively minimizes the conflict between them.

19 For example, 'Chaque chose, chaque être doit voir sa propre identité engloutie dans la différence, chacun n'étant plus qu'une différence entre des différences' (*Différence et répétition*, p. 79). Cf Nesbitt's comment that 'Glissant mentions Deleuze and Guattari as a more recent philosophical influence for the concept of relation (*PR*, p. 23), but the schematic definition of relation he offers there ('All *identity* extends itself in a relationship with the Other') is essentially the Hegelian one I am describing here' (*Voicing Memory*, p. 234, my italics).

20 'Remaining' in this sense echoes Glissant's long-standing concern with both *duration* and *endurance* – a concern which has perhaps been overshadowed by the more recent emphasis on vertiginous change that informs the 'Tout-monde'. In 'Le Roman des Amériques', for instance, he characterizes 'la poétique du continent américain' as being 'une quête de la durée' (*DA*, p. 254), before going on to emphasize the importance of landscape in American writing. In *Faulkner, Mississippi*, too, Glissant comments that 'endurance' is a central quality in Faulkner's conception of his black characters (p. 41), as Mary Gallagher remarks: 'Édouard Glissant notes the link between endurance and duration [...] and he suggests that endurance confers [...] the density of duration' (*Soundings in French Caribbean Writing since 1950: The Shock of Space and Time* (Oxford: Oxford University Press, 2002), pp. 85–86). But Faulkner's portrayal of the negroes' endurance is not, for Glissant, wholly positive, since it is linked to an incapacity for action and change (*Faulkner, Mississippi*, p. 41) and implies a kind of ahistorical objectification of them (pp. 83–84); whereas there is no trace of any such ambivalence in his own representation of the 'demeurés' in *Une Nouvelle Région*.

21 Marcuse, *Reason and Revolution* (New York: Humanities Press, 1954), p. 147.

22 Hegel, *Science of Logic* vol. 1 (New York: Macmillan, 1929), p. 132. In Glissant's earlier texts, such as *Introduction à une poétique du divers*, the phrase '*se changer en échangeant avec l'autre*' recurs repeatedly to define relational identity based on *unpredictable*, random change; it reappears in *Une Nouvelle Région* but in a significantly modified *dialectical* form: now it is a question of 'chaque variété ou chaque identité [...] vient à *changer en elle-même en échangeant avec les autres*' (p. 66, my italics).

23 E.g., 'un agencement, dans sa multiplicité travaille à la fois forcément sur des flux sémiotiques, des flux matériels et des flux sociaux' (*Mille Plateaux*, pp. 33–34). Cf also Ian Buchanan's characterization of deterritorialization: 'Deterritorialisation names the process whereby the very basis of one's identity, the proverbial ground beneath our feet, is eroded, washed away like the bank of a river swollen by floodwater' ('Space in the Age of Non-Place', in Buchanan and Lambert (eds), *Deleuze and Space*, pp. 16–35, p. 23).

24 Mary Gallagher points out the association, via the etymological link with what is 'dur', between ideas of duration or endurance and Glissant's place names, such as 'Malendure', or those which incorporate the word 'roche' (*Soundings in French Caribbean Writing*, p. 86).

25 See chapter 14 of *Mille Plateaux*.

### Appendix

1 At the time of this interview I was beginning to work on my book on community in French Caribbean fiction.

2  Condé, *Desirada* (Paris: Laffont, 1997).

3  Condé, *Célanire cou-coupé* (Paris: Laffont, 2000).

4  Condé, *La Vie scélérate* (Paris: Seghers, 1987).

5  Françoise Lionnet, '*Traversée de la mangrove* de Maryse Condé: vers un nouvel humanisme antillais?', *The French Review*, 66 (1993), pp. 475–86.

6  See Joseph Zobel, *La Rue Cases-Nègres*.

7  Fritz Gracchus, *Les Lieux de la mère dans les sociétés afro-américaines* (Paris: Éditions Caribéennes, 1986).

8  See Jacques André, *L'Inceste focal dans la famille noire antillaise*.

9  Condé, *La Belle Créole* (Paris: Mercure, 2001).

10  Condé's *La Migration des cœurs* (Paris: Laffont, 1995) is in part a rewriting of Emily Brontë's *Wuthering Heights*.

# Bibliography

Achebe, Chinua, 'The African Writer and the English Language', in his *Morning yet on Creation Day* (London: Heinemann, 1975), pp. 55–62.

Adam, Ian and Helen Tiffin (eds), *Past the Last Post: Theorizing Post-Colonialism and Post-Modernism* (Brighton: Harvester, 1991).

Affergan, Francis, *Exotisme et altérité* (Paris: PUF, 1987).

Ahmad, Aijaz, *In Theory: Classes, Nations, Literatures* (London: Verso, 2000).

Althusser, Louis, *Pour Marx* (Paris: Maspero, 1966).

——, 'Idéologie et appareils idéologiques d'État' in his *Positions (1964–1975)* (Paris: Éditions Sociales, 1976), pp. 67–125.

André, Jacques, *L'Inceste focal dans la famille noire antillaise* (Paris: PUF, 1987).

Antoine, Régis, *La Littérature franco-antillaise: Haiti, Guadeloupe et Martinique* (Paris: Karthala, 1992).

——, 'Postface', in Pfaff, *Entretiens* (1993), pp. 175–82.

Araujo, N. (ed.), *L'Œuvre de Maryse Condé: questions et réponses à propos d'une écrivaine politiquement incorrecte* (Paris: L'Harmattan, 1996).

Arnold, A. James, *Modernism and Negritude: The Poetry and Poetics of Aimé Césaire* (Cambridge, MA: Harvard University Press, 1981).

——, 'The Erotics of Colonialism in Contemporary French West Indian Literary Culture', *New West Indian Guide*, 68.1 & 2 (1994), pp. 5–22.

Ashcroft, Bill, Gareth Griffiths and Helen Tiffin, *The Empire Writes Back* (London: Routledge, 1989).

Bakhtin, Mikhail, *The Dialogic Imagination* (Austin, TX: University of Texas Press, 1981).

——, *Problems of Dostoevsky's Poetics* (Minneapolis, MN: University of Minnesota Press, 1984).

Barthes, Roland, *Mythologies* (Paris: Éditions du Seuil, 1957).

——, 'Introduction à l'analyse structurale des récits', *Communications*, 8 (1966), pp. 1–27.

——, *S/Z* (Paris: Éditions du Seuil, 1970).

——, *Le Plaisir du texte* (Paris: Éditions du Seuil, 1973).

Baudot, Alain, 'Maryse Condé ou la parole du refus', *Recherche, Pédagogie et Culture*, 57 (1982), pp. 30–35.

Belsey, Catherine, *Critical Practice* (London: Routledge, 1980).

Bernstein, Lisa, 'Demythifying the Witch's Identity as Social Critique in Maryse Condé's *I, Tituba, Witch of Salem*', *Social Identities*, 3.1 (1997), pp. 77–89.

Benveniste, Émile, *Problèmes de linguistique générale* (Paris: Gallimard, 1966).

Bernabé, Jean, *Fondal-Natal: grammaire basilectale approchée des créoles guadeloupéens et martiniquais* (Paris: L'Harmattan, 1983).

——, 'De la négritude à la créolité: éléments pour une approche comparée', *Études françaises*, 28.2–3 (1993), pp. 23–38.

Bernabé, Jean, Patrick Chamoiseau and Raphaël Confiant, *Éloge de la créolité* (Paris: Gallimard, 1989).

Bhabha, Homi, 'The Third Space', in Jonathan Rutherford (ed.), *Identity: Community, Culture, Difference* (London: Lawrence and Wishart, 1990), pp. 207–21.

Bickerton, Derek, *Dynamics of a Creole System* (Cambridge: Cambridge University Press, 1975).

Bongie, Chris, *Exotic Memories: Literature, Colonialism and the Fin de Siècle* (Stanford, CA: Stanford University Press, 1991).

——, *Islands and Exiles: The Creole Identities of Postcolonial Literature* (Stanford, CA: Stanford University Press, 1998).

——, *Friends and Enemies: The Scribal Politics of Post/Colonial Literature* (Liverpool: Liverpool University Press, 2008).

Bouraoui, Hédi, '*Tropiques* ou la découverte du temps de l'interprétation', *Éthiopiques*, 19 (July 1979), http://www.refer.sn/ethiopiques/imprimer-article.php3?id_article=968).

Boyce Davies, Carole, *Black Women, Writing, and Identity: Migrations of the Subject* (London and New York: Routledge, 1997).

Boyce Davies, Carole and Elaine Savory Fido (eds), *Out of the Kumbla: Caribbean Women and Literature* (Trenton, NJ: Africa World Press, 1990).

Brathwaite, Edward Kamau 'Houses in the West Indian Novel', *The Literary Half - Yearly* 17.1 (1976), pp. 111–21.

——, *History of the Voice: The Development of Nation Language in Anglophone Caribbean Poetry* (London and Port of Spain: New Beacon, 1984).

Braxton, Joanne M., *Black Women Writing Autobiography* (Philadelphia, PA: Temple University Press, 1989).

Britton, Celia, *Édouard Glissant and Postcolonial Theory: Strategies of Language and Resistance* (Charlottesville, VA and London: University Press of Virginia, 1999).

——, 'La Poétique du relais dans *Mahagony* et *Tout-Monde*', in Jacques Chevrier (ed.), *Poétiques d'Édouard Glissant* (Paris: Presses de l'Université de Paris-Sorbonne, 1999), pp. 169–78.

——, *Race and the Unconscious: Freudianism in French Caribbean Thought* (Oxford: Legenda, 2002).

——, *The Sense of Community in French Caribbean Fiction* (Liverpool: Liverpool University Press, 2008).

——, 'Secret worlds: Incommunicability and initiation in three novels by Ernest Pépin', *Francophone Postcolonial Studies*, 6.1 (2008), pp. 7–23.

——, 'Dual Identities: The Question of "Départementalisation" in Michel Leiris's *Contacts de civilisations en Martinique et en Guadeloupe*', *French Cultural Studies*, 22.1 (2011), pp. 61–72.

Brydon, Diana, 'The White Inuit Speaks', in Ian Adam and Helen Tiffin (eds), *Past the Last Post: Theorizing Post-Colonialism and Post-Modernism*, pp. 191–203.

Buchanan, Ian, 'Space in the Age of Non-Place', in Ian Buchanan and Gregg Lambert (eds), *Deleuze and Space* (Edinburgh: Edinburgh University Press, 2005), pp. 16–35.

Burton, Richard, '"Ki Moun Nou Ye?" The Idea of Difference in Contemporary French West Indian Thought', *New West Indian Guide*, 67.1 & 2 (1993), pp. 5–32.

——, *La Famille coloniale: La Martinique et la Mère Patrie, 1789–1992* (Paris: L'Harmattan, 1994).

Camus, Jean-Yves, 'The Commemoration of Slavery in France and the Emergence of a Black Political Consciousness', *The European Legacy*, 11.6 (2006), pp. 647–55.

Cailler, Bernadette, *Les Conquérants de la nuit nue: Édouard Glissant et l'H(h)istoire antillaise* (Tübingen: Gunther Narr, 1988).

Césaire, Aimé, *Cahier d'un retour au pays natal* (Paris: Volontés, 1939).

——, *Discours sur le colonialisme* (Paris: Présence Africaine, 1955).

Césaire, Aimé, et al., *Tropiques* (Paris: Jean-Michel Place, 1978).

Chamoiseau, Patrick, *Solibo magnifique* (Paris: Gallimard, 1988).

——, *Texaco* (Paris: Gallimard, 1992).

Chamoiseau, Patrick, and Raphaël Confiant, *Lettres créoles: tracées antillaises et continentales de la littérature: Haïti, Guadeloupe, Martinique, Guyane 1635–1975* (Paris: Hatier, 1991).

Chancé, Dominique, *L'Auteur en souffrance: essai sur la position et la représentation de l'auteur dans le roman antillais contemporain* (Paris: PUF, 2000).

Clifford, James, *The Predicament of Culture: Twentieth-Century Ethnography, Literature, and Art* (Cambridge, MA: Harvard University Press, 1988).

Chaulet-Achour, Christiane, *La Trilogie caribéenne de Daniel Maximin* (Paris, Karthala, 2000).

Condé, Maryse, 'L'Afrique, un continent difficile'. Interview with Marie-Clotilde Jacquey and Monique Hugon, *Notre Librairie*, 74 (1984), pp. 21–25.

——, *La Vie scélérate* (Paris: Seghers, 1987).

——, *Traversée de la mangrove* (Paris: Mercure de France, 1989).

——, 'Habiter ce pays, la Guadeloupe', *Chemins critiques*, 1.3 (1989), pp. 5–14.

——, *Les Derniers Rois mages* (Paris: Mercure de France, 1992).

——, 'Order, Disorder, Freedom and the West Indian Writer', *Yale French Studies*, 83.2 (1993), pp. 121–35.

——, *La Migration des cœurs* (Paris: Laffont, 1995).

——, 'Chercher nos vérités', in Maryse Condé and Madeleine Cottenet-Hage (eds), *Penser la créolité* (Paris: Karthala, 1995), pp. 305–10.

——, *Desirada* (Paris: Laffont, 1997).

——, *Célanire cou-coupé* (Paris: Laffont, 2000).

——, *La Belle Créole* (Paris: Mercure, 2001).

Confiant, Raphaël, *Le Nègre et l'amiral* (Paris: Éditions Grasset, 1988).

——, 'La Littérature créolophone des Antilles-Guyane', *Notre Librairie*, 104 (1991), pp. 56–62.

——, 'Questions pratiques d'écriture créole', in Ralph Ludwig (ed.), *Écrire la parole de nuit, la nouvelle littérature antillaise* (Paris: Gallimard, 1994), pp. 171–80.

Corzani, Jack, La Littérature des Antilles-Guyane française (6 vols.) (Fort-de-France: Désormeaux, 1978).

Cottenet-Hage, Madeleine and Lydie Moudileno (eds), *Maryse Condé. Une nomade inconvenante* (Guadeloupe: Ibis Rouge Éditions, 2002).

Crosta, Suzanne, 'Narrative and discursive strategies in Maryse Condé's *Traversée de la mangrove*', *Callaloo*, 15.1 (1992), pp. 147–55.

Crowley, Patrick, and Jane Hiddlestone (eds), *Postcolonial Poetics: Genre and Form* (Liverpool: Liverpool University Press, 2011).

Dällenbach, Lucien, *Le Récit spéculaire* (Paris: Éditions du Seuil, 1977).

Dash, J. Michael, 'Le Roman de nous', *Carbet*, 10 (1990), pp. 21–31.

Debreuille, Jean-Yves, 'Le Langage désancré de *Malemort*', in Yves-Alain Favre (ed.), *Horizons d'Édouard Glissant* (Biarritz: J. & D. Éditeurs, 1992), pp. 319–28.

Degras, Priska, 'Se nommer soi-même', *Carbet*, 10 (1990), pp. 57–64.

Deleuze, Gilles, *Différence et répétition* (Paris: PUF, 1968). English translation by Paul Patton, *Difference and Repetition* (London: Athlone Press, 1994).

Deleuze, Gilles and Félix Guattari, *Kafka. Pour une littérature mineure* (Paris: Éditions de Minuit, 1975).

——, *Rhizome* (Paris: Éditions de Minuit, 1976).

——, *Mille Plateaux (Capitalisme et schizophrénie 2)* (Paris: Éditions de Minuit, 1980).

Depestre, René, *Le Mât de cocagne* (Paris: Éditions Gallimard, 1979).

——, *Alléluia pour une femme-jardin* (Paris: Éditions Gallimard, 1981).

——, *Hadriana dans tous mes rêves* (Paris: Éditions Gallimard, 1988).

Derrida, Jacques, *De la grammatologie* (Paris: Éditions de Minuit, 1967).

——, *Passions* (Paris: Éditions Galilée, 1993).

——, *Le Monolinguisme de l'autre – ou la prothèse de l'origine* (Paris: Éditions Galilée, 1996

Dirlik, Arif, 'The Postcolonial Aura: Third World Criticism in the Age of Global Capitalism', *Critical Inquiry*, 20.2 (1994), pp. 328–56.

Eagleton, Terry, *Criticism and Ideology: A Study in Marxist Literary Theory* (London: Verso, 1976).

Fanon, Frantz, *Peau noire, masques blancs* (Paris: Éditions du Seuil, 1952).

Finkielkraut, Alain, 'Quelle sorte de Français sont-ils?' http://questionscritiques. free.fr/edito/haaretz/finkielkraut_171105.htm.

Forsdick, Charles, 'Travelling Concepts: Postcolonial Approaches to Exoticism', *Paragraph*, 24.3 (2001), pp. 12–29.

ffrench, P., 'Community in Maryse Condé's *Traversée de la mangrove*', *French Forum*, 22.1 (1997), pp. 93–105.

Frow, John, 'Intertextuality and ontology', in Michael Worton and Judith Still (eds), *Intertextuality: Theories and practices* (Manchester and New York: Manchester University Press, 1990), pp. 45–55.

Gallagher, Mary, *Soundings in French Caribbean Writing since 1950: The Shock of Space and Time* (Oxford: Oxford University Press, 2002).

——, 'Postcolonial Poetics: l'exception francophone?', *Modern and Contemporary France*, 18.2 (2010), pp. 251–68.

——, 'Lafcadio Hearn's American Writings and the Creole Continuum', in Martin Munro and Celia Britton (eds), *American Creoles: The Francophone Caribbean and the American South* (Liverpool: Liverpool University Press, 2012), pp. 19–39.

Gauvin, Lise, *Ecrire, pour qui? L'écrivain francophone et ses publics* (Paris: Karthala, 2007).

Genette, Gérard, 'Vertige fixé', in his *Figures I* (Paris: Éditions du Seuil, 1966), pp. 69–90.

Gikandi, Simon, *Writing in Limbo: Modernism and Caribbean Literature* (Ithaca, NY and London: Cornell University Press, 1992).

Gilroy, Paul, *The Black Atlantic: Modernity and Double Consciousness* (Cambridge, MA: Harvard University Press, 1993).

Giraud, Michel, 'La Créolité: une rupture en trompe-l'œil', *Cahiers d'études africaines*, 148 (1997), pp. 795–812.

Glissant, Édouard, *La Lézarde* (Paris: Éditions du Seuil, 1958).

——, *Le Quatrième Siècle* (Paris: Éditions du Seuil, 1964).

——, *L'Intention poétique* (Paris: Éditions du Seuil, 1969).

——, *Malemort* (Paris: Éditions du Seuil, 1975).

——, *La Case du commandeur* (Paris: Éditions du Seuil, 1981).

——, *Le Discours antillais* (Paris: Éditions du Seuil, 1981).

——, 'Entretien du *CARÉ* avec Édouard Glissant', *CARÉ*, 10 (1983), pp. 17–25.

——, *Mahagony* (Paris: Éditions du Seuil, 1987).

——, *Poétique de la Relation* (Paris: Gallimard, 1990).

——, *Tout-monde* (Paris: Gallimard, 1993).

——, *Introduction à une poétique du divers* (Paris: Gallimard, 1996).

——, 'L'Ecrivain et le souffle du lieu', interview with Lise Gauvin, reprinted in *Introduction à une poétique du divers*, pp. 129–35.

——, *Faulkner, Mississippi* (Paris: Gallimard, 1996).

——, *Traité du tout-monde* (Paris: Gallimard, 1997).

——, *Sartorius* (Paris: Gallimard, 1999).

——, 'Édouard Glissant avec *Les périphériques vous parlent*', novembre 2002. http://www.lesperipheriques.org/article.php3?id_article=34.

——, *La Cohée du Lamentin* (Paris: Gallimard, 2005).

——, *Une Nouvelle Région du monde* (Paris: Gallimard, 2006).

Gracchus, Fritz, *Les Lieux de la mère dans les sociétés afro-américaines* (Paris: Éditions Caribéennes, 1986).

Green, Mary Jean, Karen Gould and Micheline Rice-Maximin (eds), *Postcolonial Subjects: Francophone Women Writers* (Minneapolis, MN: Minnesota University Press, 1996).

Gyssels, Kathleen, *Filles de solitude: essai sur l'identité antillaise dans les (auto) biographies de Simone et André Schwarz-Bart* (Paris: L'Harmattan, 1996).

Haigh, Sam, 'Migration and Melancholia: from Kristeva's "dépression nationale" to Pineau's "maladie de l'exil"', *French Studies*, 60.2 (2006), pp. 232–50.

Hallward, Peter, *Absolutely Postcolonial: Writing Between the Singular and the Specific* (Manchester: Manchester University Press, 2001).

Harrison, Nicholas, *Postcolonial Criticism* (Cambridge: Polity, 2003).

Hearn, Lafcadio, *Esquisses martiniquaises*, ed. Mary Gallagher (Paris: L'Harmattan, 2004).

Hegel, G.W.F., *Science of Logic* (New York: Macmillan, 1929).

Hewitt, Leah, *Autobiographical Tightropes: Simone de Beauvoir, Nathalie Sarraute, Marguerite Duras, Monique Wittig, and Maryse Condé* (Lincoln, NE: University of Nebraska Press, 1990).

——, 'Condé's Critical Seesaw', *Callaloo*, 18.3 (1995), pp. 641–51.

Hoffmann, Léon-François, 'L'image de la femme dans la poésie haïtienne', *Présence africaine*, 34–36 (1960), pp. 183–206.

Huggan, Graham, *The Post-colonial Exotic: Marketing the Margins* (London and New York: Routledge, 2001).

Hutcheon, Linda, 'Circling the Downspout of Empire', in Ian Adam and Helen Tiffin (eds), *Past the Last Post: Theorizing Post-Colonialism and Post-Modernism*, pp. 9–16.

Jameson, Fredric, 'Third-World Literature in the Era of Multinational Capitalism', *Social Text*, 15 (1986), pp. 65–88.

Kristeva, Julia, 'Le Mot, le dialogue et le roman', in her *Recherches pour une sémanalyse* (Paris: Éditions du Seuil, 1969), pp. 82–112.

Lacan, Jacques, *Écrits* (Paris: Éditions du Seuil, 1966).

——, 'Le Stade du miroir comme formateur de la fonction du Je', in *Écrits* vol. 1, pp. 89–97.

——, *Les Quatre Concepts fondamentaux de la psychanalyse (Le Séminaire Livre XI)* (Paris: Éditions du Seuil, 1973).

Lane, Jeremy, *Jazz and Machine-Age Imperialism: Music, "Race" and Intellectuals in France, 1918–1945* (Ann Arbor, MI: University of Michigan Press, 2013).

de Lauretis, Teresa, 'Feminist Studies/Critical Studies: Issues, Terms and Contexts', in de Lauretis (ed.), *Feminist Studies/Critical Studies* (Bloomington, IN: Indiana University Press, 1986), pp. 1–19.

Lazarus, Neil, 'The Politics of Postcolonial Modernism' in Ania Loomba et al. (eds), *Postcolonial Studies and Beyond* (Durham, NC: Duke University Press, 2005), pp. 423–38.

Lecercle, Jean-Jacques, *Deleuze and Language* (Basingstoke: Palgrave Macmillan, 2002).

Leiris, Michel, *Contacts de civilisation en Martinique et en Guadeloupe* (Paris: Gallimard, 1955).

——, 'Antilles et poésie des carrefours', in his *Zébrage* (Paris: Gallimard, 1992), pp. 67–87.

Lionnet, Françoise, *Autobiographical Voices: Race, Gender, Self-Portraiture* (Ithaca, NY and London: Cornell University Press, 1989).

——, '*Traversée de la mangrove* de Maryse Condé: vers un nouvel humanisme antillais?', *The French Review*, 66 (1993), pp. 475–86.

——, *Postcolonial Representations: Women, Literature, Identity* (Ithaca, NY and London: Cornell University Press, 1995).

Lorraine, Tamsin, 'Ahab and Becoming-Whale: The Nomadic Subject in Smooth Space', in Ian Buchanan and Gregg Lambert (eds), *Deleuze and Space* (Edinburgh: Edinburgh University Press, 2005), pp. 159–75.

Lucey, Michael, 'Voices accounting for the Past: Maryse Condé's *Traversée de la Mangrove*', in Maryse Condé (ed.), *L'Héritage de Caliban* (Pointe-à-Pitre: Éditions Jasor, 1992), pp. 123–32.

Macherey, Pierre, *Pour une théorie de la production littéraire* (Paris: Maspero, 1966).

Maragnes, Daniel, 'L'Identité et le désastre (origine et fondation)', *Portulan*, 2 (1998), pp. 273–80.

Marcuse, Herbert, *Reason and Revolution* (New York: Humanities Press, 1954).

Maran, René, *Batouala* (Paris: A. Michel, 1921).

Marquez, Gabriel Garcia, 'Operation Carlotta', *New Left Review*, 101–2 (1977), pp. 123–37.

Maximin, Daniel, *L'Isolé soleil* (Paris, Éditions du Seuil, 1981).

——, *L'Île et une nuit* (Paris: Éditions du Seuil, 1995).

Mayaux, Catherine, 'La Structure romanesque de *Mahagony* d'Édouard Glissant' in Yves-Alain Favre (ed.), *Horizons d'Édouard Glissant*, (Biarritz: J. & D. Éditeurs, 1992), pp. 349–63.

McCusker, Maeve, *Patrick Chamoiseau: Recovering Memory* (Liverpool: Liverpool University Press, 2007).

Ménil, René, 'De l'exotisme colonial', in his *Antilles déjà jadis (précédée de Tracées)* (Paris: Jean-Michel Place, 1999), pp. 20–27.

Merleau-Ponty, Maurice, *Signes* (Paris: Gallimard, 1960; English translation by Richard G. McGleary, *Signs* (Evanston, IL: Northwestern University Press, 1964).

Moudileno, Lydie, 'Les Écrivains de Maryse Condé: face à la filiation et à l'affiliation', in her *L'Écrivain antillais au miroir de sa littérature* (Paris: Karthala, 1997).

Munro, Martin, *Shaping and Reshaping the Caribbean: The Work of Aimé Césaire and René Depestre* (London: MHRA Texts and Dissertations, vol. 52, 2000).

——, *Exile and Post-1946 Haitian Literature: Alexis, Depestre, Ollivier, Laferrière, Danticat* (Liverpool: Liverpool University Press, 2007).

Murdoch, Adlai, 'The Language(s) of Martinican Identity: Resistance to Vichy in the novels of Raphaël Confiant', *Esprit créateur*, 47.1 (2007), pp. 68–83.

Nesbitt, Nick, *Voicing memory: History and Subjectivity in French Caribbean*

*Literature* (Charlottesville, VA and London: University of Virginia Press, 2003).

Ngugi wa Thiong'o, *Decolonizing the Mind: The Politics of Language in African Literature* (London: James Currey, 1981].

N'Zengou-Tayo, Marie-José, 'Littérature et diglossie: créer une langue métisse ou la "chamoisification" du français dans *Texaco* de Patrick Chamoiseau', *TTR: traduction, terminologie, rédaction*, 9.1 (1996), pp. 155–76.

Pageaux, Daniel-Henri, 'Sartre, les Juifs, les Noirs … et les autres', *Portulan*, 2 (1998), pp. 229–46.

Pépin, Ernest, *L'Envers du décor* (Paris: Le Serpent à plumes, 2006).

Perrault, Jeanne, 'Autography/Transformation/Asymmetry', in S. Smith and J. Watson (eds), *Women, Autobiography, Theory*, pp. 190–96.

Perret, Delphine, 'L'Écriture mosaïque de *Traversée de la Mangrove*', in Maryse Condé (ed.), *L'Héritage de Caliban* (Pointe-à-Pitre: Éditions Jasor, 1992), pp. 187–200.

——, 'Lire Chamoiseau', in Maryse Condé and Madeleine Cottenet-Hage (eds), *Penser la créolité*, pp. 153–72.

Pfaff, Françoise, *Entretiens avec Maryse Condé* (Paris: Karthala, 1993).

Pineau, Gisèle, *L'Exil selon Julia* (Paris: Éditions Stock, 1996).

Placoly, Vincent, *La Vie et la mort de Marcel Gonstran* (Paris: Denoël, 1971).

——, *L'Eau de mort guildive* (Paris, Denoël, 1973).

Price, Richard and Sally Price, 'Shadow-boxing in the mangrove', *Cultural Anthropology*, 12.1 (1997), pp. 3–36.

Ridon, Jean-Xavier, 'Maryse Condé et le fantôme d'une communauté inopérante', in Christiane Albert (ed.), *Francophonie et identités culturelles* (Paris: Karthala, 1999), pp. 211–26.

Richardson, Michael, *Refusal of the Shadow: Surrealism and the Caribbean* (London: Verso, 1996).

Rosello, Mireille, 'Caribbean insularization of identities in Maryse Condé's work from *En attendant le bonheur* to *Les Derniers Rois mages*', *Callaloo*, 18.3 (1995), pp. 565–78.

Rouch, Alain and Gérard Clavreuil, *Littératures nationales d'écriture française* (Paris: Bordas, 1987).

Rousseau, Madeleine, 'Wifredo Lam, peintre cubain', *Présence africaine*, 4 (1948), pp. 590–94.

Sartre, Jean-Paul, *Qu'est-ce que la littérature?* (Paris: Gallimard, 1948).

——, 'Orphée noir', preface to L. Senghor (ed.), *Anthologie de la poésie noire et malgache de langue française* (Paris: PUF, 1948).

de Saussure, Ferdinand, *Cours de linguistique générale* (Paris: Payot 1968).

Scharfman, Ronnie, 'Rewriting the Césaires', in Maryse Condé (ed.), *L'Héritage de Caliban* (Pointe-à-Pitre, Guadeloupe, Éditions Jasor, 1992), pp. 233–45.

——, '"Créolité" is/as Resistance: Raphaël Confiant's *Le Nègre et l'Amiral*', in Maryse Condé and Madeleine Cottenet-Hage (ed.), *Penser la créolité*, pp. 125–34.

Schwarz-Bart, André, *Le Dernier des Justes* (Paris: Éditions du Seuil, 1959).

Schwarz-Bart, André and Simone Schwarz-Bart, *Un Plat de porc aux bananes vertes* (Paris: Éditions du Seuil, 1967).

Schwarz-Bart, Simone, *Pluie et vent sur Télumée Miracle* (Paris: Éditions du Seuil, 1972).

Scott, Joan W., 'Experience', in S. Smith and J. Watson (eds), *Women, Autobiography, Theory*, pp. 57–71.

Selvon, Samuel, *The Lonely Londoners* (London: Longman, 1956).

Simon, Claude, *Triptyques* (Paris: Minuit, 1973).

Smith, Sidonie and Julia Watson (eds), *Women, Autobiography, Theory* (Madison, WI: Wisconsin University Press, 1998).

Smock, Ann, 'Maryse Condé's *Les Derniers Rois mages*', *Callaloo*, 18.3 (1995), pp. 668–88.

Sorensen, Eli Park, *Postcolonial Studies and the Literary* (Basingstoke: Palgrave Macmillan, 2010).

Spivak, Gayatri, *The Postcolonial Critic: Interviews, Strategies, Dialogues*, ed. Sarah Harasym (New York: Routledge, 1990).

——, *Death of a Discipline* (New York: Columbia University Press, 2003).

Syrotinski, Michael, *Deconstruction and the Postcolonial: At the Limits of Theory* (Liverpool: Liverpool University Press, 2007).

Taleb-Khyar, Mohammed, 'An Interview with Maryse Condé and Rita Dove', *Callaloo*, 14.2 (1991), pp. 347–66.

Tiffin, Helen, 'Post-colonial Literatures and Counter-discourse' in Bill Ashcroft, Gareth Griffiths and Helen Tiffin (eds), *The Post-colonial Studies Reader* (London and New York: Routledge, 1995), pp. 95–98.

Toumson, Roger, 'L'Exotisme. Problématiques de la représentation de l'autre et de l'ailleurs', *Revue française d'histoire du livre*, 60–61 (1988), pp. 433–50.

——, 'Deux figures du destin', *Portulan*, 2 (1998), pp. 9–18.

Warner-Vieyra, Myriam, *Le Quimboiseur l'avait dit* (Paris and Dakar: Présence Africaine, 1980).

Webb, Barbara, *Myth and History in Caribbean Fiction* (Amherst, MA: University of Massachusetts Press, 1992).

Wing, Nathaniel, 'Écriture et relation dans les romans d'Édouard Glissant', in Yves-Alain Favre (ed.), *Horizons d'Édouard Glissant* (Biarritz: J. & D. Éditeurs, 1992), pp. 296–303.

Wilson, Betty, 'Introduction' to Miriam Warner-Vieyra, *Juletane*, translated by Betty Wilson (London: Heinemann, 1981), pp. v–xv.

Žižek, Slavoj, 'Deleuze's Platonism: Ideas as Real', http://www.lacan.com/zizplato.htm.

Zobel, Joseph, *La Rue Cases-Nègres* (Paris: J. Froissart, 1950).

# Index